Maria Shagina

JOINING A PRESTIGIOUS CLUB

Cooperation with Europarties and Its Impact on Party Development in Georgia, Moldova, and Ukraine 2004–2015

With a foreword by Kataryna Wolczuk

ibidem-Verlag
Stuttgart

Bibliografische Information der Deutschen Nationalbibliothek
Die Deutsche Nationalbibliothek verzeichnet diese Publikation in der Deutschen Nationalbibliografie; detaillierte bibliografische Daten sind im Internet über http://dnb.d-nb.de abrufbar.

Bibliographic information published by the Deutsche Nationalbibliothek
Die Deutsche Nationalbibliothek lists this publication in the Deutsche Nationalbibliografie; detailed bibliographic data are available in the Internet at http://dnb.d-nb.de.

∞

Gedruckt auf alterungsbeständigem, säurefreien Papier
Printed on acid-free paper

ISSN: 1614-3515

ISBN-13: 978-3-8382-1084-1

© *ibidem*-Verlag
Stuttgart 2017

Alle Rechte vorbehalten

Das Werk einschließlich aller seiner Teile ist urheberrechtlich geschützt. Jede Verwertung außerhalb der engen Grenzen des Urheberrechtsgesetzes ist ohne Zustimmung des Verlages unzulässig und strafbar. Dies gilt insbesondere für Vervielfältigungen, Übersetzungen, Mikroverfilmungen und elektronische Speicherformen sowie die Einspeicherung und Verarbeitung in elektronischen Systemen.

All rights part of this publication may be reproduced, stored in or introduced into a retrieval system, or transmitted, in any form, or by any means (electronical, mechanical, photocopying, recording or otherwise) without the prior written permission of the publisher. Any person who does any unauthorized act in relation to this publication may be liable to criminal prosecution and civil claims for damages.

Printed in the EU

Contents

List of Abbreviations 7
List of Tables and Figures 9
Foreword by Kataryna Wolczuk 11
Acknowledgements 13
1. Introduction 15
2. Research Framework 29
   2.1 Theoretical Framework:
       Socialisation and Norm Diffusion 29
   2.2 Explanatory Model 33
   2.3 Case Selection and Methodology 39
   2.4 Operationalisation 42
   2.5 Data Collection 45
3. Understanding the Context of Cooperation 47
   3.1 Historical and Institutional Development
       of the Europarties 48
   3.2 Party Development in Post-Communist Countries ... 57
4. Finding Each Other: Process
   of Application and Identification 71
   4.1 Application and Selection Process 71
   4.2 Identifying a Suitable Europarty 76
5. Incentive Structures for Cooperation 91
   5.1 Motives for the Europarties 92
   5.2 Motives for the non-EU parties 101
6. Impact on Ideological Profiles 111
   6.1 Ideological Match: Fitting
       into the European Party Family 112
   6.2 Analysing the Ideological Match 156

7. **Impact on Organisational Structure** 159
   7.1 Organisational Changes in Mother Parties,
        Youth and Women's Branches 161
   7.2 Analysing the Organisational Changes 173
8. **Impact on Inter-Party Behaviour** 181
   8.1 Inter-Party Relationships between Sister Parties 182
   8.2 Inter-Party Cooperation across the Europarties 196
   8.3 Analysing the Inter-Party Behaviour 206
9. **Conclusions** 211
   9.1 Key Empirical Findings 211
   9.2 Comparative Analysis 217
   9.3 Impact on the Party System 222
   9.4 Impact on the Europarties 224
   9.5 Limitations 225
   9.6 Future Research Trajectories 226

Bibliography 229
   Interviews 229
   Official Documents 232
   Party Documents 233
   Literature 236

Soviet and Post-Soviet Politics and Society (SPPS)   Vol. 172
ISSN 1614-3515

General Editor: Andreas Umland,
Institute for Euro-Atlantic Cooperation, Kyiv, umland@stanfordalumni.org

Commissioning Editor: Max Jakob Horstmann,
London, mjh@ibidem.eu

EDITORIAL COMMITTEE*

DOMESTIC & COMPARATIVE POLITICS
Prof. **Ellen Bos**, *Andrássy University of Budapest*
Dr. **Ingmar Bredies**, *FH Bund, Brühl*
Dr. **Andrey Kazantsev**, *MGIMO (U) MID RF, Moscow*
Prof. **Heiko Pleines**, *University of Bremen*
Prof. **Richard Sakwa**, *University of Kent at Canterbury*
Dr. **Sarah Whitmore**, *Oxford Brookes University*
Dr. **Harald Wydra**, *University of Cambridge*

SOCIETY, CLASS & ETHNICITY
Col. **David Glantz**, *"Journal of Slavic Military Studies"*
Dr. **Marlène Laruelle**, *George Washington University*
Dr. **Stephen Shulman**, *Southern Illinois University*
Prof. **Stefan Troebst**, *University of Leipzig*

POLITICAL ECONOMY & PUBLIC POLICY
Prof. em. **Marshall Goldman**, *Wellesley College, Mass.*
Dr. **Andreas Goldthau**, *Central European University*
Dr. **Robert Kravchuk**, *University of North Carolina*
Dr. **David Lane**, *University of Cambridge*
Dr. **Carol Leonard**, *Higher School of Economics, Moscow*
Dr. **Maria Popova**, *McGill University, Montreal*

FOREIGN POLICY & INTERNATIONAL AFFAIRS
Dr. **Peter Duncan**, *University College London*
Prof. **Andreas Heinemann-Grüder**, *University of Bonn*
Dr. **Taras Kuzio**, *Johns Hopkins University*
Prof. **Gerhard Mangott**, *University of Innsbruck*
Dr. **Diana Schmidt-Pfister**, *University of Konstanz*
Dr. **Lisbeth Tarlow**, *Harvard University, Cambridge*
Dr. **Christian Wipperfürth**, *N-Ost Network, Berlin*
Dr. **William Zimmerman**, *University of Michigan*

HISTORY, CULTURE & THOUGHT
Dr. **Catherine Andreyev**, *University of Oxford*
Prof. **Mark Bassin**, *Södertörn University*
Prof. **Karsten Brüggemann**, *Tallinn University*
Dr. **Alexander Etkind**, *University of Cambridge*
Dr. **Gasan Gusejnov**, *Moscow State University*
Prof. em. **Walter Laqueur**, *Georgetown University*
Prof. **Leonid Luks**, *Catholic University of Eichstaett*
Dr. **Olga Malinova**, *Russian Academy of Sciences*
Prof. **Andrei Rogatchevski**, *University of Tromso*
Dr. **Mark Tauger**, *West Virginia University*

ADVISORY BOARD*

Prof. **Dominique Arel**, *University of Ottawa*
Prof. **Jörg Baberowski**, *Humboldt University of Berlin*
Prof. **Margarita Balmaceda**, *Seton Hall University*
Dr. **John Barber**, *University of Cambridge*
Prof. **Timm Beichelt**, *European University Viadrina*
Dr. **Katrin Boeckh**, *University of Munich*
Prof. em. **Archie Brown**, *University of Oxford*
Dr. **Vyacheslav Bryukhovetsky**, *Kyiv-Mohyla Academy*
Prof. **Timothy Colton**, *Harvard University, Cambridge*
Prof. **Paul D'Anieri**, *University of Florida*
Dr. **Heike Dörrenbächer**, *Friedrich Naumann Foundation*
Dr. **John Dunlop**, *Hoover Institution, Stanford, California*
Dr. **Sabine Fischer**, *SWP, Berlin*
Dr. **Geir Flikke**, *NUPI, Oslo*
Prof. **David Galbreath**, *University of Aberdeen*
Prof. **Alexander Galkin**, *Russian Academy of Sciences*
Prof. **Frank Golczewski**, *University of Hamburg*
Dr. **Nikolas Gvosdev**, *Naval War College, Newport, RI*
Prof. **Mark von Hagen**, *Arizona State University*
Dr. **Guido Hausmann**, *University of Munich*
Prof. **Dale Herspring**, *Kansas State University*
Dr. **Stefani Hoffman**, *Hebrew University of Jerusalem*
Prof. **Mikhail Ilyin**, *MGIMO (U) MID RF, Moscow*
Prof. **Vladimir Kantor**, *Higher School of Economics*
Dr. **Ivan Katchanovski**, *University of Ottawa*
Prof. em. **Andrzej Korbonski**, *University of California*
Dr. **Iris Kempe**, *"Caucasus Analytical Digest"*
Prof. **Herbert Küpper**, *Institut für Ostrecht Regensburg*
Dr. **Rainer Lindner**, *CEEER, Berlin*
Dr. **Vladimir Malakhov**, *Russian Academy of Sciences*

Dr. **Luke March**, *University of Edinburgh*
Prof. **Michael McFaul**, *Stanford University, Palo Alto*
Prof. **Birgit Menzel**, *University of Mainz-Germersheim*
Prof. **Valery Mikhailenko**, *The Urals State University*
Prof. **Emil Pain**, *Higher School of Economics, Moscow*
Dr. **Oleg Podvintsev**, *Russian Academy of Sciences*
Prof. **Olga Popova**, *St. Petersburg State University*
Dr. **Alex Pravda**, *University of Oxford*
Dr. **Erik van Ree**, *University of Amsterdam*
Dr. **Joachim Rogall**, *Robert Bosch Foundation Stuttgart*
Prof. **Peter Rutland**, *Wesleyan University, Middletown*
Prof. **Marat Salikov**, *The Urals State Law Academy*
Dr. **Gwendolyn Sasse**, *University of Oxford*
Prof. **Jutta Scherrer**, *EHESS, Paris*
Prof. **Robert Service**, *University of Oxford*
Mr. **James Sherr**, *RIIA Chatham House London*
Dr. **Oxana Shevel**, *Tufts University, Medford*
Prof. **Eberhard Schneider**, *University of Siegen*
Prof. **Olexander Shnyrkov**, *Shevchenko University, Kyiv*
Prof. **Hans-Henning Schröder**, *SWP, Berlin*
Prof. **Yuri Shapoval**, *Ukrainian Academy of Sciences*
Prof. **Viktor Shnirelman**, *Russian Academy of Sciences*
Dr. **Lisa Sundstrom**, *University of British Columbia*
Dr. **Philip Walters**, *"Religion, State and Society"*, Oxford
Prof. **Zenon Wasyliw**, *Ithaca College, New York State*
Dr. **Lucan Way**, *University of Toronto*
Dr. **Markus Wehner**, *"Frankfurter Allgemeine Zeitung"*
Dr. **Andrew Wilson**, *University College London*
Prof. **Jan Zielonka**, *University of Oxford*
Prof. **Andrei Zorin**, *University of Oxford*

* While the Editorial Committee and Advisory Board support the General Editor in the choice and improvement of manuscripts for publication, responsibility for remaining errors and misinterpretations in the series' volumes lies with the books' authors.

Soviet and Post-Soviet Politics and Society (SPPS)
ISSN 1614-3515

Founded in 2004 and refereed since 2007, SPPS makes available affordable English-, German-, and Russian-language studies on the history of the countries of the former Soviet bloc from the late Tsarist period to today. It publishes between 5 and 20 volumes per year and focuses on issues in transitions to and from democracy such as economic crisis, identity formation, civil society development, and constitutional reform in CEE and the NIS. SPPS also aims to highlight so far understudied themes in East European studies such as right-wing radicalism, religious life, higher education, or human rights protection. The authors and titles of all previously published volumes are listed at the end of this book. For a full description of the series and reviews of its books, see
www.ibidem-verlag.de/red/spps.

Editorial correspondence & manuscripts should be sent to: Dr. Andreas Umland, Institute for Euro-Atlantic Cooperation, vul. Volodymyrska 42, off. 21, UA-01030 Kyiv, Ukraine

Business correspondence & review copy requests should be sent to: *ibidem* Press, Leuschnerstr. 40, 30457 Hannover, Germany; tel.: +49 511 2622200; fax: +49 511 2622201; spps@ibidem.eu.

Authors, reviewers, referees, and editors for (as well as all other persons sympathetic to) SPPS are invited to join its networks at
www.facebook.com/group.php?gid=52638198614
www.linkedin.com/groups?about=&gid=103012
www.xing.com/net/spps-ibidem-verlag/

Recent Volumes

164 *Nozima Akhrarkhodjaeva*
The Instrumentalisation of Mass Media in Electoral Authoritarian Regimes
Evidence from Russia's Presidential Election Campaigns of 2000 and 2008
ISBN 978-3-8382-1013-1

165 *Yulia Krasheninnikova*
Informal Healthcare in Contemporary Russia
Sociographic Essays on the Post-Soviet Infrastructure for Alternative Healing Practices
ISBN 978-3-8382-0970-8

166 *Peter Kaiser*
Das Schachbrett der Macht
Die Handlungsspielräume eines sowjetischen Funktionärs unter Stalin am Beispiel des Generalsekretärs des Komsomol Aleksandr Kosarev (1929-1938)
Mit einem Vorwort von Dietmar Neutatz
ISBN 978-3-8382-1052-0

167 *Oksana Kim*
The Effects and Implications of Kazakhstan's Adoption of International Financial Reporting Standards
A Resource Dependence Perspective
With a foreword by Svetlana Vlady
ISBN 978-3-8382-0987-6

168 *Anna Sanina*
Patriotic Education in Contemporary Russia
Sociological Studies in the Making of the Post-Soviet Citizen
With a foreword by Anna Oldfield
ISBN 978-3-8382-0993-7

169 *Rudolf Wolters*
Spezialist in Sibirien
Faksimile der 1933 erschienenen ersten Ausgabe
Mit einem Vorwort von Dmitrij Chmelnizki
ISBN 978-3-8382-0515-1

170 *Michal Vít, Magdalena M. Baran (eds.)*
Transregional versus National Perspectives on Contemporary Central European History
Studies on the Building of Nation-States and Their Cooperation in the 20th and 21st Century
With a foreword by Petr Vágner
ISBN 978-3-8382-1015-5

171 *Philip Gamaghelyan*
Conflict Resolution Beyond the International Relations Paradigm
Evolving Designs as a Transformative Practice in Nagorno-Karabakh and Syria
With a foreword by Susan Allen
ISBN 978-3-8382-1057-5

List of Abbreviations

AECR	Alliance of European Conservatives and Reformists
AEI	Alliance for European Integration
ALDE	Alliance of Liberals and Democrats for Europe
BEL	Bulgarian European Left
BYuT	Bloc of Yulia Tymoshenko
CDM	Christian Democratic Movement of Georgia
CDPP	Christian-Democratic People's Party of Moldova
CEE	Central and Eastern Europe
CIS	Commonwealth of Independent States
DCFTA	Deep and Comprehensive Free Trade Agreement
DPM	Democratic Party of Moldova
EaP	Eastern Partnership
ECPM	European Conservative Political Movement
EDS	European Democrat Students
EL	European Left
EL FEM	Women of the Party of the European Left
ENDYL	European Network of Democratic Young Left
ENP	European Neighborhood Policy
EP	European Parliament
EPP	European People's Party
EU	European Union
FES	Friedrich-Ebert-Stiftung
FNS	Friedrich-Naumann-Stiftung
IFLRY	International Federation of Liberal Youth
IRI	International Republican Institute
HZDS	People's Party — Movement for a Democratic Slovakia
KAS	Konrad-Adenauer-Stiftung
LDPM	Liberal Democratic Party of Moldova
LDYM	Liberal Democratic Youth of Moldova
LYMEC	European Liberal Youth
NDI	National Democratic Institute for International Affairs

NIMD	Netherlands Institute for Multiparty Democracy
OSCE	Organisation for Security and Cooperation in Europe
PCRM	Party of Communists of the Republic of Moldova
PES	Party of European Socialists
QCA	Qualitative Comparative Analysis
UNM	United National Movement
VVD	Volkspartij voor Vrijheid en Democratie (People's Party for Freedom and Democracy
YEPP	Youth of the European People's Party

List of Tables and Figures

Figure 2.1 The mechanism of the Europarties' impact on the non-EU parties 34

Table 2.1 Operationalisation of scope conditions 41

Table 2.2 Operationalisation of dependent variable 43

Table 5.1 Motivations of the non-EU parties 109

Table 6.1 Ideological congruence between the EPP and its Georgian, Moldovan, and Ukrainian sister parties ... 129

Table 6.2 Ideological congruence between the PES and its Moldovan sister party 133

Table 6.3 Ideological congruence between the ALDE and its Moldovan and Georgian sister parties 142

Table 6.4 Ideological congruence between the EL and its Moldovan sister party 151

Table 6.5 Ideological congruence between the AECR and its Georgian sister party 156

Table 7.1 Organisational changes in mother parties 176

Table 7.2 Organisational changes in youth branches 177

Table 7.3 Organisational changes in women's branches 178

Foreword

This book studies transnational influences on political parties. The author takes on the momentous task of studying why, how and with what effects political parties in Eastern Europe (Ukraine and Moldova) and the South Caucasus (Georgia) cooperate with Europarties.

As such, the book addresses three under-researched dimensions. First, it examines political parties in the post-Soviet countries in order to then understand the Europeanisation of political parties in the Eastern neighbourhood. At present there is hardly any literature on cooperation between national parties and Europarties. Second, the study is particularly important because there is relatively little written on political parties in the post-Soviet countries. Third, there is hardly any *comparative* literature on political parties across the post-Soviet space because most academic literature deals with single countries. The author therefore faced the formidable challenge of simultaneously researching parties themselves in order to gain an insight into the extent to which their cooperation with the Europarties impacted on them and how the impact differed across the countries, thereby developing comparative insights. In doing so, the book delivers on its promise to provide "cross-national, cross-partisan and cross-dimensional perspectives". This is a new research pathway in European Studies as it analyses "Europeanisation beyond enlargement" with a new set of EU and domestic actors.

Rather than a "blanket" change, the study can observe gradual forms of change in the process of selective and strategic engagement of domestic actors with external actors leads to a non-systemic impact. These complex modalities of change pose a considerable challenge for gauging the actual extent of, and mechanisms accounting for, "Europeanisation beyond enlargement". Cooperation with Europarties seems to enhance domestic processes but cannot compensate for the weakness of the domestic parties and volatility of the party system as such.

This book encompasses a great deal of research and delivers a set of strong and well-documented findings. To her credit, Maria Shagina does not shy away from a full recognition of the complexity of the findings and embraces it with a scholarly scrutiny. This is an ambitious, extensive and original study, which—despite or rather its sobering findings—pushes the frontiers of the debates on Europeanisation.

Kataryna Wolczuk
University of Birmingham, May 2017

Acknowledgements

I would like to express my deep gratitude to my supervisors Prof. Dr. Sandra Lavenex and Prof. Kataryna Wolczuk for their continuous support, patient guidance, and useful critiques. Without their enthusiastic encouragement and constructive comments, this research work would not be the same.

My sincere thanks also goes to Prof. Dr. Frank Schimmelfennig, Prof. Lars Svåsand, Prof. Dr. Daniel Bochsler, Dr. Thomas Winzen, Dr. Tim Haughton, and Prof. Dr. Dirk Lehmkuhl for their insightful and fruitful feedback at different stages of my research work, but also for their critical questions which motivated me to look at my thesis from different perspectives and to further enhance it.

I also would like to extend my thanks to the research committee of the University of Lucerne for believing in my research and for granting me a Doc.Mobility scholarship for my research stay at the University of Birmingham. Equally, I would like to thank the Graduate School of Lucerne and NCCR Democracy for the financial support. Without their generous support it would not be possible to conduct my field research.

Last but not least, I would like to express my gratitude to the CREES team for their warm welcome and engaging discussions. This research also would not have been possible without the assistance and support of many people in Belgium, Georgia, Moldova, and Ukraine those who helped me with arranging interviews and those who found time to share their thoughts during the interviews. My special thanks go to my family and friends for their endless support and patience through the process of researching and writing this thesis. In particular, I am thankful to Julia, Myriam, Nino, Valeriya, and to my mother Valentina and my husband David for their continuous encouragement and help.

Maria Shagina
Lucerne, May 2017

1. Introduction

In 2003, a new framework for relations with Eastern and Southern European Union's (EU) neighbours was developed by the European Commission. Reflected in Prodi's speech "A Wider Europe — A Proximity Policy as the key to stability", the initiative aimed to develop a zone of prosperity and a friendly neighbourhood, offering "everything but institutions".[1] Promising no EU membership perspective, in return, the EU has offered an attractive and effective framework for closer co-operation with its neighbouring countries. In its attempt to become "a real global player"[2], the EU provided new opportunities for stable and sustainable political and economic environment. The "wider Europe" initiative emphasized the importance of mutual interests existing between the EU and its neighbours and the need for sharing common values. Aimed at the promotion of the EU values beyond the Union's borders, the new framework claimed that the scope of EU impact is not necessarily limited to the EU member states and can also take place beyond the EU borders.

Being a gravity model of democracy promotion, the EU and its institutions provide a credible blueprint for transformations for its neighbouring countries. One of the avenues through which the EU norms and values are channelled is the Europarties. Being umbrella organisations at the EU level, the Europarties provide a template for the European party-building for immature post-communist parties. Based on the evidence from Central and Eastern Europe (CEE) countries, the Europarties had a substantial impact on

---

1   Romano Prodi, "A Wider Europe — A Proximity Policy as the key to stability," "Peace, Security and Stability — International Dialogue and the Role of the EU," *Sixth ECSA-World Conference*. Jean Monnet Project, Brussels, 5–6 December 2002.
2   Ibid.

CEE parties by providing ideological and material support.[3] Whereas the Europarties had rather a limited impact on party systems in established democracies[4], their involvement in new democracies proved to be more pronounced.[5] Cultural and historical rapprochement to Europe (i.e. "return to Europe" narrative) facilitated the penetration of the EU impact into the domestic arena, by demonstrating dynamics and responsiveness. For example, the Slovakian case showed that transnational links contributed to democratic consolidation and party system stabilisation. In the process of interaction with the Europarties, the Slovak parties experienced programmatic influence and reinforced their party identities, which led to the gradual standardisation of the political spectrum. Staying under a European observation, the Slovak democratic forces benefited from external solidarity and democracy-building, competing against the Mečiar government. Furthermore, the Slovak elites used transnational links as a platform for networking and unofficial lobbying in favour of EU accession.[6]

Whereas in CEE countries the cooperation with the Europarties took place under the mechanism of conditionality—the EU

---

3   Geoffrey Pridham, "Patterns of Europeanization and Transnational Party Co-operation: Party Development in Central and Eastern Europe." *Paper for Workshop on European Aspects of Post-Communist Party Development, ECPR Sessions*, Mannheim, University of Mannheim (1999); Geoffrey Pridham, "The European Union's Democratic Conditionality and Domestic Politics in Slovakia: The Meciar and Dzurinda Governments Compared," *Europe-Asia Studies* 54:2 (2002); Giorgia Delsoldato, "Eastward Enlargement by the European Union and Transnational Parties," *International Political Science Review* 23:3 (2002); Paul Lewis, "Changes in the Party Politics of the New EU Member States in Central Europe: Patterns of Europeanization and Democratization," *Journal of Southern Europe and the Balkans Online* 10:2 (2008).
4   See, for example, Peter Mair, "The Limited Impact of Europe on National Party Systems," *West European Politics* 23:4 (2000): 27–28.
5   Pridham, "Patterns of Europeanization"; Pridham, "The European Union's Democratic Conditionality,"; Delsoldato, "Eastward Enlargement"; Paul Lewis, "Changes in the Party Politics"; Maria Spirova, "Europarties and Party Development in EU-Candidate States: The Case of Bulgaria," *Europe-Asia Studies* 60:5 (2008).
6   Pridham, "Patterns of Europeanization."

membership perspective, the interaction between the Europarties and East European parties from non-candidate countries is deprived of this leverage. However, despite the lack of EU membership perspective, these countries have high aspirations for European integration, while the non-EU parties are willing to initiate cooperation and actively participate in the Europarties' joint activities. In fact, the affi-liation with the Europarties is often seen by Georgian, Moldovan, and Ukrai-nian parties as an opportunity to be accepted among European party elites and, therefore, is perceived as joining a prestigious club.[7]

This factor of prestige makes parties more exposed to the Europarties' influences, what could potentially lead to a more discernible impact on their party development. As a result of their interaction, which occurs through institutionalised programs of mutual visits, joint seminars, training, and political consulting, the non-EU party elites become exposed to the Europarties' norms and values, gradually absorbing the EU rules and practices. During this process of socialisation, the Europarties have the potential to "teach" the non-EU party elites the EU rules and norms, whereas the non-EU parties have an opportunity to adjust their party manifestos, approximate their organisational structure, and alter their political behavior in line with European party-building.

Driven by shifting the focus from CEE countries to non-EU countries, this research tackles the phenomenon of cooperation in which immediate tangible rewards are absent. It is the absence of rewards for both parties that makes their cooperation so perplexing. On the one hand, the Europarties do not obtain any additional votes in the European Parliament (EP), by incorporating newcomers from the non-EU member states. On the other hand, the non-EU parties are deprived of votes and initiative rights and have no influence within the Europarties' decision-making bodies, which makes their cooperation limited. Nevertheless, the non-EU parties willingly initiate the cooperation and participate in the Europarties'

---

[7] Dorota Dakowska, "Beyond Conditionality: EU Enlargement, European Party Federations and the Transnational Activity of German Political Foundations," *Perspectives on European Politics and Society* 3:2 (2002).

activities, whereas the Europarties compete in their network expansion and are eager to have sister parties outside of Europe.

Research questions

The aim of this research is to investigate the impact of cooperation on party development in Georgia, Moldova, and Ukraine through an affiliation with the Europarties. Applying the socialisation approach, there are two main research questions to be answered: *what are the incentives for the Europarties and the non-EU parties to cooperate with each other?* and *what impact does cooperation with the Europarties have on party development in Georgia, Moldova, and Ukraine?*

Looking at cooperation with the Europarties, the first research question aims to envisage the rationale that drives this cooperation. Applying both the "logic of consequences" and the "logic of appropriateness", the research examines the incentive structures of both the Europarties and the non-EU parties.

The second research question aims to shed some light on the causal mechanism of this puzzling cooperation and explain the "black box" of the Europarties' impact on party development. It aims to examine whether there is an impact and, if yes, to what extent cooperation with the Europarties impacts non-EU party development. The research is interested in identifying "the cogs and wheels" of cooperation that trigger the process of socialisation and transformational changes. The Europarties' impact is analysed in terms of ideological, organisational, and behavioural changes. Dealing with EU outsiders, the research is driven by looking at different faces of Europeanisation, not necessarily positive ones.

The main implications of this contribution are to analyse whether this cooperation leads to transformations in party-building and whether these reforms lead to transformations on the party system level. The decrease in ideological polarisation, increase in organisational capacity, and stability of inter-party relationships might spill over into the party system level and lead to its stabilisation, consolidation, and democratisation. In this way, the research aims to contribute to the nascent studies of Europeanisation beyond Europe and to conduct systematic cross-country, cross-partisan, and cross-dimensional comparisons of the Europarties' influence on domestic parties outside of the EU.

Europeanisation of party politics: locating the research

In a broader context, this research is deeply embedded in the realm of democracy promotion and particularly into the field of international party assistance.[8] The point of departure of this research is, however, the Europeanisation of party politics. In his seminal work, Ladrech conceptualised a theoretical framework for the analysis of the Europeanisation of political parties.[9] The Europeanisation was defined through five dimensions, namely party programmes, organisational structure, patterns of party competition, party–government relations, and relations beyond the national party system. Following his analytical framework, various studies have examined some of those dimensions.[10]

Overall, the EU's direct impact on the format and mechanics of Western party systems was rather limited, as there was no effect on domestic party competition. The explanation for this insignificant impact is rooted in the underdeveloped character of the European

---

8   See, for example, Peter Burnell, "Democracy Assistance: Origins and Organizations," in *Democracy Assistance: International Cooperation for Democratization*, ed. P. Burnell (London: Frank Cass, 2000), 34–66; Peter Burnell, "Promoting Democracy Backwards," *FRIDE Working Paper* 28, 2006; Thomas Carothers, *Aiding Democracy Abroad: The Learning Curve* (Washington, DC: Carnegie Endowment for International Peace, 1996); Thomas Carothers, *Confronting the Weakest Link: Aiding Political Parties in New Democracies* (Washington, DC: Carnegie Endowment for International Peace, 2006), Thomas Carothers, "Examining Political Party Aid," in *Globalising Democracy*, ed. P. Burnell (London: Routledge Publishers, 2006); Thomas Carothers, "Democracy Support and Development Aid: The Elusive Synthesis," *Journal of Democracy* 21:4 (2010).

9   Robert Ladrech, "Europeanization and Political Parties: Towards a Framework of Analysis," *Party Politics* 8:4 (2002).

10 See, for example, Thomas Poguntke et al., "Europeanisation of National Party Organisations: A Conceptual Analysis," *European Journal of Political Research* 46:6 (2007): 20; Paul Pennings, "An Empirical Analysis of the Europeanization of National Party Manifestos, 1960–2003," *European Union Politics* 7:2 (2008); Alex Szczerbiak and Paul Taggart (Eds.), *Opposing Europe? The Comparative Party Politics of Euroscepticism* (Oxford: Oxford University Press, 2008).

party system. The European-level elections still remain second-order elections, with blurred and weak party competition that prevents the spill-over effect into the national arena.[11] Moreover, national party systems operate as gatekeepers and define electoral agendas. Finally, the national and European political arenas are strictly divided along policy issues. While national politics seems to be the arena for contestation over European issues, European politics is becoming a playground for day-to-day decision-making.[12]

Focusing on CEE and Balkan countries, a series of studies were conducted, analysing the Europeanisation of party politics, including the influence of the Europarties on their member parties. The findings vary, depending on the assessment of the degree of Europeanisation. While some studies find a substantial impact on domestic party politics, other literature claims EU influences had no impact. The first strand of literature establishes that domestic party politics underwent significant changes under the EU impact. Thus, in his pivotal study, Pridham finds the evidence of the impact on CEE party systems after cooperation with transnational party federations. Aspiring to join the EU, unsettled CEE party systems were exposed to systemic pressure and underwent transformations on different levels such as "identity and ideology, programme, organisation, electoral politics and personnel".[13] Cooperation with transnational actors had several observable results. Firstly, cooperating with "standard" parties only, a line of demarcation was drawn by the Europarties to exclude extremist and nationalist parties. As a result, it led to standardisation of the CEE political spectrum. Secondly, lacking experience and self-confidence, the European links helped CEE parties build up political and electoral experience by boosting the party elites' confidence. Finally, cooperation

---

11 Mair, "The Limited Impact," 27–28.
12 Ibid., 45–46.
13 Pridham, "Patterns of Europeanization and Transnational Party Cooperation," 7.

was employed by non-EU parties as an unofficial channel for networking to speed up the EU accession process.[14]

In the same vein, Delsoldato argued that transnational party cooperation influenced EU candidate countries' parties. The Europarties impacted post-communist parties by transferring their own models of organisation, action, and thinking.[15] Moreover, the Europarties operated as interlocutors between domestic and European levels to build personal trust. However, due to the lack of knowledge about post-communist parties, the process of affiliation quickly started to turn into a superficial affiliation rather than a close ideological match in which the larger parties were easily recognised.[16] Dakowska's research corroborated the abovementioned observations. It found out that, driven by rational calculations, CEE parties opted for the larger and more powerful Europarties in order to achieve international recognition, domestic legitimacy, and social proof. On the other hand, facing the realities of a post-communist landscape, the Europarties lowered their expectations for close ideological matches and favoured the admission of stronger parties in order to improve their bargaining power once the enlargement was finalised.[17] The German party foundations played a crucial role in the intermediation, socialisation, and persuasion of post-communist parties. Operating as "norm entrepreneurs", they proved to be the channels for transmitting norms, values, and political contacts to CEE countries. Nevertheless, although some CEE parties adopted general discourses of European values, norm transfer via the Europarties proved to be rather intricate.[18]

Similarly, Lewis detected particular transformations in government coalitions, party-system structure, and party organisations. In line with Pridham, he observed a tendency towards the marginalisation of radical parties and its subsequent moderation in CEE countries, resulting in the changes in coalition formats. The

---

14   Pridham, "Patterns of Europeanization and Transnational Party Cooperation," 14.
15   Delsoldato, "Eastward Enlargement," 277.
16   Ibid., 281.
17   Dakowska, "Beyond Conditionality," 284.
18   Ibid., 288, 290.

mainstream parties tended to exclude extremist parties from the coalition-building process. In particular, the Slovak case was the most illustrative, when the Party of European Socialists (PES) used its leverage to affect the coalition format by excluding extremist and EU-noncompatible "Movement for a Democratic Slovakia" (HZDS) from their family. The HZDS underwent significant changes to be considered compatible for the PES again. Although it is difficult to identify any profound impact on the consolidation of CEE party systems, as a result of the EU's adaptive pressure, domestic parties became limited in their exploitation of populism. Secondly, the EU's impact on party ideology and party organisation found its evidence in terms of the introduction of gender quotas, adoption of the European party symbols and alternation of party names.[19]

Likewise, Spirova found evidence of the Europarties' impact on domestic electoral strategies in Bulgaria through the Europarties' encouragement of forging alliances and mergers. For example, the PES actively supported the creation of a new, leftist force — the Bulgarian European Left (BEL). However, observing how the BEL was gradually losing their popularity, the PES opted for the consolidation of Bulgarian social-democratic forces. The main driving force behind the engagement of the PES was electoral support rather than ideology. Due to the strong personalisation of Bulgarian party politics, the consolidation of left forces failed. In a similar case, the European People's Party (EPP) made an attempt to encourage the unification of the Bulgarian right, but also failed to achieve any success. In fact, the Europarties' encouragement for consolidation sometimes led to friction within the party, proving the Europarties' impact to be rather counterproductive.[20]

In contrast, some studies in CEE countries found that Europeanisation had little to no impact on party systems. Thus, Szczerbiak and Bil established very little evidence of EU impact on the Polish

---

19   Lewis, "Changes in the Party Politics," 158–159.
20   Spirova, "Europarties and Party," 802.

party system due to the domestic factors.[21] In a similar vein, Haughton *et al.* detected limited impact on party organisations and programmes in CEE countries after the accession. In fact, CEE parties used the links with the European level as a "badge of approval" to enhance their significance and standing for the domestic electorate.[22] Examining the role of the PES in shaping social democracy in CEE countries, Holmes and Lightfoot established "very little evidence of any impact".[23] The evidence of genuine ideological and behavioural change was absent, whereas the level of internalisation was shallow without any degree of reflection. CEE parties used the PES affiliation as an external validation of their distinction from unreformed post-communist parties and therefore indulged in role-playing.[24]

In the non-EU member states, cooperation with the Europarties has drawn very little attention and up until now was investigated based on a single case study. The first scholarly study of the Europarties' influence on non-EU parties was conducted by Timus.[25] Focusing on Ukraine, Timus investigated the affiliation of Ukrainian parties with the EPP. The main focus was on the admission process and the ideological match between the Europarty and its Ukrainian sister parties. The main findings revealed strategic incentives for cooperation, emanating from both the Europarty and

---

21 Alex Szczerbiak and Monika Bil, "When in Doubt, (re-) Turn to Domestic Politics? The (non-) Impact of the EU on Party Politics in Poland," *SEI Working Paper* No 103, *EPERN Working Paper* No 20 (2008): 8.
22 Tim Haughton, "Driver, Conductor or Fellow Passenger? EU Membership and Party Politics in Central and Eastern Europe," *Journal of Communist Studies and Transition Politics* 25:4 (2009): 421–423.
23 Michael Holmes and Simon Lightfoot, "Limited Influence? The Role of the Party of European Socialists in Shaping Social Democracy in Central and Eastern Europe," *Government and Opposition* 46:1 (2011): 54.
24 Holmes and Lightfoot, "Limited Influence," 42, 46.
25 Natalia Timus, "Coming Closer to Europe: Transnational Cooperation between EPFs and Post-Soviet Parties," *GARNET Working Paper* No 72/09, November 2009; Natalia Timus, "Transnational Party Europeanization: EPP and Ukrainian Parties," *Acta Politica* 49:1 (2014).

domestic parties. While in domestic arena, parties used engagement with the Europarties for domestic legitimacy and international recognition, for the Europarties the cooperation represented an opportunity to strengthen their positions in the neighbourhood.[26]

Only recently has there been an attempt to elaborate a comparative framework to investigate the activity of the Europarties regarding party-building in CEE democracies.[27] When examining transnational party activity, it is important to integrate such aspects as the complementary activity of the internationals and party foundations, bilateral links between the EU parties and individual parties within the Europarties, the ongoing process of democratisation and consolidation of party systems, the European integration process, and the EU's own democratic conditionality.[28]

Significance of the research

The review of previous studies points out existing research gaps within the Europeanisation studies. Whereas the abovementioned contributions are limited to a single case study, this research, in contrast, is driven by a comparative approach. It pursues the conduction of a systematic analysis of the Europarties' impact beyond the EU from cross-national, cross-partisan, and cross-dimensional perspectives. Aiming to increase the generalisability of the findings, the research includes Georgia, Moldova, and Ukraine in the analysis to establish any cross-regional patterns and similarities. Secondly, to increase the scope of analysis, the research encompasses all mainstream Europarties and relevant domestic parties. By including both strong and weak Europarties and domestic parties, the research aims at party variation in political weight. On the one hand, this allows an examination of whether there is a difference between

---

26 Timus, "Coming Closer".
27 See, for example, Benjamin von dem Berge and Thomas Poguntke, "The Influence of Europarties on Central and Eastern European Partner Parties: A Theoretical and Analytical Model," *European Political Science Review* 5:2 (2013).
28 Geoffrey Pridham, "Comparative Perspectives on Transnational Party-Building in New Democracies: The Case of Central and Eastern Europe," *Acta Politica* 49:1 (2014): 32–37.

stronger and weaker Europarties in establishing cooperation and in their potential to influence non-EU parties. On the other hand, incorporating strong and weak domestic parties allows the analysis of whether there are some commonalities in their incentive structures and whether there is a difference in susceptibility to the Europarties' impact. Finally, the examination of the Europarties' impact on three dimensions is inclusive and encompasses party development from its main standpoints: identity and party ideology, organisational structure, and inter-party relationships. This kind of research design allows comparisons of the significance of ideological, organisational, and behavioural changes both within and across parties, and across countries.

Given the extensive fieldwork data, the main contribution of the research is first-hand insights into the motives driving cooperation and into the precise mechanism of the admission of non-EU parties. Having international party assistance as a control variable, the research aims to single out the Europarties' net impact on non-EU party development. Rooted in domestic politics, the cases reveal publicly inaccessible storylines behind each party's cooperation and the factors that informally influence it. Extending beyond the party level, the research pursues the analysis of whether the Europarties' influence contributes to the standardisation, consolidation, and democratisation of party systems in Eastern Europe. Last but not least, considering constant party system instability in East Europe, the research indirectly uncovers the effectiveness and sustainability of the Europarties' engagement and points out the potential shortcomings and limitations of the Europarties' activities in the region.

Itinerary of the book

Chapter 2 describes the theoretical and conceptual frameworks of the research. In particular, it starts with the concepts of socialisation and norm diffusion and continues with the introduction of the explanatory model of the Europarties' impact on party development and its scope conditions that may trigger socialisation. The second half of the chapter engages with the methodology, operationalisation and data gathering.

Chapter 3 explains the historical context and institutional development of both the Europarties and the non-EU parties. The first part of the chapter introduces the historical and institutional development of the Europarties, their functions and organisational structure. The second part focuses on the particularities of party development in post-communist countries. It starts with a discussion of different cleavage structures, public distrust, and high electoral volatility and continues with the excessive personalisation of party politics, and the lack of internal party democracy.

Chapter 4 highlights the selection and application process for the non-EU parties. Based on the EPP example, the chapter sheds some light on the formal steps of application and, more importantly, identifies the informal factors which influence the chances of being accepted into the Europarty. This chapter will help to understand how the Europarties find their potential partners and which criteria they use to identify a proper match.

Chapter 5 examines the motivational structures of both the Europarties and the non-EU parties which trigger cooperation between them. This chapter constitutes a crucial part of the analysis, as it touches upon the core of the puzzling phenomenon of cooperation: why do the Europarties and the non-EU parties cooperate with each other if tangible rewards are absent? It identifies a set of motives for both Europarties and non-EU parties and illustrates it in practice by analysing each case of cooperation in greater detail.

Chapter 6 assesses the ideological match between the Europarties' and the non-EU parties' profiles. Firstly, the chapter identifies the Europarties' fundamental ideological principles. Secondly, using this "ideological checklist", the ideological congruence between the Europarties and their sister parties is measured on economic, social, and European dimensions. It aims to evaluate to what extent the affiliated non-EU parties fit into their chosen European party families.

Chapter 7 focuses on the organisational approximation between the Europarties and the non-EU parties. It estimates the degree of organisational changes the non-EU mother parties and its youth and women's branches introduced after cooperation the Europarties. The evaluation of the impact is examined in terms of changes in internal decision-making, transfer of know-how, promotion of youth to the mother party, introduction of gender quotas on the electoral lists, and female political empowerment.

Chapter 8 examines the behavioural changes of the non-EU parties after cooperation, particularly analysing the cases of cooperation between domestic sister parties. It aims to assess to what extent the Europarties' endorsement of cooperation influenced the non-EU parties' behaviour and led to coalition-building, government formation, or party mergers.

Chapter 9 summarises the key findings revealed from the analysis of cooperation. Moreover, it draws a systematic comparative analysis from cross- and within-dimensional, cross-partisan, and cross-national perspectives. It analyses which dimension — ideological, organisational or behavioural — proved to be the most susceptible to the Europarties' norms and values, which parties — strong or weak — proved to be the most successful in implementing changes and which country — Georgia, Moldova or Ukraine — proved to be the most influenced by the cooperation with the Europarties. Subsequently, it discusses the implications on the party system level and reflects on the implications for the Europarties.

2. Research Framework

Inspired by the appeal of "going empirical", this research aims to depart from a traditional "rationalist-constructivist" divide and to move further, by offering a fine-grained explanation of the puzzling phenomena of cooperation between Europarties and non-EU parties. Bridging both approaches, this research is interested in revealing why actors are willing to undergo the costly process of adaptation and how actors internalise new norms. It is interested in portraying the "cogs and wheels" of the causal mechanism of socialisation and in defining the scope conditions stipulating the internalisation.

Combining both rationalist and constructivist logics to party politics, this research focuses on the driving forces behind domestic change as the result of cooperation between Europarties and non-EU parties. Why do political parties decide to comply with norms and implement changes? Is domestic change driven by parties' noble beliefs or by their pragmatic power tactics? How does norm diffusion occur, and under what conditions does it penetrate the domestic level? These questions can be addressed from both rational and normative perspectives, emphasising a "logic of consequences" and a "logic of appropriateness" in the process of Europeanisation.

2.1 Theoretical Framework: Socialisation and Norm Diffusion

According to Checkel, socialisation is "the process of inducting new actors into the norms, rules, and way of behaviour of a given community".[29] As members of a certain community, actors share an identity, beliefs, values, and norms, which spread through the socialisation mechanism and thus impose certain expectations on ac-

---

[29] Jeffrey T. Checkel, "International Institutions and Socialization in Europe: Introduction and Framework," *International Organization* 59:4 (2005): 804.

tors' behavioural patterns. This definition implies an uneven "master-novice" relationship, where newcomers become integrated into an established group and change their behaviour in line with the group's rules through social interaction.[30] As Johnston put it succinctly, "socialization is aimed at creating membership of a society where the intersubjective understandings of the society become taken for granted".[31] As a result, socialisation enables conformity to norms and its internalisation.

Socialisation facilitates norm diffusion. For new norms to be fully institutionalised and internalised, the whole "lifecycle" must take place, which includes three stages: "norm emergence", "norm cascade" and internalisation.[32] The first stage occurs when an established set of norms faces a destabilising shock that undermines the legitimacy of the norms. Confronted with a new si-tuation, the old set of norms fails to offer a satisfying solution to new challenges and problems. This leads to an "ideational vacuum", in which actors are no longer satisfied with the status quo and start looking for a new set of norms that will solve the uncomfortable situation.[33]

The second stage begins once the set of norms is selected. At the "norm cascade" stage, the norm entrepreneurs try to convince the actors to comply with their rules and practices through arguing or persuasion. In fact, this stage is characterised by an active phase of socialisation when the norm leaders are trying to induct actors into their system of values. The "norm cascade" occurs under certain circumstances that trigger the norm adoption by actors. The conditions vary depending on the situation but encompass features of

---

30   Trine Flockhart, "Masters and Novices: Socialization and Social Learning through NATO Parliamentary Assembly," *International Relations* 18 (2004): 366.
31   Alistair Johnston, "Treating International Institutions as Social Environments," *International Studies Quarterly* 45 (2001): 494.
32   Martha Finnemore and Kathryn Sikkink, "International Norm Dynamics and Political Change," *International Organization* 52:4 (1998).
33   Flockhart, "Masters and Novices," 362.

institutional design, properties of the actors to be socialised, and properties of the socialising actors.[34]

Finally, at the last stage, actors internalise new norms and perform them on a habitual basis. New norms are taken for granted and are no longer subjected to a public debate. As a result, norms are viewed as right, appropriate, and intersubjective.

The intricate process of socialisation requires the analysis of the microfoundations which, in turn, predetermines the sustainability of internalisation. The shift from a "logic of consequences" to a "logic of appropriateness" might be triggerred by two microprocesses — persuasion or social influence.[35]

Persuasion is an idealistic form of internalisation when newcomers ge-nuinely change their beliefs and attitudes, resulting in "deep" socialisation and sustainable change of behaviour. This type of microprocess leads to a genuine attitude change through high intensity cognition, reflection, or argument.[36]

In contrast to persuasion, social influence triggers "pro-norm behaviour through the distribution of social rewards and punishments".[37] The social-influence method employs a variety of rewards, including psychological well-being, increased status, and a sense of belonging, achieved through confor-mity with role expectations. Punishments, on the other hand, might include shaming, exclusion, demeaning, or cognitive dissonance derived from inconsistent behaviour vis-à-vis the new role and identity.[38]

Described as "public conformity without private acceptance", social influence underlines an unfinished process of internalisation,

---

34 Michael Zürn and Jeffrey T. Checkel, "Getting Socialized to Build Bridges: Constructivism and Rationalism, Europe and the Nation-State," *International Organization* 59:4 (2005): 1050.
35 Flockhart, "Masters and Novices," 366.
36 Johnston, "Treating International Institutions as Social Environments," 498.
37 Ibid., 499.
38 Ibid., 499.

in which the actor does not internalise new rules and norms, but alters its behaviour due to group pressure.[39] Of crucial importance in the microprocess of social influence are the maximisation of status, honour, and prestige, and the desire to avoid losing reputation and public image through humiliation and shaming. The desire to maximise reputational attributes converts the status into an instrument. The membership in a high-status group unleashes leverage over the actor's attitude. Pursuing self-esteem, actors comply with norms, as they want others to think well of them and they want to think well of themselves.[40]

Depending on the microprocesses underlying the socialisation, internalisation might result in strategic calculation, role adoption, or normative suasion. Having its roots in rationalist theory, strategic calculation takes place when the promised rewards are expected to be greater than the cost of compliance.[41] In contrast to pure instrumental rationality, "strategic social construction" argues that despite the actors' desire to maximise their utility, they might move from behavioural adaptation to a sustained compliance, reflecting the normative commitments of the norm-promoting agency. Embedded in organisational theory and cognitive psychology, role-playing occurs when actors change their beliefs and actions to appear to comply with the norm-promoting agency's requirements. The shift from a "logic of consequences" towards a "logic of appropriateness" commences in role-playing, but lacks any reflective internalisation.[42] Finally, normative suasion indicates complete internalisation. It takes place when actors "actively and reflectively internalise new understandings of appropriateness".[43] The normative suasion excludes a rational cost-benefit calculus.

---

39 F. J. Booster, "Commentary on Compliance-gaining Message Behavior Research," in *Communication and Social Influence Processes,* ed. C. R. Berger and M. Burgoon (East Lasting: Michigan State University Press, 1995), 96.
40 Finnemore and Sikkink, "International Norm Dynamics and Political Change," 903.
41 Ibid., 903.
42 Checkel, "International Institutions and Socialization in Europe," 809–810.
43 Ibid., 812.

Through arguing and persuasion, a new set of rules is taken for granted and is no longer a matter of public discussion.[44]

2.2 Explanatory Model

Operating as sites of socialisation, the Europarties can be considered "epistemic communities" that provide expertise knowledge in a voluntary manner.[45] Being in a "group with a common style of thinking", domestic actors are socialised in line with European beliefs, values, and practices, and on the other hand, are exposed to peer pressure to comply with their normative commitments.[46] Through mutual events and activities, inter-elite socialisation triggers the mechanism of "norm cascade" and facilitates the penetration into the domestic arena (Figure 2.1).

---

44 Checkel, "International Institutions and Socialization in Europe," 813.
45 Ernst Haas, "Introduction: Epistemic Communities and International Policy Coordination," *International Organization* 46:1 (1992).
46 Haas, "Introduction," 3.

Figure 2.1 The mechanism of the Europarties' impact on the non-EU parties

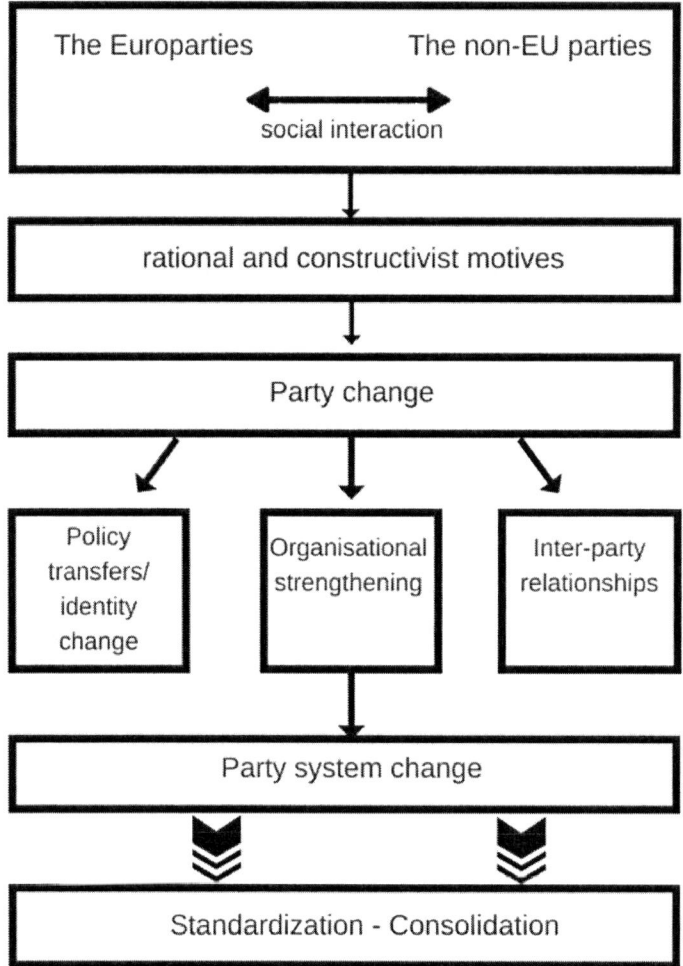

The socialisation of the non-EU parties is facilitated through certain environmental features of European and domestic levels. The precondition for cooperation between the Europarties and the non-EU parties lies in the ideational vacuum caused by an exogenous shock. Being recently established, post-communist parties are immature and undeveloped in party-building. Having only experienced the rule of the single communist party, the European party-building is a novel and uncertain domain for them. With no long historical records, post-communist parties are still undergoing the process of identification and possess few ingrained beliefs and values. Moreover, due to the historical absence of a pluralist system, the beliefs and practices of post-communist parties vary significantly from those of the European ones. Looking for the European experience and its knowledge, the non-EU parties turn to the Europarties, which they perceive as being authoritative and prestigious. After the cooperation is established, the Europarties organise mutual workshops and trainings, through which the non-EU parties become engaged in a social learning process in a deliberative manner. Operating outside the mainstream of European politics, the Europarties deliver their knowledge and expertise in less politicised and insulated settings.

Scope conditions

What factors are conducive to successful socialisation, which in turn leads to further transformations on ideological, organisational, and behavioural dimensions? This study argues that socialisation via cooperation with Europarties is triggered by scope conditions such as the length and intensity of contact, party position, and motivations.

As socialisation does not happen overnight, the time factor is important to consider in evaluating the Europarties' impact. As a long-lasting process, both the duration and intensity of the contact are necessary conditions for socialisation.[47] The party position — strong or weak — influences the bargaining process vis-à-vis the Europarties and their willingness to embark on transformations. The parties with a strong position are likely to have better stakes than the parties with a weak position in the application process. As desirable partners, strong parties thus have better leverage against the Europarty's decision in the admission procedures. Finally, the set of

---

47   Jan Beyers, "Multiple Embeddedness and Socialization in Europe: The Case of Council Officials Authors," *International Organization* 59:4 (2005), 911.

motivations for establishing cooperation is crucial. Driven by ideational motives, parties seek to oblige to the rules and practices of the Europarties as they find this behaviour appropriate.

Hypotheses

The effect of the abovementioned scope conditions has different effects on ideological, organisational, and behavioural dimensions.

Ideological dimension

On the ideological dimension, the time factor is expected to have a positive effect on the ideological congruence over the course of the affiliation. The changes are expected to be driven not merely by lengthy contact, but rather by the quality of the contact.[48] Frequent and intense contacts with the Europarties contribute to full embeddedness of the domestic parties into the Europarty's norms and practices:

> H1: The longer and the more intensely an observer party cooperates with the Europarty, the closer the ideological match is expected.

With regard to the party position, strong parties—which are usually government and/or catch-all parties—are expected to be less congruent with the Europarty, as their ideological profile aims to encompass broader social groups. In turn, weak parties—which are usually opposition and/or minor parties—are expected to have a closer fit with the Europarty, as their ideological profiles are more consolidated:

> H2: Weak political parties are expected to have a better ideological match vis-à-vis the Europarty than strong political parties.

Finally, the motivation factor behind the affiliation is expected to have an impact on the congruence. Depending on the incentive structure, the ideological match is likely to be closer when the non-EU parties join the Europarties due to their convictions and beliefs.

---

48 Jeffrey T. Checkel, "'Going Native' in Europe?: Theorizing Social Interaction in European Institutions," *Comparative Political Studies* 36:1/2 (2003), 210.

In contrast, the predominance of rational considerations is expected to lead to lower congruence between the party profiles:

> H3: Parties with ideational motives are likely to have a better ideological match with the Europarties than parties with strategic motives.

Organisational Dimension

Looking at the various factors that might impact the organisational compatibility, the time factor is expected to positively influence the non-EU party structures:

> H4: The longer and more intense the cooperation between the Europarty and an observer party, the more structural adjustments are expected to be implemented.

Depending on the party's position, strong parties are expected to be structurally more compatible with the Europarties. Because they have more resources, strong parties have more opportunities to better develop their party structures and to implement structural changes following the Europarties' template, respectively:[49]

> H5: Strong parties are likely to implement more structural adjustments than weak parties.

In a similar vein to the ideological dimension, ideational motives for cooperation are expected to have a positive impact on organisational compatibility. Genuine motivations for cooperation are likely to trigger more borrowing of practices in the European party-building:

> H6: Parties with ideational motives are likely to implement more structural changes than parties with strategic motives.

Behavioural Dimension

On the behavioural dimension, the time factor is likely to have a positive impact on parties' readiness to cooperate with each other. The long-standing sister parties are expected to cooperate with each

---

[49] James G. March and Johan P. Olsen, "The Logic of Appropriateness," *ARENA Working Paper* 04/09, Center for European Studies, University of Oslo (2009): 21.

other more willingly, in comparison to those parties that only recently joined the Europarties:

> H7: The longer sister parties have been affiliated and the more intense their cooperation with the Europarties, the closer the relationships between sister parties.

In the affiliation process, different party types have different forms of leverage vis-à-vis the Europarties, which might potentially influence the Europarties' decision to accept another sister party and consequentially affect sister parties' willingness to cooperate. Two effects on the inter-party relationships are expected, depending on the party's position as strong or weak. Strong parties usually have more leverage on the Europarties' decision in the application process and might influence the Europarties' admission of another sister party. As viable and credible political forces, strong parties obviously enjoy stronger interest from the Europarties, which puts them in a better negotiating position vis-à-vis the Europarties:[50]

> H8: Strong parties are likely to block the admission of another sister party if they disapprove of it.

On the other hand, cooperation tends to occur between strong and weak sister parties rather than between two strong parties. In cooperation between strong and weak parties, both parties profit by supporting each other. By forging cooperation with weak parties, strong parties can profit from staying in power, whereas weak parties can win from international recognition domestically. In contrast, cooperation between strong parties is likely to lead to rivalry, as both parties target the same electoral field and compete for unique relationships with the Europarty:

> H9: Cooperation is likely to happen between strong and weak parties rather than between two strong parties.

Finally, the set of motivations that the non-EU parties considered in the wake of establishing cooperation is crucial for assessing the

---

50 von dem Berge and Poguntke, "The influence of Europarties on Central and Eastern European partner parties," 324.

impact of cooperation on the inter-party relationship. Parties with ideational considerations perceive the Europarties' calls for cooperation with other sister parties as expected and rightful behaviour:

> H10: Parties with ideational motives are likely to cooperate willingly with other sister parties than parties with strategic motives.

2.3 Case Selection and Methodology

The selection of case studies follows a two-step approach. On the country level, the selection is based on the "most-similar-systems" design.[51] Having high aspirations to joining the EU, Georgia, Moldova, and Ukraine, share historical, economic, sociological, and political commonalities what enables to compare them in terms of cause-and-effect mechanisms while omitting country-specific conditions.

In the second step, the level of analysis descends to political parties and concentrates on the Europarties and the national parties in Georgia, Moldova, and Ukraine. The unit of analysis is the established affiliations between the Europarties and their non-EU sister parties. It encompasses the affiliations with the European People's Party (EPP), the Party of European Socialists (PES), the Alliance of Liberals and Democrats for Europe Party (ALDE, the former ELDR), the European Left (EL), and the Alliance of European Conservatives and Reformists (AECR). Aiming at the variation on the independent variable, the research design strives to include cases with various scope conditions—parties that have long-standing affiliation with the Europarties and those which recently joined, parties with high and low intensity of activities, parties with strong and weak positions and parties with rational and ideational motives (Table 2.1).

The timeline of the study is case-specific and is defined for each party individually. Altogether the study covers the time interval of 2004–2015. The timeline for each case of cooperation follows

---

51 Adam Przeworski and Henry Teune, *The Logic of Comparative Social Inquiry* (New York: Wiley-Interscience, 1980).

the logic of the three-stage process—interaction, cooperation, integration.[52] The starting point is the first informal contacts between the Europarty and the non-EU party, when each party identifies possible partners for cooperation. At the second stage, the formal application process is under review and the Europarty evaluates "the goodness of fit" with an applicant party. The endpoint of the study—the third stage—is when the non-EU party is granted observer status or full membership and is completely integrated into the Europarty family.

---

52   Oskar Niedermayer, *Europäische Parteien? Zur grenzüberschreitenden Interaktion politischer Parteien im Rahmen der Europäischen Gemeinschaft* (Frankfurt: Campus, 1983).

Table 2.1 Operationalisation of scope conditions

The Europarty	The non-EU parties	Length of contact (2004–2015)	Intensity of contact	Party position
EPP	People's Union "Our Ukraine" (UA)	9 years (2005–2013)	Low	Strong (2004–2008), weak (2008–2013)
EPP	The *Batkivshchyna* party (UA)	8 years (since 2008)	High	Strong
EPP	People's Movement of Ukraine *Rukh* (UA)	11 years (since 2005)	High	Weak
EPP	United National Movement (GE)	8 years (since 2008)	High	Strong
EPP	New Rights Party (GE)	Pending application since 2003	----	Weak
EPP	Liberal Democratic Party (MD)	5 years (since 2011)	High	Strong
EPP	Christian Democratic People's Party (MD)	8 years (2005–2012)	Low	Weak
PES	Democratic Party (MD)	6 years (since 2010)	Low	Strong
ALDE	Republican Party (GE)	9 years (since 2007)	High	Weak
ALDE	Our Georgia-Free Democrats (GE)	5 years (since 2011)	Low	Weak
ALDE	Liberal Party (MD)	6 years (since 2010)	High	Weak
AECR	Christian-Democratic Movement (GE)	4 years (since 2012)	Low	Weak
EL	Party of Communists (MD)	9 years (since 2007)	High	Strong

Note: GE – Georgia, MD – Moldova, UA – Ukraine.
Source: Author's own compilation based on the interviews and desk research.

The comparative case study and process-tracing are the main research methods for hypotheses-testing. The comparative case study method is justified due to the underexplored area of the Europarties and their affiliation with the non-EU parties, which helps to uncover the "black box" of the causal mechanisms. In a rapidly changing environment, particularly in the post-Soviet countries, case study research design allows for flexibility and adaptation. Process-tracing was employed to reveal the motivations that nudged both actors to cooperation and to identify conducive factors for the impact of socialisation to happen. This research utilised explaining-outcome process-tracing, focusing on puzzling historical outcomes.[53] To supplement this set of methods, a counterfactual analysis was added to the research's tool kit. The counterfactual analysis helpfully reinforces the causal explanation in two respects. First, the logic of counterfactual analysis helps to isolate the impact of cooperation with the Europarties from other exogenous factors, i.e., other international institutions involved in party assistance such as the Organisation for Security and Cooperation in Europe (OSCE), the Council of Europe, the National Democratic Institute (NDI), the International Republican Institute (IRI), and the Netherlands Institute for Multiparty Democracy (NIMD). Secondly, by including the cases with non-X — parties with no cooperation with the Europarties, it aims to explore whether the ideological, organisational, and behavioural development of those parties that are not engaged with the Europarties is similar to that of those that are affiliated with them. As it might be an effect of general democratic party development that is not inherent to the Europarties, this counterfactual argumentation helps to avoid overdetermination of the impact of cooperation on party development.

2.4 Operationalisation

In order to evaluate the impact of cooperation on domestic party development, the process of operationalisation is divided into two

---

53 Derek Beach and Rasmus B. Pedersen, *Process-tracing Methods: Foundations and Guidelines* (Ann Arbor: The University of Michigan Press, 2013), 11.

steps. Examining the incentive structure for cooperation, the first stage of research is concentrated on answering the "why" question. The set of motives is captured through elite interviews with party officials from the Europarties and domestic parties. In the second stage, the research dwells on investigating the "how" question. For this purpose, the independent and dependent variables as well as the scope conditions are operationalised as follows (Table 2.2):

Table 2.2   Operationalisation of dependent variable

Dependent Variable	Indicators	Sources
Ideological changes	- congruence of party profiles; - incorporation of Europarties' norms and values into party manifestos; - party identity change	The Europarties' core documents; party documents of domestic parties; elite and expert interviews; media coverage
Organisational changes	- references to the affiliation with Europarties in party statutes; - changes in the mechanism of internal party democracy; - participation of youth in decision-making; - introduction of gender quotas on electoral lists	Elite and expert interviews; party statutes; reports on capacity-building and organisational strengthening
Behavioural changes	- inter-party cooperation (e.g. government formation, coalition-building, party mergers, etc.)	Elite and expert interviews; media coverage; reports on coalition-building and/or multiparty dialogue

Ideological changes

Ideological changes can be operationalised, first of all, through the congruence of party profiles.[54] The application of the ideological checklist aims to show "the goodness of fit" on fundamental principles between the sister party and its chosen European party family. While the Europarties' core principles will be derived from their core ideological documents, the domestic parties' fundamental

---

54   Vit Hloušek and Lubomir Kopeček, *Origin, Ideology and Transformation of Political Parties: East Central and Western Europe Compared* (Surrey: Ashgate Publishing, 2010).

principles will be captured via party documents, expert interviews, and media coverage. The triangulation of the sources aims to capture "real" profiles of domestic parties as opposed to the merely formal inclusion of the Europarties' core principles. Another type of evidence for ideological change is the incorporation of the Europarties' norms and values into domestic party manifestos. Finally, modifications of a party's name and symbols as well as changes to the party identity are considered another indicator of the Europarties' impact on the ideological dimension.

Organisational changes

Organisational changes are captured through the analysis of internal party structure. Firstly, the structural embeddedness of domestic parties' branches into the Europarties' organisational fabric is examined, i.e. affiliation with the Europarties' youth and women´s branches and other associations. Secondly, the organisational structure of the mother party is analysed with regard to whether it includes references to its affiliation in the party statutes, introduces procedural changes into the internal decision-making processes, and transfer of expertise and knowledge. Thirdly, the structural changes in youth and women's branches after the cooperation with the Europarties' youth and women's associations are analysed. The changes in the youth branch's position vis-à-vis the mother party in internal decision-making processes and examples of youth being promoted to the mother party are examined. Similarly, evidence of organisational changes is tracked in the women's branches. It examines whether domestic women's branches introduced gender quotas on the candidate lists or enhanced the gender balance through the political empowerment of women in parliament and the government.[55]

---

[55] Since the aim of organisational dimension is to examine the embeddednes of observer parties in the Europarties' organisational structures, youth and women's branches were added to capture the organisational match of affiliation. Youth and women's branches were not included into ideological and be-

Behavioural changes

On the behavioural dimension, the relationships between sister parties and the inter-party relationships across the European party families are in the focus. Endorsing cooperation between like-minded parties, the Europarties aim to consolidate democratic and pro-European domestic forces. The forms of cooperation between the sister parties vary, ranging from government formation, coalition-building, the formation of an electoral block, the nomination of a single presidential/parliamentary candidate to party mergers between sister parties. Secondly, the analysis of inter-sister party relationships across the Europarties is undertaken. Of particular interest is the inter-party cooperation within the Moldovan "Alliance for European Integration", whose three coalition partners were all affiliated with the Europarties and the Georgian inter-party conflict between the EPP-affiliated United National Movement (UNM) and the Georgian Dream.

2.5 Data Collection

Data collection was gathered primarily via semi-structured interviews with European and domestic party elites. Altogether, eighty interviews were conducted in Belgium (Brussels), Ukraine (Kyiv and Donetsk), Georgia (Tbilisi), Moldova (Chisinau), Lithuania (Vilnius), Sweden (Stockholm), and the UK (London and Birmingham), covering the time span from October 2013 to July 2015.[56]

---

havioural dimensions, because of their underdevelopment. Due to weak institutionalisation, the inclusion of youth and women's branches into the analysis of ideological match and inter-party cooperation would be futile and shallow. The majority of youth and women's branches closely follow the mother party in ideological orientation and do not have separate programmatic documents as well as rarely have cooperation with respective branches of other parties.

56 The interviewees were selected based on their direct involvement in the process of affiliation or participation in the joint activities or the organisation of trainings and workshops on party development. On the European level, three potential groups of interviewees were selected: official representatives from the Europarties, party representatives from the youth and women's branches,

Other information comes from various types of party documents such as the core documents from both the Europarties and the domestic parties and evaluation reports from party foundations and different institutions for party assistance. Finally, the last source includes the media coverage by local and European newspapers, particularly focused on party statements and interviews with party representatives.

For each of these dimensions, the researcher combined those sources of information to analyse the Europarties' impact on the party development. The ideological level was mainly assessed by comparing Europarties' and domestic parties' documents, official reports, and the evaluation of trainings and workshops on programmatic development. In addition, interviews with academics and experts on ideological matching were used to corroborate the information. On the organisational level, the researcher relied on the interviews with party representatives, party statutes, official reports, evaluations of capacity-building programmes, and data from the party websites and international organisations. The analysis of the behavioural level was based on the interviews with both Europarty and domestic party representatives, official reports, evaluations of programmes for coalition-building and multiparty dialogue, and media coverage.

---

and representatives from the party foundations. Likewise, three groups of interviewees were targeted on the domestic level: party representatives from the central office — secretary generals and/or international secretaries, the representatives of the party foundations, and acade-mics and experts. In addition, as a part of counterfactual analysis, representatives from other institutions involved in party assistance were interviewed, such as the National Democratic Institute (NDI), the International Republican Institute (IRI), the Netherlands Institute for Multiparty Democracy (NIMD), and the Westminster Foundation for Democracy.

3. Understanding the Context of Cooperation

Currently, 15 recognised Europarties operate on the EU level. The most significant ones are the European People's Party (EPP), the Party of European Socialists (PES), the Alliance of Liberals and Democrats for Europe (ALDE, formerly ELDR), the European Green Party, the Party of the European Left (EL) and the Alliance of European Conservatives and Reformists (the AECR).

Recently, the European party federations have started gaining relevance among EU institutions. Turning from marginal into powerful political actors, they have developed into agents of EU norms and values promotion not only in Western Europe but also outside the EU. In the last decade, the Europarties increased their representation in Eastern Europe by establishing affiliations with like-minded parties. The EPP possesses the widest and strongest representation, through its cooperation whereby it currently cooperates with the Ukrainian *Batkivshchyna*, *Rukh*, UDAR, the Georgian UNM and the Moldovan Liberal Democratic Party (LDPM) parties. Until 2012 and 2013, respectively, the Christian Democratic People's Party and "Our Ukraine" were integrated in the EPP family as well. By comparison, the European Socialists and the European Liberals have weaker representation in the region. Due to difficulties in finding credible partners, the PES cooperates only with the Moldovan Democrats and very recently with the Georgian Dream, while the ALDE has established affiliations with the Georgian Republicans, the Moldovan Liberal Party, and the Ukrainian European party. Finally, the European Left has a strong communist partner in Moldova, and the Alliance for Conservatives and Reformists in Europe cooperate with a marginal right-wing party in Georgia — the Christian-Democratic Movement and Conservative Party.

Structurally, this chapter firstly analyses the evolution of the Europarties' institutionalisation in recent decades. The historical and institutional development sheds light on the Europarties' role and functions in the EU institutions and on the process of European integration. Moreover, it focuses on the Europarties' internal structures and their main organisational bodies. The second part of the chapter examines the particularities of post-Soviet party-building and its functioning, and identifies the discrepancies between Western and Eastern European parties. It provides a general overview of the party development in the post-communist countries, drawing commonalities inherent to political parties in Georgia, Moldova, and Ukraine.

3.1 Historical and Institutional Development of the Europarties

The European party federations or the Europarties are umbrella organisations comprising like-minded national parties and representing ideological alliances on the supranational level. Historically, the process of transnational party cooperation began in the 1950s, when the traditional Internationals were founded. Beginning in the 1970s, the process of politicisation changed the EU-wide transnational party cooperation in two ways. Firstly, the transnational cooperation of national parties started forming: the Confederations of Socialist Parties of the European Community (1974), the Federation of European Liberal and Democratic Parties in the European Community (1976) and the Federation of Christian Democratic Parties in the European Community (1976).[57] Secondly, the three-component structure of the Europarties became crystallised, with growing interlinkage between EP party groups, extra-parliamentary federations and national parties.[58]

Institutionally, the strengthening of the Europarties began with the devolution of powers to the EP and the European Council, in particular, with the empowerment of the EP. It was only after the

---

[57] Simon Hix and Christopher Lord, *Political Parties in the European Union* (Basingstoke: Palgrave Macmillan, 1997), 168.
[58] Geoffrey Pridham and Pippa Pridham, *Transnational Party Cooperation and European Integration: The Process towards Direct Elections* (Boston: George Allen & Unwin, 1981), 2.

introduction of direct elections to the EP in 1979 that the party federations gained institutional relevance in the EU structures. Though described as institutional catalysts, direct elections failed to transform the Europarties into viable political actors that interlinked national and supranational levels. Their role was reduced to that of clearing houses responsible for "providing information and campaign materials, and organising (poorly attended) conferences".[59] Moreover, the party federations failed to adopt detailed manifestos for European elections due to disagreements on programmatic principles. Instead, the introduction of the intergovernmental conferences triggered a new phase of party federation development. The institutionalisation of the Party Leaders' Meetings around the meetings in the European Council aimed to increase the Europarties' influence in the decision-making process. Although the number of party congresses decreased, the Party Leaders' Meetings evolved from ad hoc events to the party federations' official decision-making organ.[60]

The next institutional impetus was triggered by the Party Article (138a) of the Maastricht Treaty (1991). Initiated by EPP former leader Wilfried Martens, the Party Article was broadly supported by the Socialist and Liberal party federations.[61] Inspired by the Party Article 21 of the German Basic Law, the party federations were officially recognised as an important "factor for integration within the Union" in "forming a European awareness" and "expressing the political will of the citizens of the Union".[62] Although it gave a significant impulse for further development of the Europarties, the Party Article 138a was rather an "incomplete contract".[63] It was a mere declaration of principle without any juridical basis for its

---

59   Hix and Lord, *Political Parties in the European Union*, 169.
60   Ibid., 186.
61   Karl Magnus Johansson and Tapio Raunio, "Regulating Europarties: Cross-Party Coalitions Capitalizing on Incomplete Contracts," *Party Politics* 11:5 (2005): 522.
62   The Treaty of Maastricht, Article 138a.
63   Johansson and Raunio, "Regulating Europarties," 522.

funding. Similarly, the article failed to specify the Europarties' role in the European elections and nomination procedures.[64]

Acknowledging the declarative character of the Party Article, the Tsatsos Report reiterated the problem with absent legal and financial basis for the party federations' funding.[65] Likewise, the report from the Court of Auditors criticised the state of the party finance.[66] The situation in which no direct funding was allocated for the Europarties and in which the Europarties tended to rely on the EP party groups' budget was identified as illegal.[67] This gave a new momentum to solve the issue of party finance. The Treaty of Nice amended incomplete legislation and provided legal grounds for the Europarties' funding (Article 191).[68] Additionally, the Treaty introduced the co-decision-procedure—a qualified majority voting in the Council on issues of the Europarties. This amendment made passing the legislation on the Europarties easier, as previous decisions had been blocked by the unanimous voting requirement in the Council. As a result, the EP's position was strengthened to that of co-legislator.[69]

With the Treaty of Nice coming into force, Article 191 required operationalisation of its provision. The regulation of the Europarties was based on the Leinen Report, which specified legal and financial

---

64 Johansson and Raunio, "Regulating Europarties," 522.
65 Dimitris Tsatsos, "Bericht über die konstitutionelle Stellung der Europäischen Politischen Parteien," *European Parliament Institutional Affairs Committee Report* No. A4-0342/96 (10 December 1996).
66 Court of Auditors Special Report No. 13/2000, OJ C181/1 (28 June 2000).
67 Simon Lightfoot, "The Consolidation of Europarties? The '"Party Regulation" and the Development of Political Parties in the European Union," *Representation* 42:4 (2006): 305; Johansson and Raunio, 524.
68 The Treaty of Nice, 2000.
69 Brendan Donnelly and Mathias Jopp, "European Political Parties and Democracy in the EU," in *Democracy in the EU and the Role of the European Parliament*, ed. Gianni Bonvicini (Rome: Quaderni IAI, 2009), 27.

provisions.[70] A European political party was defined as an "association of citizens which pursue political objectives and which is either recognised by, or established in accordance with, the legal order of at least one member state".[71] The amended regulation introduced several conditions for a European political party to be recognised. A Europarty either must "have elected members to the EP, the national parliaments or regional parliaments in at least one-quarter of the member states *or* have obtained at least 3% of support in one-quarter of the member states in the last EP elections".[72] Furthermore, party programmes and activities were expected to be in line with the values and principles of the European Union and to respect the fundamental rights and the rule of law. A Europarty also must participate in elections to the EP or have expressed the intention to do so. In 2007, the newly amended regulation EC No. 1524/2007 envisaged the funding for the European party foundations to be for "analysing and contributing to the debate on European public political issues" by "orga-nising and supporting seminars, training, conferences and studies".[73]

With the Lisbon Treaty and the EP's further empowerment, the position of the Europarties has been strengthened. According to the new provision, the EP elects the President of the EU Commission based on the proposal made by the EU Council, taking into the account the results of the European elections.[74] Although for the first time the Europarties were allowed to actively participate in the election campaign and to propose their candidates for the President of the EU Commission, as the European elections in 2014 showed, a vague formulation watered down the provision and preserved

---

70   Committee on Constitutional Affairs, "Proposal for a European Parliament and Council Regulation on the Statute and Financing of European Political Parties," Report No. A5-0170/2003 (Rapporteur: Jo Leinen, 21 May 2003).
71   Commission of the European Communities (CEC), Regulation No. 2004/2003 (Brussels: Official Journal, 2003).
72   EC Regulation No. 2004/2003.
73   Ibid.
74   Donnelly and Jopp, "European Political Parties and Democracy in the EU," 31.

the status quo in which the EU Council had the upper hand in the nomination.

In April 2011, based on the Giannakou Report, the regulation of the Europarties was again debated and adopted as a non-binding resolution. It reiterated the importance of the European political parties "as a means of enhancing participatory governance in the EU and finally strengthening democracy" and pledged for a statute for the Europarties.[75] The Report suggested the introduction of a uniform European Legal Status as a precondition for EU funding. The proposed regulation also called for stricter conditions for obtaining EU funding and for a more flexible system.[76] Based on the recommendations in the Giannakou Report, the last institutional development envisages the registration of the Europarties as organisations under EU law and adjusts the financial regulations on spending and donations.[77] Until now, the Europarties have operated as non-profit organisations. The newly amended regulation, which came into force in January 2017, provides a uniform EU-level legal status to increase Europarties' visibility and their links to the citizens. In addition, the regulation implements more flexible rules on spending and donations, allowing parties to use the sources from previous years.[78]

Functions of the Europarties

At the beginning, the Europarties were perceived as "transmission belts",[79] which meant to link the European citizens and European

---

[75] Committee on Constitutional Affairs, "Report on the Application of Regulation (EC) No 2004/2003 on the Regulations Governing Political Parties at European Level and the Rules Regarding Their Funding," Report No. 2010/2201(INI) (2011).

[76] European Scrutiny Committee, House of Commons (2012).

[77] EU Regulation No …/2014.

[78] "Parliament Agrees on New Rules to Beef up EU Parties," *EurActiv*, 16 April 2014.

[79] Pascal Delwit, Erol Külahci, and Cédric Van de Walle, "The Europarties: Organisation and Influence," *CEVIPOL*, Brussels, Centre d'étude de la vie politique of the Free University of Brussels (ULB), 2004, 33.

institutions in an effort to reduce the EU's democratic deficit. However, due to the strong resistance from national parties, the position of the Europarties remains very weak in terms of internal organisation and decision-making. Moreover, the failed linkage function of the Europarties only questioned their legitimacy and relaunched the debate on the democracy deficit within the EU institutions. The Europarties fail in terms of representation, aggregation and articulation of voters' interests.[80] They possess no direct links to electoral campaigning and society. National parties have the upper hand in elections by controlling the composition of electoral lists, EP candidate selection and media access.[81] Furthermore, the Europarties possess less control over the EP party groups' behaviour in the parliament. Concomitantly, emphasising its low importance among the public, the European elections are seen as second-order elections in which domestic rather than European issues are debated. Moreover, placed in the middle of an electoral cycle, the European elections appear to be more of a litmus test for national governments than for EU issues. In this situation, governmental parties tend to obtain a vote sanction, whereas minor parties largely benefit from protest voting.[82]

Due to their supranational position, the Europarties have a broader range of functions than their national counterparts. The Europarties do not establish traditional organisational ties between society and government but interlink European- and national-level organisations. Since the Europarties are umbrella organisations in which nomination, election campaigning and internal decision-making belong to national parties, they fail to perform such tradi-

---

[80] Peter Mair, "Representative versus Responsible Government," *MPIfG Working Paper* 09/8 (2009).

[81] Stefano Bartolini, *Restructuring Europe: Centre formation, system building and political structuring between the nation-state and the European Union* (Oxford: Oxford University Press 2005), 331.

[82] Karl Heiz Reif and Hermann Schmitt, "Nine Second-Order National Elections. A Conceptual Framework for the Analysis of European Election Results," *European Journal for Political Research* 8 (1980): 8.

tional functions as representation, mobilisation, recruiting and legitimation. Instead, the Europarties fulfil a new set of functions: communication, coordination, inclusion and networking[83]; they are therefore sometimes described as "networks facilitators" or "party networks".[84] They make "the professional intermingling of national, transnational, and supranational actors all the routine".[85] Operating in multilevel settings, the Europarties provide structures for communication and information exchange. The Europarties regularly organise the party congresses, the Party Leaders' Meetings which unite representatives from national parties and EP party groups, ministers and heads of government, and non-EU representatives. In turn, the gathering events help the Europarties to generate and coordinate their common positions and resolutions prior to the EP sessions and the EU Council meetings.[86] Furthermore, including a number of like-minded parties in a particular party family, the Europarties contribute to the process of learning and socialisation of their members. Through the coordination and communication, the function of inclusion aims to build trust and foster the integration process.[87]

Organisational structure

Organisationally, transnational party federations are composed of three elements: national parties on the domestic level, EP party groups and extra-parliamentary organisations. Transferring these

---

[83] Jürgen Mittag and Janosch Steuwer, *Politische Parteien in der EU* (Wien: Facultas Verlag- und Buchhandels AG, 2010). Clemens, Zur Hausen, *Der Beitrag der "Europarteien" zur Demokratisierung der Europäischen Union* (Marburg: Tectum Verlag, 2008).

[84] Robert Ladrech, "The European Union and Political Parties," in *Handbook of Party Politics,* ed. Richard S. Katz and William Crotty (London: Sage Publications, 2004), 495.

[85] Robert Ladrech and Phillippe Marlière (ed.), *Social Democratic Parties in the European Union* (Basingstoke: Palgrave Macmillan, 1999), 108.

[86] Stephen Day, "Between 'Containment' and 'Transnationalization' — Where next for the Europarties?" *Acta Politica* 1:4 (2013): 14.

[87] Mittag and Steuwer, *Politische Parteien in der EU,* 118.

"three faces" of party organisations to the European level, the components of transnational party federations can be compared as follows. National parties correspond to the "party on the ground", the EP party groups are equivalent to the "party in public office", and the extra-parliamentary organisations can be seen as the "party in central office".[88] Recently, the term "Europarties" has become widely used to refer to the EU-level components: the EP party groups and the extra-parliamentary federations.[89]

In the process of professionalisation, the Europarties managed to develop their internal organisation. Each Europarty has similar organisational units: the party congress, the party assembly and the general secretariat. Some of the Europarties also have established a meeting of partisan leaders.

Taking the EPP's example of internal structure, its party congress constitutes the fundamental institution and represents the main highlight in the party activities. At the EPP Party Congress, members make important decisions such as the adoption of a new political line, an electoral manifesto or amendments to the statute. Moreover, the EPP leadership is elected, and new party members are introduced. Usually, the EPP Party Congress is held once every three years, and it meets both in plenary and in working groups. The party congress gathers delegates from full, associated and observer members; from affiliated associations' members; from the EPP party group in the EP; from European Commissioners who belong to the party; and from heads of national parties and governments.[90]

The EPP Political Assembly is the strategic organisational element and its tasks are to unite the party and to influence the EU

---

88 Luciano Bardi, "European Party Federations' Perspectives," in *The Europarties: Organisation and Influence*, ed. Delwit et al. (Brussels: Centre d'étude de la vie politique, 2004), 312.
89 In this book, the term "Europarties" refers to the extra-parliamentary federations only.
90 Thomas Jansen and Steven van Hecke, *At Europe's Service: The Origins and Evolution of the European People's Party* (Berlin: Springer-Verlag, 2011), 109.

agenda in line with the EPP's programme and policies.[91] The assembly is composed of full and associated party members as well as ex officio members.[92] Gathering approximately every two months, the assembly represents the EPP's main decision-making body and is responsible for the adoption of the annual budget, the admission and exclusion of party members, the election of the deputy Secretary General on the recommendations of the presidency, the recognition of associations and the determination of the Congress's agenda and regulations.[93]

The EPP's General Secretariat is the central body of the party's daily business, and it has a permanently employed staff. The secretariat's activities include administrative, financial and organisational ones. The day-to-day management includes supervising the cooperation between the full, associated and observer members; convening the meetings; drafting the meetings' agendas and writing the meetings' minutes.[94] Apart from these managerial tasks, the secretariat performs a communicational function. It is responsible for the dissemination of information to the member parties through the EPP's media sources.

Since 1990, the role of the presidency changed from merely being ceremonial towards monitoring. According to the EPP Statute, the EPP Presidency ensures the implementation of the decision made by the EPP Political Assembly, oversees the work of the EPP General Secretariat (in particular, budget management) and ensures the permanent political presence of the EPP.[95]

In 1990, the Conference of Party and Government Leaders was incorporated into the EPP's structure, and in 1995, it was officially renamed as the EPP Party Summit. As informal ministerial meetings, these summits serve as platforms for non-binding negotiations and for the elaboration of common positions prior to EU

---

91   Jansen and van Hecke, *At Europe's Service*, 138.
92   EPP Statute (Marseille: EPP, 2011).
93   Jansen and van Hecke, *At Europe's Service*, 138.
94   EPP Statute (Marseille: EPP, 2011).
95   Ibid.

Council meetings.⁹⁶ The summits provide forums for exchanging ideas and insights, testing reactions to proposals, and building solidarity and integrity among members. During the EPP Party Summits, the delegates discuss intra-party issues, the EU institutional reforms and the EU enlargement process.⁹⁷ Since 2007, the meetings have been extended to the members of the Council of Ministers and have been successfully integrated into the EPP structure as "Ministerial Meetings".⁹⁸

3.2 Party Development in Post-Communist Countries

Shaped by the legacy of patrimonial communism, the patterns of party development in Georgia, Moldova, and Ukraine share a common set of features. In these countries, party systems hinge on "vertical chains of personal dependence between leaders in the state and party apparatus and their entourage, buttressed by extensive patronage and clientelist networks".⁹⁹ A durable period of a one-party system under communism distorted the classical view of political parties as the link between state and society. The evolution of post-Soviet party systems paved its own way for development, characterised by the erosion of social cleavages, eradication of ideological underpinnings, weak anchorage in society and strong entanglement with the state. Unlike the Western parties, which mobilise, aggregate and represent societal interests and demands, post-communist parties operate differently.

Different cleavage structures

Due to different historical and cultural development, the social structure of (civil) societies in the post-Soviet countries does not correspond with the Western one. Social cleavages in Georgia, Moldova, and Ukraine were shaped differently than those in the West

---

96 EPP's website, http://www.epp.eu/structure/summit/
97 Jansen and van Hecke, *At Europe's Service*, 151.
98 Ibid., 162.
99 Herbert Kitschelt et al., *Post-Communist Party Systems: Competition, Representation, and Inter-Party Cooperation* (Cambridge: Cambridge University Press, 1999), 23.

because of the overlapping processes of nation-building and economic transition. In Ukraine, for example, society is divided by socio-cultural differences such as language, history and assessment of particular historical figures, and the attitude towards Ukraine's foreign policy. While in 1998 the main cleavage was between the left and national-democratic forces, reflecting the process of nation-building, by 2004, the "left-right" cleavage was entirely substituted by a "pro-presidential–anti-presidential" one. As a result of the politically fierce 2004 presidential campaign, cultural and linguistic distinctions were meticulously emphasized.[100] During 2005–2010, the socio-cultural division stabilised and became deeply anchored in the party system. The geographical division overlapped with the foreign policy division. While voters in Western Ukraine supported "orange" parties which favoured the pro-European orientation, Eastern Ukraine supported the pro-Russian opposition.

Similarly, in Georgia societal cleavages were eroded during the communist regime. Historically, Georgian parties did not aim to represent interests of particular social groups, but rather aimed to distinguish themselves from the Communist regime and represent national interests. After the independence, "parties of power" that were initiated from the top dominated Georgian political life. "Parties of power" structured the political life in Georgia, whereas the opposition was represented by a large number of small parties confronting the regime. As a result, political parties are primarily divided by "pro-regime–anti-regime" line, whereas ideological polarisation is quite low.[101]

In the same vein, the structuring of political life in Moldova is not reflected in ideological "left-right" terms. The Moldovan party cleavage is predominantly structured around geopolitical lines. According to Botan, the Moldovan parties can be divided into (1) pro-

---

100   Центр Разумкова, "Еволюція партійної системи України: основні етапи," *Національна Безпека і Оборона* 5 (2010): 8. [Razumkov Center, "The evolution of party system in Ukraine: the main stages," *National Security and Defence* 5 (2010): 8].

101   Gia Nodia and Àlvaro Pinto Scholtbach, *The political landscape of Georgia. Political Parties: Achievements, Challenges and Prospects* (Eburon: Delft 2006), 99–100.

Russian, pro-Commonwealth of Independent States (CIS) and anti-NATO; (2) pro-Moldova, pro-CIS, pro-neutrality; and (3) pro-Romanian, pro-EU, pro-NATO and anti-CIS.[102] Leftist parties are pro-Russian, supporting the restoration of some form of Soviet regime, whereas rightist parties are pro-Romanian, favouring unification with Romania and considering Moldova's independence an intermediate stage in the country's development. Centre-right and centre-left parties are pro-Moldovan, combining two opposite orientations.[103]

Failed linkage with society

The post-Soviet parties are weakly anchored in society, as indicated by their low public trust, high electoral volatility and small party membership. After communism, political parties were left with citizens who had weak partisan identity and deep apathy about party politics. As an example of difficult mobilisation, in the 1990s the ideological and political orientations of Ukrainian citizens were marked by high uncertainty or sceptical attitude. Thus, 33.4% of respondents were undecided, whereas 25.6% supported no ideology.[104] Moreover, even in 2010 the political socialisation of Ukrainian citizenry did not change to a great extent: 60% of citizens could not distinguish between left and right parties, while only 5.4% of those polled were well-informed about the differences.[105]

In a similar vein, the Georgian parties are loosely rooted in society. A recently conducted National Democratic Institute's (NDI) poll established a deep dissatisfaction with the Georgian parliamentarians and their inability to represent voters' interests. Thus, a negligible 2% of those polled have been contacted by their MPs since

---

102 "Is there any ethnic cleavage in the Moldovan society?" *Alianta.md*, 10 March 2009.
103 Ibid.
104 Центр Разумкова, "Чинники, що впливають на еволюцію партійної системи України," *Національна Безпека і Оборона* 5 (2010): 18. [Razumkov Center, "Factors that influence the elovution of party system in Ukraine," *National Security and Defence* 5 (2010): 18].
105 Ibid., 25.

the 2012 elections. Only 31% can correctly name their majoritarian representatives, while 70% do not know how to reach their MPs. The figures indicate a significant disconnect between the citizenry and its parliamentarian representatives.[106]

High apathy to elections is established in Moldova as well. In 1998, the percentage of the population that has a clear electoral preference has been rather low: 22% of those polled were not determined, and 12% could not name any party they would vote for.[107] In 2002, the situation hardly changed. Roughly 31% of the respondents would not know whom to vote for or would not vote at all.[108]

Low public trust

Due to citizens' negative experiences with partisan affiliation, interest and public trust remains consistently low in all three countries. As a result of parties' estrangement from voters and close interlocking with business, public distrust is perpetuating. In Ukraine, public distrust in political parties from 2001 to 2010 was strikingly high, ranging from 62% to 86%.[109] In 2010, according to public opinion polls, 63.4% of citizens believed that political parties were "political tools" for financial and business groups, whereas only 9.8% were convinced that they represented the voters' interests.[110] In Georgia in 2006, 60% of the respondents declared their lack of trust in political parties, whereas in 2012 only 18% of respondents trusted political parties.[111] The latest opinion poll, conducted by NDI in 2016, showed similar low trust in political figures—64% of respondents

---

106   NDI Poll, Low Trust in Parliament and Political Figures; Most Georgians Politically Undecided, 13 April 2016.
107   Barometer of Public Opinion, Institute for Public Policy, November 2001.
108   Barometer of Public Opinion, Institute for Public Policy, April 2002.
109   Центр Разумкова, "Сучасний стан політичних партій та партійної системи. Головні проблеми та недоліки," *Національна Безпека і Оборона* 5 (2010): 27. [Razumkov Center, "The current state of political parties and party system. The main problems and flaws," *National Security and Defence* 2 (2010): 27].
110   Ibid., 20.
111   CRRC Caucasus Barometer 2012 Georgia.

believe that members of parliament care about their own interests, while only 24% think that Georgian MPs represent public interests.[112] The situation in Moldova echoes the wide distrust in political parties among the population. Parties consistently enjoyed the least of citizens' trust among other public institutions. In 2015, distrust in governing parties grew, amounting to 70% of respondents.[113]

Broad public distrust affects the membership-electorate ratio. In all three countries, the share of population belonging to a political party is negligible. Thus, in Georgia, according to the GORBI opinion poll in 2001, only 4.4% were members of a political party. By 2004, the percentage dropped to 2.6.[114] Similarly, in Ukraine, the membership-electorate ratio reached 5.8%.[115] In contrast, in Moldova, around 10.6% of the eligible voters are members of political parties[116], which is one of the highest figures among CEE countries.[117]

Electoral volatility

Due to the low public trust, electoral volatility is respectively very high. During the 1990s and 2000s, Moldova possessed the highest volatility score among the post-Soviet countries. In the 1994–1998 election cycle, 36% of votes went to newly established parties. In the 1998 elections, a dramatic shift in the political landscape occurred with the re-emergence of the Party of Communists. As a re-

---

112 NDI Poll, Low Trust in Parliament and Political Figures; Most Georgians Politically Undecided, 13 April 2016.
113 Igor Botan, Barometer of Public Opinion about the social-cultural situation before the local elections, *E-democracy*, 25 May 2015.
114 Nodia and Scholtbach, *The political landscape of Georgia*, 105.
115 Priit Kallakas, "Membership Developments in Political Parties in Estonia, Moldova and Ukraine," *Politics*, 206.
116 Ibid., 204.
117 Ingrid van Biezen, Peter Mair and Thomas Poguntke, "Going, going, ... gone? The decline of party membership in contemporary Europe," *European Journal of Political Research* 51 (2012).

sult, the volatility dropped by one-third due to the party's consolidating effect on the electorate.[118] In Ukraine, only 35% of citizens are consistent with their party choice at elections, whereas 48% of respondents support political force to some extent and 36% are looking for "a better political choice".[119] In Georgia, electoral volatility reached 75% in 1992–1995 but then dropped to 46% in 1995–1999 electoral cycle.[120]

On the other hand, electoral volatility is stipulated by short party age and permanent fluctuations in party creation and dissolution. The proliferation of parties is enormous. Thus, in 2006 the Ministry of Justice in Georgia re-gistered 183 parties,[121] and there were 138 in Ukraine in 2007.[122] In 2014, the number of legally registered parties in Ukraine grew — 225 parties with 27 new parties.[123] In Moldova, the number of registered parties is considerably lower than in Ukraine and Georgia. In 1994–1998, there were only 9 parties registered to participate in the elections. However, the fluidity of the party system was reflected in the number of independent candidates. Whereas 20 candidates with no party affiliation were registered in 1994, by 1998 the number grew to 60. Over the course of 1994–2014, the number of parties increased to 20 and 19 in 2010 and 2014 respectively, while the number of independent candidates diminished to 4 in 2014.[124]

---

118   Erik S. Herron, *Elections and Democracy After the Communism?* (New York: Palgrave Macmillan, 2009), 83–84.
119   Центр Разумкова, "Сучасний стан політичних партій та партійної системи. Головні проблеми та недоліки," *Національна Безпека і Оборона* 5 (2010): 23. [Razumkov Center, "The current state of political parties and party system. The main problems and flaws," *National Security and Defence* 2 (2010): 23].
120   Nodia and Scholtbach, *The political landscape of Georgia*, 104.
121   Ibid., 152.
122   Андрей Голубитский, "Виртуальная двухпартийность," *Комментарии.UA*, 2007. [Andrei Golubitskii, "Virtual two-party system," *Kommentarii.UA*, 2007].
123   Sarah Whitmore, Political party development in Ukraine, *GSDRC, Applied Knowledge Service, Helpdesk Research Report* (2014): 3.
124   Parliamentary Elections in the Republic of Moldova, *E-democracy.md*.

High personalisation

Parties' estrangement from (civil) society alongside low public trust in parties triggers a vicious cycle. Low popularity of parties causes high electoral volatility, low membership-electorate ratio and general apathy towards political parties. As a result, parties operate as elite-driven projects detached from society, where ideological attachment is artfully replaced by high affiliation to party leaders. The lack of demands from society allows political parties to diminish their level of political accountability and apply unpretentious charismatic and clientelistic types of relations.[125]

Structurally, parties in Georgia, Moldova, and Ukraine all resemble personalised projects rather than proper representative organisations. Political parties are often created around a party leader, and their survival is heavily dependent on his/her charismatic personality and employment of populist promises for prosperity and stability in a time of crisis. In other words, the Ukrainian *Batkivshchyna*, "Our Ukraine", the Moldovan Party of Communists, the Liberal Party and the Georgian Labour Party would not last long without their party leaders. Deprived of strong links with society and developed party structure, such parties cease to exist once the party leader leaves.

The strong presidentialism which prevails in the post-Soviet countries encourages the personalisation of politics. The politics of personalities concentrated around winning the presidential elections dominates. The exaggerated focus on the presidential post hinders the development of political parties, as their role in politics is constrained. The individual candidates possess few motives to invest in political parties, as the principal arena for policy-making is vested in the executive and not in the legislative.[126] In the presidentialist system, parties operate rather as "electoral machines", seeking to get into office.

---

[125] Kitschelt, *Post-Communist Party Systems*, 450.
[126] John T. Ishiyama and Ryan Kennedy, "Superpresidentialism and Political Party Development in Russia, Ukraine, Armenia and Kyrgyzstan," *Europe-Asia Studies* 53: 8 (2001), 1179.

In addition, voters' lack of political culture reinforces this trend of personalisation. In highly personalised politics of the post-Soviet countries, voters shape their electoral preferences looking at the party leader. Thus, 58.1% of Ukrainian citizens consider the leader's personality to be of primary importance when voting for a certain party.[127] Similarly in Moldova, the rating of political personalities replicates the rating of political parties. This is often the case when the party leader's rating is higher than that of the party itself. Once the party leader is distrusted, so is the whole party.

Dependency on oligarchs and administrative resources

The post-communist parties are tightly linked to the business circles. Both tend to profit from such symbiosis. While political parties cover their enormously expensive campaign costs and daily expenses, oligarchs secure their business by controlling the policy-making process. Because the weak links with society membership or affiliation fees are negligible, the post-communist parties rely on oligarchic financial support. On the other hand, being aware of constantly changing rules, oligarchs try to secure their business either by directly participating in politics or by having proxies in (sometimes several) parties.[128] As oligarchs are only interested in protecting their own business, there is usually no ideological alignment between them and their parties. Moreover, once the party ceases to exist, oligarchs move their financial support to another party.

The close interconnection of parties with business and state turns them from representative agencies to instruments for oligarchs' lobbying or self-serving agencies. As a result, it distorts the function of political representation and inevitably leads to rampant corruption. In Ukraine, for example, the oligarchic system was fully

---

[127] Центр Разумкова, "Сучасний стан політичних партій та партійної системи. Головні проблеми та недоліки," *Національна Безпека і Оборона* 5 (2010): 29. [Razumkov Center, "The current state of political parties and party system. The main problems and flaws," *National Security and Defence* 5 (2010): 29].

[128] Whitmore, "Political party development in Ukraine," 3.

completed during the term of Leonid Kuchma, Ukraine's second president. At this time—the second half of the 1990s—business and politics started to intertwine. The *nomenklatura* profited from financial support that oligarchs provided them with, and in return, members of the state apparatus covered the oligarchs' opaque privatisation methods.[129] During 2005–2010, the industrial financial groups dominated all the mainstream parties, regardless of their ideological or pro- or anti-regime position.[130]

For example, the Party of Regions emerged on the nexus of the largest financial-industrial group, based in Donbas, and the local *nomenklatura*.[131] In contrast to the Party of Regions, in the *Batkivshchyna* party and "Our Ukraine" leaders' personalities were the main party's capital, while the influence of oligarchs was significantly smaller than in the Party of Regions. This can be partly explained through more limited potential of "orange" oligarchs in contrast with the industrialised Donbas clan.[132]

In Moldova, the extent of oligarchic influence is rather limited compared to Ukraine. Due to the absence of a large industrial sector, the Moldovan oligarchy boils down to two personalities—Vlad Plahotniuc, the current leader of the Democratic Party of Moldova, and Vlad Filat, the former prime-minister and the former president of LDPM. Both are longstanding competitors in politics and business, who gained their capital during the early period of privatisation.

In Georgia, the situation is similar to the Moldovan one. Two close rivals represent the country's political heavyweights: Mikheil Saakashvili, the former prime-minister and former UNM party leader and Ivanishvili, the former leader of the Georgian Dream.

---

129 Slawomir Matuszak, "The oligarchic democracy. Influence of business groups on Ukrainian politics," *Center for European Studies* 42 (2012): 13.

130 Центр Разумкова, "Еволюція партійної системи України: основні етапи," *Національна Безпека і Оборона* 5 (2010): 11. [Razumkov Center, "The evolution of party system in Ukraine: the main stages," *National Security and Defence*, No 5 (2010), 11].

131 Henry E. Hale, "Formal Constitutions in Informal Politics: Institutions and Democratization in Post-Soviet Eurasia," *World Politics* 63:4 (2011).

132 Matuszak, "The oligarchic democracy," 28.

Public funding

Until recently, there were no provisions for state funding to political parties in Georgia, Moldova, and Ukraine. Heavily funded by the oligarchs and using administrative resources, parties were not obliged to disclose any information about their sources of funding. Described as a "fight of purses", the contestation was defined by money instead of political ideas.

In the last years, all three countries have passed legislation to introduce state funding to political parties. The new amendment to the Georgian Organic Law of Political Union of Citizens introduced direct transfers, funding via the Center of Electoral Systems, Development, Reforms and Trainings, and funding for TV advertisements during the campaigning period as a form of state funding. Parties which receive at least 4% at the national level and at least 3% at the local level are eligible for public funding.[133] In addition, the law imposed regulations on private funding, prohibiting donations from foreign and state entities and defining a ceiling on donations from individual donors.[134] Following GRECO's recommendations, Moldova also introduced public funding to political parties. According to the new Moldovan legislation, parties which obtained at least 3% in the previous elections became eligible for state funding. The law also provided equal media access for political parties during elections.[135] Finally, in October 2015, the Ukrainian parliament approved amendments to legislative acts on preventing and combatting corruption by introducing state funding of political parties. Similarly to Georgia and Moldova, the law defined the provision of public financing to parties which pass the 5% threshold at parliamentary election. The newly adopted law introduced obligatory financial reports every four months and required external financial

---

133 The Organic Law of Georgia on Political Unions of Citizens, Article 30, paragraph 3.
134 Ibid., Article 26.
135 The Law of Moldova on Political Parties, Article 28, 2012.

audit. The maximum size of donations from individual and legal entities was limited to 800 minimum salaries.[136]

Although it was designed to diminish the dependency on private donors, the public financing hardly prevented parties from being influenced by oligarchs. Since state funding provides limited financial support, in hybrid regimes only parties with oligarchic backing are capable of challenging the status quo of parties in power.[137]

Lack of intra-party democracy

Due to the personality-centred nature of post-communist parties, the majority of them experience a lack of internal democracy. Formally democratic, parties are designed as "personal vehicles" for the party leader to seek, obtain or regain the power, where all power is concentrated at the top. A change of leadership is quite rare, as it almost inevitably leads to the party's demise. Regardless of party type and ideological position, parties by inertia follow the principle of "democratic centralism". Borrowed from the Communist party, this term means that the decisions are formed at the top and internal party debates are limited. Once a decision is made, party members are not allowed to question it.[138] The party leader has excessive control over party management, decision-making and outside communication. As a personal project, the party leader decides over the party's vision and election platforms, nominates candidates for elections, allocates the organisational resources within the party and speaks to the wider public.[139] Consequentially, "democratic centralism" leads to organisational rigidity and hierarchy. Party leaders, who were socialised in Soviet times, are not very well informed about other party organisation principles, and party

---

136   Anton Marchuk, "The Law on Financing of Political Parties: Changing the Rules of Political Game," *VoxUkraine*, December 2015.
137   Ketevan Bolkvadze, "Drams, Laris and Politics. Political Funding Regulations in Armenia and Georgia," *NIMD South Caucasus*.
138   Nodia and Scholtbach, *The political landscape of Georgia*, 154.
139   Tatiana Kostadinova and Barry Levitt, "Towards a Theory of Personalist Parties: Concept Formation and Theory Building," *Politics and Polity* 42:4 (2014): 500.

members do not perceive the lack of internal democracy as an urgent issue.

Conclusions

Both party development on the European and domestic levels has its implications for the impact of cooperation. On the one hand, the relatively weak position of the Europarties in the EU architecture affects their potential to impact non-EU parties. Being merely umbrella organisations with limited powers within the EU architecture, the Europarties do not have a traditional veto power through which the non-EU parties could directly influence the EU decision-making. Moreover, as supranational groupings with loose internal structures, the Europarties are hardly viewed by the non-EU parties as a direct template from which to borrow a party structure. In contrast, it is the Europarties' members — the national parties — who are the gatekeepers, possessing more influence within and outside the EU and representing a model of the European party-building which the non-EU parties copy. Nevertheless, the role of the Europarties in this process is quintessential. Operating as network facilitators, the Europarties provide opportunity structures for the non-EU parties to cooperate with the national parties of the respective Europarties.

On the other hand, the peculiarities of Georgia, Moldovan, and Ukrainian party development impose their own limitations on the penetration of socialisation effect. On the ideological dimension, due to the concomitant processes of nation-building and economic transition, the party programmes are vague and inconsistent, often combining values of different ideologies. Furthermore, the dominating personalisation of party politics endangered the development of ideological platforms and made it cumbersome to apply the classic "left-right" scheme. The names of the parties do not reflect their de facto political stances and do not provide any proxy for belonging to a certain party family. Parties apply a catch-all approach to target different societal groups, which makes their programmes eclectic and indistinguishable.

In organisational terms, the personalisation of party politics causes the over-centralisation of party structures, where the power is fully concentrated in the hands of party leader who controls all of the decision-making. A skewed distribution of responsibilities between the top leadership and the rank-and-file members leads to ineffective party management and underdevelopment of local branches.[140] As a result, party discipline is very poor, which has a corrosive effect on the party structure.[141] Since the party unity is imposed from above, the rigidity and hierarchy of the party structure often causes splits and internal conflicts. As a common solution to intra-party tension, party members either switch to another party or establish their own personal project. The personalistic character of party-building hinders the development of party structure and blocks open debate within the party. The lack of intra-party democracy, in turn, further exacerbates the development of youth and women's branches and impedes their equal participation in decision-making.

On the behavioural dimension, high personalisation hinders the cooperation between the parties. Lacking the experience of a well-functioning multi-party democracy, the European-style grand coalitions are rare, as they require one party leader to step down.[142] In contrast, the formation of electoral blocks is more widespread. So are parties' ad hoc coalitions or alliances, regardless of their ideological underpinnings. Unlike their Western counterparts which cooperate based on their ideological alignments, Georgian, Moldovan, and Ukrainian parties are often engaged in "floor-crossing". The widespread switching between factions has opened the gate to

---

140   Nodia and Scholtbach, *The political landscape of Georgia*, 213.
141   Aurel Croissant and Wolfgang Merkel, "Political Party Formation in Presidential and Parliamentary System," Institute of Political Science at the University of Heidelberg, *Online Papers* (2001), 10.
142   Croissant and Merkel, "Political Party Formation in Presidential and Parliamentary System," 7.

enormous political corruption, when members of parliament are offered generous sums of money to join a particular faction.[143] Presidentialism further impedes the cooperation among parties by fostering competition among them. As the presidency is the highest goal for a party leader to achieve, it turns the party into a political vehicle to attain this post. This tendency has a negative effect on the party system, as it further exacerbates its instability and fosters its fragmentation.[144]

---

[143] Max Bader, *Against All Odds. Aiding Political Parties in Georgia and Ukraine* (Amsterdam: Amsterdam University Press, 2010): 95.
[144] Ibid., 94.

4. Finding Each Other: Process of Application and Identification

4.1 Application and Selection Process

The major Europarties share a similar approach to the identification of their members and to the selection and application procedures. In general, the application procedure proceeds in a similar manner in the EPP, the PES, and the ALDE. The domestic party sends an official application which is reviewed by the Europarty on the subject of its congruence with their norms and values defined in the Statute. In the next step, the Europarty organises a fact-finding mission to the country to explore its political landscape. During the mission, the Europarty's representatives meet with party members, NGOs, experts, journalists, etc. On this basis, an assessment of the political situation is made, after which the Europarty's presidency decides whether to accept an applicant party.

As a detailed example, the application procedure to the EPP has the following mechanism. As a rule, the initiative to join the European party family emanates from domestic parties. Firstly, they send an official request to the president, including their agreement to comply with the by-laws and internal regulations. In the first reading, the Political Assembly conducts a legal check on compliance between the applicant's principles and values and the EPP Statute and Programme. At this stage, the EPP formally assesses whether a party can be potentially associated with its party family. If the party fulfils these criteria, the assessment is continued. The EPP Working Group on Membership (WG3) sends a fact-finding mission to the country to assess political situation. The WG3 aims to receive encompassing information on applicants by setting up meetings with party representatives, activists from youth and women's branches, local party, party foundations, and international aid donors, journalists and experts. The aim of the fact-finding mission is to examine the applicant's party ideology, organisation, and intra-party democracy. Afterwards, based on this assessment, the recommendations are sent to the Political Assembly for the second reading. It decides whether to approve or reject the party's application. There is no deadline for submitting an application and there is no fixed timeframe for the evaluation of an application.

As selection criteria are loose and flexible, there are several informal factors that increase the chances for a party to be accepted. First, established *mutual trust* is a significant facilitating factor in political communication. Representing "sites of socialization"[145], the Europarties create a "sense of community"[146], where political parties operate in transparent and loyal settings. As Deutsch et al. put it, "the kind of sense of community... turned out to be rather a matter of mutual sympathy and loyalties; of 'we-feeling', trust, and mutual consideration; or partial identification in terms of self-images and interest".[147] Loyalties and trust, in turn, create a transparent political communication that fosters the process of application. Knowing party leadership personally bolsters the Europarty's confidence in an applicant party's credibility: "This is the only way to get a feeling whether this party is credible or not. Otherwise, on paper all the applicant parties are perfect, if you read their political programmes and statutes".[148] As a consequence, personal communication helps to avoid or to mitigate any possible risks for the Europarties.

Building mutual trust presumes a two-way process. The mutual trust is crucial, on the one hand, between the Europarties and the applicant parties, and, on the other hand, between the Europarties' local partners and the applicants. From this perspective, *personal contacts* between party leaderships are of paramount importance. Having trust and support of major parties from the European party family can change attitudes of negatively positioned parties in an applicant party's favour. Thus, strong bilateral party contacts may be a way to facilitate an application. On the other hand, trustworthy

---

145 Checkel, "International Institutions and Socialization in Europe," 807.
146 Karl Deutsch et al. *Political Community and the North Atlantic Area: International Organisation in the Light of Historical Experience* (Princeton: Princeton University Press, 1957).
147 Deutsch et al., *Political Community*, 36.
148 Interview with the EPP representative, 7 October 2013.

information flow between the Europarties and their local partners is of significance as well. Rarely do those fact-finding missions to the country start from scratch. As politicians in Brussels are not always aware of developments in countries, they usually rely on their partners' recommendations and evaluations. Prior to sending the mission, the Europarty checks the relevance of applications with their local partners. Therefore, good relations with the Europarties' partners is another facilitating factor for domestic parties in the application procedure.

Traditionally, the German party foundations are highly involved in the assessment process. Operating as transnational intermediaries, the foundations proved their assistance to the Europarties in following political developments in CEE countries.[149] Similarly, they fulfil the same role in the non-EU countries. They operate as interlockers and mediators, creating "opportunity structures" for informal communication. On the one hand, they send reports about political developments, party landscape, and internal political tensions to the Europarties. They advise the Europarties on potential applicants and on their liabilities and readiness. On the other hand, they provide channels for direct communication between domestic parties and the Europarties. Foundations often organise meetings on the European agenda and gather together domestic political elites with representatives from Europarties and European institutions. As a result, foundations create a communicational platform where personal contacts can intensify and mutual trust might emerge.

For the EPP, the most credible partner on the ground is Konrad-Adenauer-Stiftung (KAS). The foundation operates on behalf of the German Christian Democratic Union (CDU) and thus it is indirectly connected to the EPP. The relationships between KAS and the EPP are intense, based on mutual trust and shared common norms and values. Usually, KAS is the first contact for the EPP to help identifying and selecting potential partners. The foundation often advises the EPP on the expediency of further consideration of

---

149 Dakowska, "Beyond Conditionality," 287–288.

a party's application. During fact-finding missions, KAS often initiates the organisation of round tables, meetings, and conferences between different domestic party members, European representatives, country's experts, and journalists. They provide the EPP representatives with first-hand information on a party's ideological match, but also on a party's behaviour in parliament and on inter-party relations. In turn, this information gives the EPP a clearer picture of a political force's viability. For instance, prior to the formal application of UDAR, the Ukrainian KAS office organised a visit of the German CDU's headquarter in Berlin. During this visit, UDAR party representatives had an opportunity to gain informal contacts with the EPP former President Martens and the German EPP members.[150] Afterwards, when initial contacts were established, it was KAS again who pushed the dialogue further and helped in organising mutual events. In this way, already prior to the application submission, UDAR gained broad support—mainly through the CDU—within the EPP, which explains its fast-tracked application. The party was granted an observer membership in less than a year. As this example illustrates, by establishing trustworthy personal contacts with national parties from respective Europarties, a non-EU party can lobby its application in a subtle way. Ideally, it should be a national party with strong position within the Europarties. Having the CDU's backing, UDAR had an influential party among its supporters.

As the Europarty is interested in dealing with sustainable political parties, *viability* is of great importance in the selection process. Viability is not bound to a certain percentage threshold, but rather relates to participation and/or representation on national and local levels. In this way, the EPP wants to avoid affiliation with minor and/or unfledged parties. Investing in the promotion of their ideological commitments and European values, the Europarty is interested in stable and credible partners. Having negative experiences with fluid post-communist party systems, the Europarties prefer to exclude cooperation with unreliable partners that might

---

150   Interview with the former KAS representative, 5 November 2013.

disappear after one term. Due to this reason, frequently the Europarties look at *election results* before making any decisions on acceptance. Election results give the Europarties a proxy for party's viability. Usually, this happens in a case where mutual trust between the Europarty and applicant party is lacking. For example, the EPP was cautious to proceed further with the Georgian Christian Democratic Movement's application before the parliamentary election results in 2012.[151] Together with European Democrats of Georgia, the party won a marginal 2.05% of the vote, which halted the application's further review. Similarly, the New Right Party's application was held under review prior to the election results 2008. The EPP planned to make a final decision on the application after the party's ability to enter the parliament.[152]

Finally, the decision of acceptance might be influenced by *other sister parties* from the same country. Other parties' applications to the same Europarty are usually considered as a threat to the exclusive affiliation of already observer members. Often, other sister parties are treated as adversaries and not as like-minded partners. As the affiliation is perceived with high appreciation and prestige, other sister parties act as countervailing forces, preventing other parties from joining. After a certain negative experience with the CEE parties, it has become an informal rule for the Europarty to obtain approval from already affiliated sister parties regarding new applicants. It is believed to help avoid obstructive behaviour between sister parties and to help consolidate democratic forces. For example, the Christian Democratic Movement's and the New Rights Party's applications were placed on a slow track because of the UNM's objection towards both applications. The UNM's non-approval of other potential sister parties in the EPP kept the applicants in the waiting room despite the fulfilment of the EPP's general requirements.[153]

---

151 Interview with the KAS representative, 23 April 2014.
152 Timus, "Coming Closer to Europe."
153 Ibid.

4.2 Identifying a Suitable Europarty

Taking the non-EU parties' perspective, this part will concentrate on the process of identifying suitable European party families for applicant parties. Firstly, it will focus on parties' motives for the affiliation in greater detail. Of particular interest are switches from one Europarty to another in the pre- and post-application periods. Secondly, it will examine the application process of each party and analyse its facilitating and countervailing factors. Of particular focus will be the bilateral relations between the non-EU parties and the Europarties' members, and their role in the application process.

The EPP and the People's Movement of Ukraine Rukh (Ukraine)

The party applied for observer status in 2002. Only after the Orange Revolution the party's application was evaluated jointly with the application of "Our Ukraine". In January 2006, both parties were granted observer membership. The EPP's lack of knowledge about the Ukrainian political landscape and *Rukh's* marginal position within it debilitated the whole process. As the party was lacking domestic and international credibility, it had yet to establish trustworthy relations with the EPP. After *Rukh's* active participation in the Orange Revolution and support for Yushchenko's political orientations, the party was acknowledged as a democratic and a pro-European force.

The EPP has not conducted any fact-finding missions; instead, the Europarty has largely relied on its intermediaries and interpersonal contacts. KAS played a leading role in mediating the process. The German foundation conducted evaluations and initiated negotiations between the EPP and *Rukh*. The party leader Borys Tarasiuk, then the minister of foreign affairs, was invited to the EPP summits in 2004 and 2005. In his interview, he acknowledged the EU's increased interest in Ukraine after the Orange Revolution and highlighted the significance of informal visits such as the EPP summits, referring to 12 prime ministers from the EU countries who attended the summit.¹⁵⁴ In December 2005, the Working Group recommended granting the party observer membership. The application process was complicated as Yushchenko's "Our Ukraine" comprised different wings of *Rukh*. The EPP proceeded with its application after the collusion was eliminated and the People's Union "Our Ukraine" was established as a political party. In January 2006, the Political Assembly officially accepted *Rukh* to its family.

The EPP and the People's Union "Our Ukraine" (Ukraine)

The opposition "Our Ukraine" electoral bloc began its contacts with the EPP during the YEPP delegation in Kyiv in 2003. The application of "Our Ukraine" was reviewed in light of the Orange Revolution's achievements. During the revolution, the party proved its democratic credentials and strong pro-European stance, so, as in the previous case, no fact-finding mission had been conducted. Instead, the "Our Ukraine" delegation participated in the EPP summit in 2004, to which Yushchenko was invited as a guest speaker. The parties discussed Ukraine's political situation and the country's European choice. The EPP expressed its full support to President Yushchenko and to the government in shaping Ukraine's European future: "Ukraine's new President has a very realistic project to bring his country close to the EU and clearly shares European principles and values".¹⁵⁵ In this way, "Our Ukraine" was recognised as the first Ukrainian party to share European values and norms. In September 2005, the bloc was restructured into a new political party — People's Union "Our Ukraine" (NSNU) — and repeatedly applied for the EPP membership, while preserving its status as the successor of "Our Ukraine" electoral bloc.¹⁵⁶ In January 2006, People's Union "Our Ukraine" was officially accepted into the EPP family.

---

154 Борис Тарасюк, "Мрію побачити Рух повноправним членом ЕРР," *E-News*, 16 грудня 2005. [Borys Tarasiuk, "I dream to see Rukh as a full member of the EPP," *E-News*, 16 December 2005].
155 EPP Press Release (Brussels: EPP, 15 February 2005).
156 Timus, "Transnational Party Europeanisation," 2014.

Similar to the previous case, KAS contributed significantly to the negotiation and evaluation processes. Since 2001, the "Our Ukraine" bloc has enjoyed privileged attention from KAS, whereas *Rukh* was treated as a secondary partner.[157] After the 2002 elections, KAS also encouraged the bloc to form a united party. After "Our Ukraine" formation, KAS named it as a "natural partner" and sent its recommendation to the EPP. Under the KAS' auspices, many seminars, trainings, and study visits were organised with the CDU's members, thus fulfilling the mediating function between the applicant party and the EPP. Apart from KAS' mediation role, the foundation not only contributed to the sharpening of the party profile, but also facilitated the establishment of the party as such. Together with other international actors, KAS contributed to the formation of "Our Ukraine" as a political force.[158]

The EPP and the Batkivshchyna party (Ukraine)

In August 2007, the third Ukrainian party—the *Batkivshchyna* party—sent its application to the EPP. However, prior to its EPP affiliation, the party had informal talks with the Social International and the PES. Moreover, in May 2006, during the party's congress, Tymoshenko announced a strategic choice to join the Social International and proclaimed "solidarism" as the party's ideology: "We are looking towards the Social International, as they are the strongest alliance of parties", said Tymoshenko.[159] The choice was consistent with Tymoshenko's previous rhetoric and with the bloc's composition. The ideologically diverse bloc was divided on the matter of international affiliation. One group led by Hryhoriy Nemyria pleaded for the EPP, while the other one headed by Iosyp Vinsky favoured the affiliation with the Socialists. The position of

---

157 Bader, *Against All Odds*, 120.
158 Interview with the former KAS representative, 5 November 2013; Ralf Wachsmuth "Ukraine," in *Parteienzusammenarbeit der KAS in Mittel-, Ost- und Sudosteuropa*, ed. P. Fischer-Bollin (Berlin: Konrad-Adenauer-Stiftung e.V., 2006), 66.
159 "Тимошенко змінює орієнтацію," *Українська правда*, 7 серпня 2007. ["Tymoshenko changes her orientation," *Ukrainska Pravda*, 7 August 2007].

Nemyria, a well-networked diplomat, eventually prevailed within the party. Despite being in the socialist grouping in the Council of Europe, Nemyria lobbied for the EPP affiliation, arguing that it would provide better opportunities to promote Ukraine's European integration and to establish informal connections with European party leaders like Angela Merkel and Nicolas Sarkozy.[160]

The selection process within the party aimed to mirror European party traditions. At the party congress, both the PES' and the EPP's party programmes were distributed before the vote on a final decision. However, described as an example of internal party democracy, the voting procedure was not unbiased. Just before the voting started, then EPP President Martens gave a speech in which he encouraged *Batkivshchyna* to join the EPP and underlined the party's commitments to European values and principles.[161] The speech tacitly pointed out to the final outcome. Moreover, the party members never had a chance to discuss their given choices publicly.

Unlike for the previous Ukrainian applications, the EPP organised a fact-finding mission in November 2007. During the visit, the EPP representatives assessed the party's programme and conducted negotiations with "Our Ukraine" and *Rukh*, already the EPP sister parties. As an informal part of the application, "Our Ukraine's" and *Rukh*'s stakes in *Batkivshchyna*'s application were taken into account. Both sister parties supported the party's application. In January 2008, despite the party's poor ideological match, the party was accepted into the EPP family. Instead, weak ideological congruence was substituted by Tymoshenko's good personal relations with the Europarty. Through Nemyria, Tymoshenko gained access to the EU's top politicians and the EPP's leadership. As the leader of the Orange democratic forces, she was profiled as a European politician "who will give new impetus to Ukraine's European drive".[162] Thus, the EPP's strategy pursued two goals in taking the *Batkivshchyna* party on board. By integrating another

---

160 "Про «зміну орієнтації» партії Батьківщина," *Українська правда*, 8 серпня 2007. ["Of Batkivshchyna's change in orientation," *Ukrainska Pravda*, 8 August 2007].
161 EPP Press Release (Brusels: EPP, 5 August 2007).
162 EPP Press Release (Brussels: EPP, 18 December 2007).

Ukrainian party, the EPP could consolidate all democratic forces of the Orange coalition into one party family. On the other hand, the EPP could proceed with its expansionist strategy by incorporating a viable force. The *Batkivshchyna* party met the EPP's criteria in terms of viability and credibility. As highlighted in the EPP report, the broad public support for Tymoshenko domestically served the EPP's goal in finding sustainable partners.[163]

The EPP and the United National Movement (Georgia)

In 2008, the UNM obtained an observer status in the EPP. Prior to this decision, the UNM had informal contacts with the Liberals through different fora. Some of the party representatives were in the liberal faction in the Council of Europe. The German Friedrich-Naumann-Stiftung (FNS) and the Dutch People's Party for Freedom and Democracy (VVD) party foundations considered the UNM as a potential partner after the party voiced its intention to join the Liberal International. Both foundations terminated the cooperation with the UNM after its final decision to join the EPP.[164] The switch from the Liberals to the EPP was not perceived by the party representatives as problematic. The UNM members explained this shift was due to the party's new establishment and self-identification process.[165]

Within the party, the position on international affiliation was divided. A group close to Zurab Zhvania favoured the establishment of contacts with the Liberals, whereas the other group loyal to Giga Bokeria strongly supported the EPP affiliation. The Russian-Georgian war in 2008 shifted the party's position in favour of the EPP. The EPP's adamant position on Georgia's aspirations to join the EU and NATO as well as strong criticisms towards the Russia's aggression outweighed other potential partners. It was believed within the party than the Liberals' stance towards Russia would be less strong and critical. As one of the party representatives argued,

---

163   Timus, "Transnational Party Europeanisation," 60.
164   Bader, *Against All Odds*, 114.
165   Interview with the UNM representative, 14 April 2014.

the foreign policy position within the Liberals drifted away from the position the party would share.[166] In this situation, the country's geopolitical interests predetermined the party's interests.

Unlike the Ukrainian cases, KAS did not participate in the selection and mediation processes. Until 2007, there was no permanent KAS office in Tbilisi. After its establishment, KAS struggled to identify a viable party compatible with KAS values that limited the foundation's activities for party assistance.[167] Only since 2007, KAS started to organise activities for political parties, among which the Christian Democratic Movement enjoyed KAS' preference. During the UNM's application to the EPP, KAS barely contributed to the mediation of negotiation process. To a large extent, the contacts with the EPP were established through Saakashvili's personal contacts. Furthermore, KAS identified its partner party reversely — based on the affiliation with the EPP.[168]

Within the EPP, the decision to accept the UNM as a family member was quite controversial. Some EPP members were rather sceptical of the applicant, but the geopolitical situation influenced the EPP's decision in the UNM's favour.[169] Similar to the *Bat kivshchyna's* case, the party's credibility after the Rose Revolution and its governmental position matched with the EPP's expansionist strategy in the region.

The EPP and the Liberal Democratic Party (Moldova)

In 2009, the Liberal Democrats applied for EPP affiliation and in February 2011 the party was granted an observer status. The driving force behind a fast-track application was the German foundation. The former KAS leadership introduced the LDPM to the opportunities of organisational development and networking the EPP was offering and encouraged it to apply for the affiliation. In the next step, KAS traditionally fulfilled its role as an intermediary. Through the foundation, the LDPM was introduced to the EPP

---

166   Interview with the UNM representative, 18 April 2014.
167   Bader, *Against All Odds*, 115.
168   Interview with the KAS representative, 23 April 2014.
169   Interview with the EPP representative, 10 October 2013.

leadership and was invited to visits in Brussels and Berlin in February 2010. In October 2010, the assessment mission was sent to Chisinau headed by the EPP Vice-President Corien Wortmann-Kool. The fact-finding mission was held together with the meeting of foreign ministers of the EU member states. The timing of the mission perfectly coincided with the pre-election campaign in Moldova, where the EPP representatives expressed their full support of the government's European reform agenda. "It is impressive to see the strong commitment of the LDPM and Filat government to implement essential reforms, to ensure the development of genuine democracy in your country, to reinstate democratic values and freedoms of citizens", Wortmann-Kool noted.[170] Despite the assessment period, the EPP representatives were confident in the party's match. "LDPM desire to join the EPP is determined by the fact that we share the same set of values and policies. Both within the government and as a party with strong identity we have pleaded for bringing Moldova closer to the European value space", Wortmann-Kool underlined.[171] Later, the EPP President Martens expressed his full support and trust of Prime Minister Filat, reiterating that his party shares "the values of the EPP and we will support his effort to put Moldova on the European path".[172]

Nevertheless, the LDPM's application was doomed by the Christian Democratic People's Party's (CDPP) retreat. The Moldovan Christian Democrats were accepted to the EPP in 2005. The relationships between two Moldovan parties became rather tenuous after the LDPM became the main alternative to the Communists. While the Liberal Democrats were gaining vast support as a leading pro-European force, the Christian Democrats were losing their status as the main opposition party. Being already an EPP observer member, the CDPP possessed strong links with member parties and affiliated foundations and had a say on the LDPM's application.

---

170 LDPM Press Release (Chisinau: LDPM, 2 October 2010).
171 Ibid.
172 LDPM Press Release (Chisinau: LDPM, 30 November 2010).

Nonetheless, after the cooperation with the Communists, the Christian Democrats lost their support both within the EPP and in the country. During the 2009 parliamentary elections, the party gained a marginal 3.04% of voter's support.[173] Their unwillingness to work with the LDPM cooled down the EPP's attitude towards the party. In June 2012, the Christian Democrats announced their withdrawal from the EPP.[174] After the CDPP's withdrawal, the Liberal Democrats enjoyed the EPP's full support as a party and as a leading force in the pro-European coalition.

The PES and the Democratic Party (Moldova)

Prior to the PES affiliation, the Democratic Party of Moldova (DPM) tried to establish contacts with the Socialist International. The process of acknowledgement by the Socialist International was rather tedious and lengthy. In 2002, the Democratic Party applied to the Socialist International and only later in 2010 the party was granted a consultant membership. By 2011, the party obtained full membership, and the party leader Marian Lupu was elected as the vice-president of the Socialist International.

In 2006, the DPM started negotiations on observer membership with the PES. Similar to the previous affiliations, the negotiation process was long and cumbersome. As the left political spectrum in Moldova is quite diverse, the decision about which party to take on board decelerated. The DPM was competing with the Social Democratic Party for a common electorate and for international recognition. However, when the Social Democrats proved their anti-European position, the party was discarded from the PES' list and excluded from the cooperation with Friedrich-Ebert-Stiftung (FES).[175] On the other hand, the strong position of the Communists in the country aggravated the PES' final decision on the party's affiliation. By 2007, the Party of Communists shifted its foreign policy's stance and started utilising a pro-European narrative. Initiated

---

173 "Parliamentary Elections in Moldova," *E-democracy*, April 5, 2009.
174 CDPP Declaration (Chisinau: CDPP, 18 June 2012).
175 Interview with the FES representative, 20 January 2014.

by the Swedish Socialists, there have been discussions about starting a dialogue between the Democratic Party and the Party of Communists with the prospects of merging.[176] Nonetheless, the attempt was unsuccessful and the idea of party merger failed.

The affiliation to the PES was facilitated through bilateral contacts the Democratic Party already possessed. In the pre-application period, the party conducted informal talks with Zita Gurmai, of the Hungarian Socialist Party, Christoph Zöpel, of the German SPD, Peter Schieder, Chair of the PES and a member of the Austrian SPÖ, Titus Corlatean, of the Romanian Socialist Party, and Tadeusz Iwinski, of the Polish Democratic Left Alliance.[177] Equally, the European Forum for Democracy and Solidarity facilitated the application through their active support. Interestingly, the FES was not engaged as a mediator in the negotiations, but merely supported in organisational issues.

In 2006 and 2010, the PES and the European Forum organised their fact-finding missions, involving all the Moldovan leftist parties. During the fact-finding mission in 2010, the new party leadership was praised by the PES President Rasmussen. "Under the leadership of Marian Lupu, the Democratic Party has contributed to the historical political change Moldova witnessed in 2009. The party has become a force for all Moldovans, the force for higher living standards, more social justice and for fairer growth. Under the leadership of Marian Lupu, the Democratic Party has fought for responsible economic and social policies within the governing coalition, and it has brought Moldova closer to Europe", noted Rasmussen.[178]

ALDE and the Republican Party (Georgia)

In 2007, the Republican Party obtained its membership in the ELDR (former ALDE) family. Earlier, in 2006, the party joined the Liberal International as an associate member and in 2013 the Republicans obtained full membership there. In January 2015, Tinatin Khidasheli was elected Vice-President of the Alliance of Liberals

---

176 Interview with the DPM representative, 15 January 2014.
177 Ibid.
178 PES Press Release (Brussels: PES, 14 October 2010).

and Democrats for the Europe faction of the Parliamentary Assembly of the Council of Europe. At the same time, she became a member of the ALDE Bureau.

The affiliation process with the ALDE was propelled by the support of the German Free Democratic Party (FDP) and the Dutch VVD. Equally, FNS facilitated the application and mediation processes. The earlier acceptance into the Liberal International served as an important proxy for the party's liberal credentials. Both the Foundation and the Liberal International recommended the Republican Party to the ALDE.[179] However, the application was complicated by the UNM's engagement with VVD and FNS. At the moment of application, the UNM was trying to establish some contacts with the Liberals as well. It caused confusion within the European Liberals. Yet, after the UNM's official application to the EPP, the conflict was resolved and the Republicans were accepted.[180]

ALDE and the Liberal Party (Moldova)

In November 2011, the party obtained full membership at the ALDE Summit in Helsinki. In striking contrast to other parties in the region, the driving forces behind the cooperation were youth and women's branches of the Liberal Party. Earlier, the youth organisation started the cooperation with European Liberal Youth (LYMEC), a youth organisation of the ALDE, and with International Federation of Liberal Youth (IFLRY), an international liberal youth organisation. Prior to the final decision to join the European Liberals, some party members were lobbying for the affiliation with the EPP. Due to close relationships with the Romanian Democratic Liberal Party, the Moldovan Liberals considered it as a fast track to the EPP affiliation.[181] Among the proponents of the EPP was Dorin Chirtoaca, the vice-president of the party. The members of the newly split Liberal Reformist Party (established in April 2013) were also among the supporters of the EPP affiliation. However, the strong position of Corina Fusu, deputy minister of the Liberals, in

---

179   Interview with the Republican Party representative, 14 April 2014.
180   Bader, *Against All Odds*, 115.
181   Interview with the Liberal Party representative, 23 January 2014.

favour of ALDE and existing contacts of youth and women's organisations with European liberal branches overweighed other choices.

During the fact-finding mission, FNS became an important source of information for the party's assessment. However, it was the Dutch VVD who helped to facilitate the application process.[182] Whereas FNS and VVD served as intermediaries establishing trust between the Moldovan Liberals and the ALDE, the party's solid election results gave the application certain credibility. In the 2007 local elections, the party candidate, Chirtoaca, gathered 61.17% of voter support and won over Veaceslav Iordan, the Communist candidate, to the Chisinau mayor's office.[183] The Moldovan Liberals used their sound results in the 2009–2010 elections as well as their participation in the pro-European coalition as fine arguments for their application.[184] After three years of observer membership, the party was granted full membership status in 2011.

Among the European partners, the Moldovan Liberals named the Romanian National Liberal Party as the closest like-minded partner who switched in May 2014 from the ALDE to the EPP because of a better "doctrine compatibility".[185] Additionally, the British Liberal Democrats and the Dutch VVD were identified as close partners. Locally, the Liberal Party actively cooperates with FNS and the Westminster Foundation for Democracy. After the affiliation with ALDE, the Liberal Party applied to the Liberal International, but the application was postponed due to the party leader's critical statement about sexual minorities. The relationships were considerably damaged and the Liberals tried to whiten their image by organising the IFLRY Congress in Chisinau in 2012.[186]

---

182   Interview with the Liberal Reformist Party representative, 18 January 2014.
183   "Local Elections," *E-democracy*, 2007.
184   Interview with the ALDE representative, 7 October 2013.
185   "Romanian Liberals Seek EPP affiliation," *EurActiv*, 26 May 2014.
186   Interview with the Liberal Party representative, 23 January 2014.

The EL and the Party of Communists (Moldova)

In 2006, the Party of Communists (PCRM) applied to the EL and after a year was accepted as a full member. Prior to the decision to join the EL, the Communists were searching for an appropriate partner in the European arena. While staying in power since 2001, the Moldovan Communists alleviated their position on anti-Western rhetoric and in 2007 even announced a "liberal revolution".[187] Due to deteriorated relationships with Russia, the Communists started looking for alternative partners, this time in Europe. At the beginning, the party was also considering whether to join the Social International and its close partner the PES. The French Jacque Jearés Foundation together with the Swedish and the Greek Socialists were lobbying the party's affiliation with the PES.[188] However, the requirements from the Socialists demanded more transformations within the party which the Communists could not fulfil. Insufficiently reformed in terms of ideology and structure, the party was pushed further to the left — to the Eurosceptic EL.

Among the EL parties, the Moldovan Communists identify themselves with the German *Die Linke* and with the Italian and French Communists. Interestingly enough, the PCRM possesses no close links to the Russian and Ukrainian Communists.[189] In contrast, the party established cooperation with the Chinese Communists through educational exchanges for experience in social-economic modernisation. Additionally, the party cooperates with *transform!* europe, an organisation affiliated to the EL, and its local branch, *transform!* moldova. Recently, the party established a new contact with Rosa-Luxemburg-Stiftung in Moscow.

The AECR and the Christian Democratic Movement (Georgia)

Prior to the affiliation with the AECR, the party in vain tried to establish cooperation with the EPP. Formally, the application to the EPP failed because the party had already become a member of the European Conservative Political Movement (ECPM), another, far

---

187 Interview with the ADEPT expert, 20 January 2014.
188 Ibid.
189 Ibid.

more marginal Europarty, which contradicted the EPP's internal regulations. Informally, the UNM's stance on the Christian Democrats' application played a decisive role. Allegedly, the UNM was blocking Christian Democratic Movement's (CDM) application to remain the only Georgian party in the EPP. The relationships between the CDM and the EPP became somewhat emotional. From the EPP's perspective, they were waiting for the election results to make an ultimate decision on the CDM's application. Afterwards, they were planning to send a fact-finding mission to Georgia. Two weeks prior to the scheduled mission, the CDM announced in a press release that they had joined the European Conservatives. The application to the EPP was suspended and all events with local KAS were cancelled.[190] From the CDM's perspective, the EPP unconditionally favoured the UNM and neglected the party's needs. The Christian Democrats found communication from the EPP and KAS poor and unclear, whereas they noted a very good friendship with the former foundation's leadership. In their view, they were ready to withdraw their membership from the ECPM if the membership in the EPP were promised.[191]

Identifying themselves as a centre-right party, the Christian Democrats considered only two options for their affiliation on the EU level—either the EPP or AECR. Hence, joining the European Conservatives became the second-best choice for the party. Operating rationally, Euroscepticism of the AECR did not deter the party from the cooperation. The Christian Democrats acknowledged that the reason was mainly power-driven. They aspired to become part of a more powerful family, while the ECPM had shown little prospect for growth over the last decade. As a result, the party joined the more prestigious AECR.[192]

In bilateral party relations, the Christian Democrats pointed out close cooperation with the UK Conservatives (through the Westminster Foundation) and the Dutch Christian Democrats. Previously, in 2009–2012, relations with the German CDU were very

---

190   Interview with the KAS representative, 23 April 2014.
191   Interview with the CDM representative, 29 April 2014.
192   Ibid.

active on a party-to-party basis. Additionally, the party is a member of the International Democratic Union (IDU) family.

Conclusions

Being aware of dealing with immature and unfledged political parties in the non-EU countries, the Europarties employ a different approach in CEE countries. Apart from the Europarty's formal internal regulations, informal factors play a more important role in the application and selection procedures. In fact, the Europarties diminish the strictness of their formal requirements and rely predominantly on informal ones. Instead of searching for classical conservative, socialist, or liberal parties, the Europarties are more interested in an applicant party's sustainability and viability. In order to promote their norms and values, stable and credible parties are of particular interest for the Europarties. In addition, the Europarties are looking for democratic credentials and pro-European stances of the applicant parties. In a highly volatile post-communist environment, established mutual trust and personal contacts act as a reliable proxy for driving cooperation further and usually predetermine the outcome of the application's review. Local partners usually — the German party foundation — play an indispensable role in channeling trust between the Europarties and applicant parties. Operating as interlockers, the German party foundations provide reliable information to the Europarties about the applicants, whereas domestic parties can utilise the foundations' "opportunity structures" in obtaining direct contact with the Europarties' leadership.

Analysing the patterns of cooperation cross-nationally, there are several comparative conclusions to be made. Firstly, each country differs in the coverage of the European party families. In Ukraine, centrist and centre-right parties established cooperation only with the EPP, while the Moldovan parties covered the whole political spectrum, including the affiliation with the European Communists. In Georgia, cooperation has been established with three European party families — the EPP, the ALDE, and the AECR. Secondly, the empirical evidence shows that major or catch-all parties usually prefer to establish affiliations with the EPP and the PES.

Here the political weight of political party matters. Often forming the government or being a strong opposition, catch-all parties aspire to cooperate with the prestigious EPP and PES, whereas minor parties are usually affiliated with the ALDE, the EL, and the AECR. As the major Europarties are interested in viable political forces, their incentive structures coincide with the motives of catch-all non-EU parties. The EPP and the PES tend to cooperate with governmental or influential parties that can trigger changes in countries. The UNM, the *Batkivshchyna* party, and the LDPM as leading forces of countries' revolutions are the EPP sister parties.

On the other hand, being a viable political force, it gives a domestic party certain leverage in the bargaining process. Thus, despite its leftist leaning, the *Batkivshchyna* party was incorporated in the EPP family as a credible party. Similarly to the EPP, driven by strategic considerations the PES also searched for influential parties. However, operating in a post-communist environment, the PES' affiliations were overshadowed by links to oligarch-driven parties. For example, the PES established links to the DPM ruled by de facto oligarch and had some informal dialogue with the Party of Regions and the Georgian Dream — parties with strong oligarchic structures. In contrast, the minor parties are limited in their bargaining power. In this situation, minor parties sometimes favour their second-best decision and try to find an unoccupied niche. As a result, the Ukrainian *Rukh's* application was only reviewed together with the then-more-influential "Our Ukraine", whereas applications from the marginal New Rights and Christian Democrats have been blocked by the UNM. The long-lasting UNM's objection to support the CDM's application to the EPP caused the party's shift to the European Conservatives.

5. Incentive Structures for Cooperation

Joining a particular European party family, political party indicates its ideological preferences. The affiliation with European *familles spirituelles* signalises parties' shared values and beliefs.[193] However, the affiliation process for the non-EU parties is not necessarily based on ideological commitments alone. Frequently, the non-EU parties join the Europarties for instrumental reasons or due to the prestigious and reputational status of cooperation.

On the one hand, the Europarties do not obtain any additional votes in the EP by incorporating newcomers from the non-EU member states. On the other hand, observer parties are deprived of votes and initiative rights, which makes the cooperation limited. Nevertheless, despite the absence of immediate rewards, the Europarties willingly grant memberships to parties outside the EU, while the non-EU parties eagerly initiate cooperation with the Europarties. Thus, this chapter aims to envisage the incentive structures that trigger this cooperation by addressing the interplay of rational and ideational motivations. It seeks to answer the first research question: *what are the incentives for the Europarties and domestic parties to cooperate with each other?*

The reason for taking both perspectives is twofold. Firstly, as the establishment of cooperation is a process of interaction and bargaining, it is important to reveal the costs and benefits for both sides. Secondly, considering the bargaining process of cooperation at the pre-acceptance stage, it is crucial to understand which resources can be exchanged in this interaction and what motivations both actors have. Using their resources as leverage, domestic parties might influence the process of the Europarties' selection.

This chapter focusses on the Europarty families and their affiliated sister parties, and is structured in the following way. Firstly, it examines the motivations for both the Europarties and domestic

---

[193] Klaus von Beyme, *Political Parties in Western Democracies* (Aldershot: Gower, 1985), 444.

parties that drive cooperation. Secondly, it takes domestic parties' perspectives and elucidates their identification and selection processes of a potential European party family. In the concluding remarks, the chapter summarises parties' motivations and draws commonalities in the application and selection procedures across the Europarties and domestic parties.

5.1 Motives for the Europarties

By establishing links with parties from outside the EU, the Europarties are deprived of one of their main interests for transnational cooperation: the maximisation of parliamentary influence.[194] Due to the limited status of their observer membership, the non-EU parties are restrained in their vote and initiative rights, and are detached from the EP Groups. Thus, when cooperating with the non-EU parties, the Europarties do not obtain any additional seats in the EP and possess no *direct* influence on national policy-making. Nevertheless, despite the absence of straightforward benefits, the Europarties willingly cooperate with like-minded non-EU parties. There are multiple motives for establishing cooperation.

Promotion of norms and values

First of all, the primary objective of cooperation for the European party families is bound to *the promotion of norms and values*. The Europarties are interested in forming an ideational network that does not necessarily end at the EU's borders. They are keen to sustain and strengthen their network of like-minded partners, which is based on common values. By expanding their networks, the Europarties aim to promote their party family's ideological commitments both within and beyond Europe.

Each Europarty explicitly mentions promoting norms and values in their statutes. The EPP's statutes point out the promotion of

---

[194] Karl Magnus Johansson, *Transnational Party Alliances: Analysing the Hard-Won Alliance between Conservatives and Christian Democrats in the European Parliament* (Lund: Lund University Press, 1997), 128.

"free and pluralistic democracy" and "respect for human rights, fundamental freedoms and the rule of law".[195] The Europarty's promotion is not solely confined by the party family's ideological values, such as Christian democracy, European federalism, social market economy or subsidiarity. In fact, the EPP had already embarked on a wide-open strategy during the CEE enlargement process. The EPP took "a very broad definition of Christian democracy" in disseminating its values.[196] Leaving its Christian Democratic framework, the EPP focussed on the inclusion of conservative- and liberal-leaning groups, which diluted the core of its identity.[197] The strategy proved to be quite practical in the non-EU countries, where the tradition of Christian democracy is even weaker. Hence, the EPP is more focussed here on spreading democratic standards and freedoms. Guided by these rather general values, the Europarty aimed to "expand its influence to the post-Soviet space as well".[198] Together with the promotion of democratic values, equally important for the centre-right party is the promotion of deeper European integration, which helps the EPP to approximate neighbouring countries closer to the EU.[199]

The PES' commitment in the region overlaps with the EPP's views. The Socialists stand for "the promotion of democratic values and fight for the respect of fundamental freedoms"[200] as well as the countries' rapprochement to the EU. Yet in its statutes, the PES is more explicit about promoting the party family's values. The PES aims to "strengthen the socialist, social democratic, labour and

---

195 The EPP Statute (Marseille: EPP, December 2011).
196 David Hanley, "Christian Democracy and the Paradoxes of Europeanisation. Flexibility, Competition and Collusion," *Party Politics* 8:4 (2002): 473.
197 Pascal Delwit, "The European Peole's Party stages and analysis of a transformation," in *The Europarties: Organisation and Influence*, ed. Pascal Delwit, Erol Külahci, and Cédric Van Walle (Brussels: ULB, 2004), 141.
198 Interview with the EPP representative, 15 October 2013.
199 Interview with the EPP representative, 10 October 2013.
200 PES Press Release (Brussels: PES, 25 June 2014).

democratic progressive movement and its values in the Union and throughout Europe".[201]

In the same vein, the European Liberals state their purpose as being "to strengthen the liberal, democrat and reform movement in the European Union and throughout Europe".[202] With regard to the non-EU countries, the ALDE shares the view of the major Europarties. In the Eastern Partnership, the Europarty aims to guard democratic values such as "the sustainable development of democracy, human rights and the rule of law".[203] The European Liberals are interested in ensuring that "all partners of the Eastern Partnership live up to these commitments"[204] as well as their participation in this process. ALDE shares the idea of promoting European and liberal values.

Similarly, the aim of the European Left is to "promote the social, emancipatory, ecological, peace-loving as well as democratic and progressive thinking and acting".[205] The European Left seeks the realignment of left forces against neoliberal policies and institutions. In CEE countries, due to their strong communist legacy, the European Left highlights its commitment towards anti-Stalinism and democratic pluralism.[206]

Channels of access and influence

The Europarties invest in the future by finding potential partners. By integrating like-minded partners into their party families, the Europarties will have direct links to political elites and will gain access to key decision-makers; subsequently, they can indirectly influence national policy-making. In this respect, an expansionist strategy is conducive to yielding access and influence, by incorporating as many partners as possible. Through the Europarties acting

---

201 PES Resolution (Brussels: PES, September 2012).
202 ELDR Statute (Brussels: ALDE, April 2004).
203 ALDE Press Release (Brussels: ALDE, April 2013).
204 Ibid.
205 EL Statute (Rome: EL, May 2004).
206 Richard Dunphy and Luke March, "Seven Year Itch? The European Left Party: Struggling to Transform the EU," *Perspectives on European Politics and Society* 14:4 (2013): 528.

by inertia, the expansionist strategy was transferred to the non-EU countries as well.

In contrast to cooperation with CEE parties, there is a lack of conditionality and leverage associated with the EU membership perspective. Yet, despite vaguely defined EU prospects, the Europarties are still keen to establish links in the EU neighbouring states and thus expand their influence into post-Soviet space. The Europarties rely on their local partners to have indirect access to domestic policy-making. While mediating political crises, the Europarties have direct access to political elites to facilitate and/or influence political solutions. As a result, the Europarties' access can potentially contribute to reduced transaction costs in terms of political risks and instabilities. As Martens put succinctly:

> My long experience with the parties in Central and Eastern Europe has taught me that to create partnerships in politically unstable countries is very difficult and full of risks. But for a pan-European party like the EPP that is eager to disseminate its programme and values across the continent cannot wait. [...] We have always taken risks, and that is why we are the largest political movement in Europe. At the same time, I am convinced that the engagement of pan-European parties in countries like Ukraine actually contributes to political stability and democratic maturity.[207]

In this respect, the Europarties' policy towards identifying likeminded partners is of significant importance. Building links with sustainable and viable parties promises lasting access and influence in the countries for the Europarties. In particular, the EPP officially embarked on an expansion strategy to build channels for governing and/or promising governing parties.

The EPP had already highlighted its strategic considerations at the earlier stages of the EU's enlargement. The EU enlargement process and the EPP's expansion strategy happened simultaneously. After turning to a pragmatic approach, the EPP was not "a storehouse for Christian Democratic ideas" anymore.[208] The inclusion of the Greek New Democracy and Spanish People's Party proved the EPP's interest in parties with real political influence. As

---

207 Wilfried Martens, *Europe: I Struggle, I Overcome* (Brussels: Springer, 2008), 216.
208 Johansson, *Transnational Party Alliances*, 135.

potential government parties, these Greek and Spanish applicant parties were accepted to the EPP despite their non-traditional Christian Democratic party profiles. Torn between the "widening vs deepening" dilemma, the EPP made a decision in favour of attracting new allies. In fact, the German CDU/CSU pushed for the viewpoint of power politics to become the strongest party in the EP.[209] In his speech, Thomas Jansen, a former EPP Secretary General, stressed that the EPP's "credibility and influence demands that we be presented in all the countries which belong or will belong to the European Union. That also applies to countries where, for historical and cultural reasons, there have been no Christian Democratic parties or where the political culture has prevented the emergence of a broad-based People's Party with Christian Democratic orientation".[210]

Later, in the 1990s, this expansion strategy was transferred to next candidate countries. Parties from new target states — ranging from conservatives to liberals — were encouraged to become EPP associate members. Promoting a "familiarisation strategy", the EPP opened access to various EPP bodies. As a result, the EPP expanded its presence in Central Europe by granting seven associate memberships to its former observers. At the end, the EPP possessed direct access to the parties in governments in Hungary, Romania, Bulgaria, Poland, and Slovakia.[211]

The EPP applied the same expansionist strategy to the EU neighbouring countries. The Europarty was interested in parties with political weight, namely parties that participate in national and local elections and/or are represented in the parliament, which gave the Europarty better access and influence in the domestic arena. Underlining its pragmatic approach, the EPP is not be keen to support a purely Christian Democratic party that wins marginal percentages of vote shares.[212] Rather, the EPP looks beyond distinc-

---

209 Johansson, *Transnational Party Alliances*, 152.
210 Ibid., 137.
211 Hanley, "Christian Democracy," 474.
212 Interview with the former KAS representative, 5 November 2013.

tive Christian Democratic parties to search for parties with real political power. In this respect, the promotion of norms and values is bound to the sustainability of political parties. The Europarty sees stable and viable parties as the best way to promote its norms and values.

The PES' rationale proves to be very similar to the EPP's. Politics outweighed ideological proximity as the PES was also keen to accept influential parties.[213] With direct access to party elites, the PES could influence the partisan composition of domestic governments as well as influence the "balance of power" in the enlarged EU.[214] The enlargement of the EU put the PES in jeopardy of losing a social democratic majority. In terms of political relevance, most of the CEE parties possessed conservative profiles.[215] To some extent, this fact changed the PES' engagement in the region by making it discard its purist ideological approach. The PES became interested in finding access to electoral heavyweights and ensuring majorities in the EP after the accession of the new CEE countries.[216] For example, in Bulgaria, the PES attempted to consolidate the social democratic forces to create a strong leftist party. However, after failing to achieve its goal, the PES favoured electoral relevance over ideological proximity: "The PES switched its support from the BEL to the BSP [The Bulgarian Socialist Party] when it became clear that the BEL was no longer a major electoral contestant although it continued to maintain the principles of social democracy".[217]

The PES could not easily apply its expansionist strategy to dealing with the party successors of the communist parties. Doomed by its negative experiences in Slovakia and Romania, the

---

213 Delsoldato, "Eastward Enlargement," 281.
214 Robert Ladrech, "Programmatic Change in the Party of European Socialists," in *Social Democracy in Europe,* ed. Pascal Delwit (Brussels: ULB, 2005), 52–53.
215 Robert Ladrech, "The Party of European Socialists: Networking Europe's Social Democrats," *Journal of Policy History* 15:1 (2003): 126.
216 James Sloam, "West European Social Democracy as a Model for Transfer," *Journal of Communist Studies and Transition Politics* 21:1 (2005): 78.
217 Spirova, "Europarties and Party," 802.

PES became more cautious with potential damage to its image.[218] While using their PES affiliation as a "badge of approval",[219] CEE parties failed to adopt ideological or behavioural changes.[220] In Slovakia, SMER—using the PES' social democratic credentials—shifted its ideological orientations by forging a coalition with the far-right Slovak Nationalist Party. The PES excluded SMER for non-compliance with its declaration, which excludes "any form of political alliance or cooperation at all levels with any political party incites or attempts to stir up racial or ethnic prejudices and ethnic hatred".[221] In Romania, the PES promptly granted associate membership to the Party of Social Democrats. Due to its political weight, the party was favoured within the PES.[222] Led by Nastase, the party emulated progress in conducting reforms. However, instead of the democratisation declared on paper, political interference in the judicial system and physical harassment of the journalists took place.[223] In the non-EU countries, whereas the EPP put emphasis on viability, the PES concentrated on sustainability. Before accepting any parties, the PES needed to check the sustainability of its applicant parties. The PES was looking for powerful parties within the CEE countries: "We want to cooperate with some parties that are in the parliament and that have some influence".[224] Nevertheless, the negative experience with the Europarty's image being misused in the past put certain restrictions on their expansionist strategy. The PES categorically refused to deal with the Ukrainian Socialist Party after its betrayal of the Orange forces and its collaboration with the

---

218 Interview with the European Forum for Democracy and Solidarity representative, 5 October 2013.
219 Tim Haughton, "Driver, Conductor or Fellow Passenger?" 413.
220 Holmes and Lightfoot, "Limited Influence?" 42.
221 PES General Resolution (Warsaw: PES, October 2010).
222 Zolt Enyedi and Paul Lewis, "The Impact of the European Union on Party Politics in Central and Eastern Europe," in *The European Union and Party Politics*, ed. Paul Lewis and Zdanka Mansfeldova (Basingstoke, United Kingdom: Palgrave Macmillan, 2006).
223 Tom Gallaher, "The European Union and Romania: Consolidating Backwardness?" *Open Democracy* 26 (September 2006).
224 Interview with the PES representative, 15 October 2013.

Party of Regions. Despite its leftist label, the Georgian Labour party was denied any cooperation because of its notoriously authoritarian party leader.[225]

The post-Maastricht developments and the Eastern enlargement changed the European Liberals' approach as well. In 2004, the Europarty's leader Sir Graham Watson explicitly embarked on an expansionist strategy, acknowledging the importance of size in the EP.[226] As a result, the centrist French *Mouvement Démocrate* and Italian *Margarita* forces joined to strengthen the liberal party family. In order to become the third-largest party in the EP, ALDE aimed to yield access and influence from new joining countries. In this situation, ideological cohesion was sacrificed to a wide-ning strategy. The emerging new post-communist parties gave the Liberals new momentum for expansion. ALDE was interested in exerting influence on local political situations and public opinion.[227] Due to the high fluidity of political parties and weak liberal tradition in CEE countries, ALDE loosened its requirements towards ideological commitments. To attract new members, ALDE had to remain open, as the ideologically close EPP lured more applicants because of its powerful position in the EP.

In the same vein, the EL embarked on a pragmatic approach by widening its network. The EL decided to favour geographical expansion over ideological cohesion. In this respect, the Eastern enlargement promised the Europarty good chances to follow its expansionist strategy. From its 15 founding members in 2004, by 2012 the EL comprised 27 full members. Among the most significant partners were the communist parties from the Czech Republic, Moldova, and Finland. Prioritising quantity over quality, the EL also accepted PAS, the former Romanian Communist Party, and the Hungarian Communist Workers' Party (which left in 2009). Both

---

225 Interview with the European Forum for Democracy and Solidarity representative, 5 October 2013.
226 Julia Smith "Between Ideology and Pragmatism: Liberal Party Politics at the European Level," *Acta Politica* 49 (2014): 112.
227 Interview with the ALDE representative, 7 October 2013.

partners failed to comply with anti-Stalinism and commitment to democratic pluralism. Yet, disregarding ideological proximity, the EL aimed to absorb as many parties as possible.[228]

Competition between the Europarties

Connected to the previous motive, the *competition* among the major Europarties triggered the expansion of cooperation further eastwards. The competitive logic of the Europarties' development remains encapsulated in terms of widening their networks. Propelled by inertia after the enlargement process, the Europarties employed the widening approach in the neighbouring countries as well. Once each country is integrated into the EU, the Europarty will already have links to a stable and viable partner. In turn, the strategies of rival Europarties influence other Europarties' decisions regarding expansion. Although the Europarties cannot increase their parliamentary influence by engaging with the non-EU parties, it is also prestigious for the Europarties to have a broad network of likeminded parties beyond the EU. Having partners outside Europe can increase the influence of the Europarties internationally and enhance their image as Europeanists and promoters of democracy. As will be shown in the empirical chapters later, the competition among the Europarties has had its own effect on the Europarties' impact on the ideological, and behavioural dimensions.

As the main arena of competition within the non-EU countries is outside of parliament, the rivalry among the Europarties also takes place elsewhere. In order to prevent the incorporation of new, incoming parties into rival party families, the Europarties can mitigate their selection criteria or introduce attractive membership benefits. The Europarties are fully aware of the weak ideological commitments among post-communist parties and apply less strict programmatic requirements. While spreading its ideas in the region, ALDE competes with the EPP, whereas, on the left, the PES competes with the EL. For example, the EPP does not have the goal to find a distinctive Christian Democratic party, but a viable pro-European political force. It is always a compromise between the

---

228   Dunphy and March, "Seven Year Itch?" 528.

party's values and its political weight. Similarly, the ALDE is ready to compromise on certain issues and loosen its criteria. Acknowledging the high sensitivity of sexual and ethnical rights in the region, the ALDE would not exclude a party for misbehaviour or the application of anti-liberal policies in the LGBT sphere.[229] In the same way, the European Left is reluctant to impose strict conditions. The EL observes the processes of parties' transition and transformation patiently and is less stringent regarding the lack of internal party democracy.[230]

Similarly, different membership options are offered to compete with more influential and prestigious Europarties. For example, the ALDE decided to abandon its degrees of membership and to offer full membership to the non-EU countries. Additionally, the Europarty actively utilises individual membership "to reach out to people of liberal disposition in countries where there is no member party".[231] As the EPP's types of membership are still structured into the EU members, candidate states, and non-candidate states, ALDE's approach seems to be more inclusive and thus more attractive for new incoming parties. By granting full membership to the non-EU parties, ALDE gives them a prestigious opportunity to participate on the same footing with the EU parties. The EL has employed the same approach. The Europarty draws no distinction between its EU and the non-EU members, thus, for example, equalising the German *Linke* and the Moldovan Communists.[232]

5.2 Motives for the non-EU parties

While CEE countries were given a credible EU membership perspective, countries from the Eastern Partnership do not possess

---

229 Interview with the ALDE representative, 7 October 2013.
230 Interview with *transform!* europe representative, 3 February 2014.
231 Camilla Sandström, "The European Liberal, Democrat and Reform Party: From Co-operation to Integration," in *The Europarties: Organisation and Influence*, ed. Pascal Delwit, Erol Külahci and Cèdric van de Walle, (Brussels: ULB, 2004), 171.
232 Dunphy and March, "Seven Year Itch?" 524.

such a "carrot". Nevertheless, despite the lack of the EU membership perspective, domestic parties from non-EU countries willingly initiate cooperation with the Europarties. The motives of domestic parties to establish links with the Europarties vary based on their cost–benefit analyses.

Domestic legitimacy and international recognition

First, domestic parties benefit from the cooperation by acquiring domestic legitimacy and international recognition.[233] In the domestic arena, parties use European affiliation as a benchmark for serious, trustworthy, and genuinely pro-European parties. Political parties in this region are unsustainable and volatile, and undergo transitions and transformations. In this respect, they use international recognition as a proxy for their seriousness and credibility. Parties aim to secure their reputation domestically via external acknowledgement and convert trust and recognition accrued on the international arena into domestic legitimacy. Domestic parties aim to compensate for their immaturity and provincialism by having European partners. In domestic parties' views, their affiliation with Europarties by default means adherence to a club of credible and reputable parties. As an illustration, the LDPM portrayed Merkel's and Barroso's visits to Chisinau in August and November 2012, respectively, as acceptance into the EU party elites and as an important sign of successful European integration.[234] For the Georgian Republicans, their affiliation was proof of their seriousness as a liberal and pro-European force.[235] As a party representative put it, "the affiliation shows our voters and our opponents where we belong to, so that nobody can doubt our ideology".[236] Alternatively, international affiliation helps domestic parties to raise awareness among the population and thus to overcome the party's marginality, especially when in opposition. For the marginal Ukrainian People's

---

233 Delsoldato, "Eastern Enlargement," 275; Pridham, "The European Union's Democratic Conditionality and Domestic Politics in Slovakia," 198.
234 Interview with the ADEPT expert, 20 January 2014.
235 Interview with the Republican Party representative, 18 April 2014.
236 Interview with the Republican Party representative, 14 April 2014.

Movement, *Rukh*, its affiliation with the EPP was perceived as very prestigious. Internally, adherence to the influential Europarty family helped to buttress self-esteem among the party's members. Externally, reporting about the EPP's resolutions and decisions, *Rukh* could obtain more credibility domestically and highlight its party profile publically.[237]

In other cases, the usage of the European affiliation not only helped domestic parties to bolster their identity but also to separate themselves from populist and technical parties or to delegitimise the positions of their opponents.[238] For instance, for the Georgian Republican Party, the cooperation gave the party more substance and helped to separate them from populist parties with declarative statements. In the case of the Democratic Party of Moldova, which aspired to break away from its post-communist legacy, the party strived to enhance their image through recognition by the European party elites. For the DPM, the affiliation with European Socialists was important to separate themselves from the Communists and to show that they represent the only left-wing party in the country. Utilising the PES affiliation, the DPM positioned itself as a truly social democratic party, whereas the Communists and the Social Democratic Party were portrayed as marginal forces.[239]

Electoral and political support

During electoral campaigning, representatives from the Europarties actively support their potential partners or already-accepted sister parties. For example, in the Moldovan case, the EPP supported Filat enormously during the 2010 parliamentary campaign. Prior to the elections, Martens visited Chisinau and basically campaigned for the LDPM. During a joint press conference, he openly supported the LDPM's electoral programme and team; also, he

---

237   Interview with the *Rukh* representative, youth branch, 21 November 2013.
238   Arne Niemann, *Explaining Decisions in the European Union* (Cambridge: Cambridge University Press, 2006), 42.
239   Interview with expert, Moldova State University, 16 January 2014.

voiced his conviction that "the country has a clear European vocation".[240]

On the other hand, domestic parties actively mention their affiliation in their campaigns. They often refer to it in their public statements and electoral campaigns to emphasise their links with the Europarties. The affiliation serves as a proxy for the party's seriousness and credibility, and also helps to attract new or preserve old pro-European voters. For example, in 2005, over 77% of the Moldovan population expressed their support for European integration.[241] In this situation, the Moldovan Communists shifted towards pro-Europeanism, as campaigning on its pro-Russian message alone could have weakened their electoral base. As a result, a change in the population's attitude partly triggered the party's move to Europeanism, backed by its affiliation with the EL.

Apart from when appealing to voters, parties frequently instrumentalise their affiliation in their inter-party debates. While addressing voters, domestic parties underline the fact of their *European* affiliation; among domestic party elites, however, they emphasise their affiliation with *major* Europarties. In fact, voters rarely even know about the existence of the Europarties at all, let alone the ability to distinguish between them. In contrast, for domestic parties themselves, being affiliated with the prestigious EPP and PES is an important argument for proving their credibility and legitimacy. In the interviews, party representatives — cross-nationally and regardless of left-right positions — underlined an issue of prestige embodied in their Europarty's observer memberships.

Equally important, the affiliation promises political support for parties' activities, both in government and in opposition. Whereas parties in government can substantiate their reforms and policies by getting the Europarties' approval, parties in opposition can obtain an additional channel through which they can raise their

---

240 EPP Group Press Release (Brussels: EPP Group, 21 October 2010).
241 Luke March, "From Moldovanism to Europeanisation? Moldova's Communists and Nation Building," *Nationalities Papers: The Journal of Nationalism and Ethnicity* 35:4 (2005): 617.

voices and obtain international support. For instance, the EPP vocally supported the governments of Vlad Filat, Yulia Tymoshenko, and Mikheil Saakashvili and their progress on the path towards European integration. In the *Batkivshchyna* case, the EPP fully supported Tymoshenko as prime minister. Martens and Daul expressed their confidence that "prime-minister Tymoshenko will give new impetus to Ukraine's European drive—needless to say, the EPP will be ready to assist her in this process".[242] Likewise, the UNM leader Saakashvili received the EPP's unwavering support. In his letter in *Le Monde*, Martens expressed his support for Georgia on its reforms and European integration: "I know that I can count on President Saakashvili to strengthen democracy in Georgia", added Martens.[243] In Moldova, after the non-confidence vote in 2013, the EPP reassured that "Vlad Filat enjoys the full support and trust of the whole EPP political family. [...] I am confident that under the leadership of Vlad Filat the pro-European forces will be able to form as soon as possible a functioning government which will implement the remaining necessary reforms for the country's European agenda".[244]

Likewise, while in opposition, domestic parties have enjoyed substantial support from their European party families. In particular, the EPP backed its sister parties by providing enormous vocal support against the imprisonments of Yulia Tymoshenko, the then already ex-prime-minister, and Vano Merabishvili, the UNM ex-Secretary General. The EPP frequently declared its full support and solidarity with the former opposition leader Tymoshenko and expressed its condemnation of the aggressive, politically motivated pressure against its sister party's leader.[245] The EPP vocally criticised the Yanukovich government for curtailing democratic free-

---

242   EPP Press Release (Brussels: EPP, 18 December 2007).
243   Wilfried Martens, "Confortons la démocratie in Géorgie," *Le Monde*, 4 July 2012.
244   EPP Press Release (Brussels: EPP, 17 April 2013).
245   EPP Press Release (Brussels: EPP, 17 December 2010).

doms and spreading authoritarian practises exemplified by the imposition of a travel ban on Tymoshenko.²⁴⁶ Later, after Tymoshenko's imprisonment, the EPP gathered broad support among the EU's leaders to strongly condemn the politically motivated trial.²⁴⁷ Similarly, the EPP equivocally expressed its support for the UNM ex-Secretary General and ex-Interior Minister Merabishvili after his detention. The EPP MEP Saryusz-Wolski condemned Ivanishvili's government for backsliding on democracy and warned against following a path of "selective justice, revenge and repression of the opposition".²⁴⁸ In both cases, domestic parties utilised the Europarty's platform to raise the awareness internationally and to gain more support domestically.

Geopolitical advantage

Affiliation with major Europarties is sometimes perceived from a geopolitical perspective. The cooperation with the Europarties — which is often challenged by pro-Russian forces — promises the backing of domestic parties from the European party elites in geopolitical issues. For the UNM, the EPP affiliation meant support in its geopolitical conflict. In 2008, the Russian–Georgian war significantly cooled down the pro-American orientations of Saakashvili's party. The remoteness of the United States from the region led to reconsiderations of the country's allies. The UNM's expectations of the EPP's tougher position on Russia than that of the Liberals predetermined the party's choice.²⁴⁹ In this situation, geopolitical considerations overruled the party's choice. In turn, the EPP constantly expressed its support and assistance for the UNM, by criticising Russia's aggressive actions in the Georgian territories. To a similar extent, the decision of the Moldovan Communists to join the Europarty was indirectly influenced by geopolitical factors. After the

---

246 EPP Press Release (Brussels: EPP, 2 February 2011).
247 EPP Press Release (Brussels: EPP, 4 May 2011).
248 "Usupashvili Meets MEPs from Foreign Affairs Committee," *Civil Georgia*, 18 June 2013.
249 Interview with the Republican Party representative, 18 April 2014.

Russia-backed Kozak Memorandum favouring the federalisation of Moldova, the Moldovan Communists abandoned its pro-Russian vector and pledged to support European integration. Realising "Russia's malign intent"[250], Voronin turned the party's rhetoric towards European integration. After gaining momentum from the public popularity of its European orientation, the Moldovan Communists joined the EL.

Lobbying of EU integration
The affiliation with the Europarties is perceived as a platform for advancing the country's European aspirations. During regular mutual meetings and visits, the domestic parties become familiar with the European institutions and obtain an informal opportunity to lobby for EU integration. Aside from formal negotiations on the governmental level, party networking provides a new "opportunity structure", as an alternative to diplomatic channels. Moreover, direct access to the European party elites offers an opportunity to discuss the matter personally and in a trustworthy manner. For the opposition parties, especially, the affiliation with major Europarties increases the chances of promoting EU integration. Domestic parties have more opportunities to foster their EU aspirations by being affiliated with the influential EPP and PES, which define the EU neighbourhood policy. The interplay among partisan and governmental channels reinforces domestic parties' efforts to propel the EU issue effectively.

In addition, for many parties, their affiliation substantiates their European choice. In the interviews, party representatives often referred to cooperation as a logical step, while promoting their European agenda. In claiming their Europeanness, the affiliation of the parties — ranging from the centre-right "Our Ukraine" to the leftist PCRM — gives more substance and credibility to their European orientation. As a PCRM representative put it, "being in power and promoting European standards without any affiliation on the European level seemed

---

250 Vladimir Socor, "The Regional Impact of Moldova's Elections," *Eurasia Daily Monitor*, 9 March 2005.

to be illogical.²⁵¹ As an illustration of this motive, lobbying for EU integration was the major motive for the *Batkivshchyna* party. Despite being in the socialist grouping in the Council of Europe, with the EPP, the party saw a better opportunity to promote Ukraine's European integration and to build bilateral partnerships with influential European politicians such as Angela Merkel and Nicolas Sarkozy.²⁵² The main incentive for the Georgian UNM to join the EPP was its consistent support for the country's Euro-Atlantic aspirations. In this sense, for the UNM, the EPP represented a platform for pushing its national interests further.²⁵³ For the Moldovan Liberals, its affiliation with the prestigious ALDE was also closely connected with an opportunity to promote EU integration. The Liberals actively utilised their cooperation domestically, by reporting about their mutual events in the media and by using ALDE logos in their domestic activities. For instance, in December 2012, together with ALDE, the Liberal Party organised the conference "Liberals—The Engine of European Integration of Moldova", where they discussed the role of liberal reforms on the path to European integration.²⁵⁴

Knowledge and expertise

Last but not least, the cooperation gives domestic parties an opportunity to obtain knowledge and expertise in European party-building. Through their affiliation with ideologically close European party families, domestic parties position themselves on the political spectrum. In this way, ideologically weak post-communist parties try to crystallise their own identities and sharpen their programmatic profiles.²⁵⁵ A series of trainings and workshops on policy and programme development contribute to knowledge transfer and to solid party profiles. For instance, Filat reiterated that the EPP's values and ideals are "an infinite source for inspiration and optimism for the future".²⁵⁶ For the

---

251 Interview with the Party of Communists representative, 22 January 2014.
252 "Про «зміну орієнтації» партії Батьківщина," *Українська правда*, 8 серпня 2007. ["Of Batkivshchyna's change in orientation," *Ukrainska Pravda*, 8 August 2007].
253 Interview with the UNM representative, 18 April 2014.
254 ALDE News (Brussels: ALDE, 18 December 2012).
255 Pridham 1999, 4, Delsoldato 2002, 275.
256 LDPM Press Release (Chisinau: LDPM, 8 December 2011).

LDPM, the main rationale behind the cooperation was the knowledge exchange in party-building, which led to congruence in their values and organisational structure. In the party's opinion, it facilitated the dialogue with their European partners.[257] In particular, in case of catch-all parties with especially vague party profiles, the European affiliation serves as an anchor for approximating their ideological positions and as guidance for adjusting their organisational structure. All of the catch-all parties (*Batkivshchyna*, the UNM, and the LDPM) mentioned the role of their EPP affiliation in the process of self-identification and crystallisation.[258]

The incentives of each domestic party which triggered the affiliation with the Europarties are summarised below:

Table 5.1 Motivations of the non-EU parties

The Europarty	The non-EU parties	Motivations
EPP	People's Union "Our Ukraine" (UA)	Rational and ideational
EPP	*Batkivshchyna* (UA)	Rational
EPP	People's Movement of Ukraine *Rukh* (UA)	Ideational
EPP	United National Movement (GE)	Rational
EPP	New Rights Party (GE)	Ideational
EPP	Liberal Democratic Party (MD)	Rational and ideational
EPP	Christian Democratic People's Party (MD)	Rational
PES	Democratic Party (MD)	Rational
ALDE	Republican Party (GE)	Ideational
ALDE	Our Georgia-Free Democrats (GE)	Rational and ideational
ALDE	Liberal Party (MD)	Rational
AECR	Christian-Democratic Movement (GE)	Rational
EL	Party of Communists (MD)	Rational

Source: Based on author's interviews

Conclusions

Political weight and prestige penetrate the relationships between the Europarties and domestic parties. As Lebow succinctly noted,

---

257 Interview with the LDPM representatives, 13 January 2014.
258 Ibid; interview with the UNM representative, 15 April 2014; "Про «зміну орієнтації» партії Батьківщина," *Українська правда*, 8 серпня 2007. ["Of Batkivshchyna's change in orientation," *Ukrainska Pravda*, 8 August 2007].

"acquiring prestige is essential for being a great power, just as becoming a great power confers prestige".[259] On the one hand, driven by their motivations of expansion and competition, the Europarties frequently decide in favour of viable political force to substantiate their influential position in the EP. Striving for broader networks and viable partners, it is also prestigious for the Europarties to have sustainable parties with strong political weight, preferably parties in government. On the other hand, political weight of the Europarties and their strong position in the EP are crucial for domestic parties to prove their "great power" status. While selecting among different Europarties, domestic parties analyse their potential benefits from the cooperation and its added value. Interested in lobbying for European integration and acquiring domestic legitimacy, domestic parties usually prefer cooperation with powerful Europarties such as the EPP and the PES.

As each case of the affiliation showed earlier, the incentive structures for both the Europarties and the non-EU parties are multifaceted. In each case, it is a combination of strategic and ideational motives that trigger the cooperation. The Europarties and domestic parties employ both rational and constructivist arguments to engage with each other. Moreover, the predominance of either rational or ideational motives can have different effects on the degree of socialisation and subsequently on the impact on party development. Whereas the predominance of entirely rationalist considerations tends to end up in role playing, genuinely ideational motives tend to lead to normative suasion. Bearing in mind the Europarties' and the non-EU parties' incentive structures, the next chapters will analyse the impact and its level of penetration on party development on the ideological, organisational, and behavioural dimensions.

---

259 Richard Ned Lebow, *A Cultural Theory of International Relations* (Cambridge: Cambridge University Press, 2008), 487.

6. Impact on Ideological Profiles

This chapter aims to assess the congruence of party profiles between the European party federations and their non-EU sister parties. Bearing in mind the low ideological profiles of Eastern European parties and the diluted ideological cores of the Europarties, full congruence of party policies is not expected, but rather an ideological match on *fundamental principles*. The identified fundamental principles and values, which are retrieved from the Europarties' founding documents, serve as a measuring tool for assessing ideological matches. This "ideological checklist" is employed with the aim of showing "the goodness of fit" between an observer member and its chosen European party family. The congruence of party profiles is measured based on *economic* and *social* dimensions. Moreover, the *European* dimension is added to examine each party's stance on European integration. In this respect, the chapter aims to analyse to what extent the affiliated non-EU parties fit into their chosen European party families and under what circumstances the Europarties are ready to make concessions on the ideological dimension and accept newcomers despite obvious ideological misfit.

With regard to the scope conditions, the time factor is expected to have a positive effect on the ideological congruence over the course of affiliation. It is hypothesised that the longer an observer party is affiliated with the Europarty, the greater the ideological match will be (H1). Secondly, strong parties are expected to be less congruent with the Europarty because their ideological profile is broader. In contrast, weak parties are expected to have a closer fit with the Europarty, as their ideological profiles are more consolidated (H2). Thirdly, the motivation factor behind the affiliation is expected to have an impact on the congruence as well. Depending on the incentive structure, the ideological match is likely to be higher when parties join due to their convictions and beliefs, whereas in the case of rational considerations, the congruence is expected to be rather low (H3).

The chapter is structured in the following way. Firstly, it proceeds by summarising the Europarties' fundamental principles.

Secondly, the ideological match between the Europarties and their observer members are assessed using the ideological checklist. Moreover, as the composition of the Europarties is quite diverse, close partners for the non-EU parties are identified within the Europarties. Finally, in the concluding part, it analyses the extent to which the scope conditions affected the "goodness of fit".

6.1 Ideological Match: Fitting into the European Party Family

The European People's Party (EPP)

As the most influential force, the EPP is an attractive choice for many non-EU parties because it gives them an excellent opportunity for the promotion of European integration and for networking with powerful EU politicians. Among all the Europarties, the EPP has a leading position in attracting the non-EU parties — 6 observer parties out of 11 analysed cases of affiliations in total. Over the last decade, the EPP remarkably managed to increase its presence in Moldova, Georgia, and Ukraine. In these neighbouring countries, the EPP possesses strong links with all major political forces which led the Rose, the Orange, and the Twitter Revolutions, respectively.

Ideologically, the EPP comprises conservative and centre-right parties among others, including the German Christian Democratic Union, the French Union for a Popular Movement, and the Polish Civic Platform. Despite its wide composition, the EPP core values can be boiled down to Christian democracy, social market economy, traditional family values, and the principle of subsidiarity.

The EPP's core values and principles are laid down in the 1992 Athens Basic Programme and in the EPP Basic Document, "A Union of Values".[260] Deeply shaped by its historical origin, one of the EPP's core fundamentals is *Christian democracy*. As a political movement and a political philosophy, Christian democracy is reflected

---

[260] EPP Basic Document "A Union of Values," adopted by the Fourteenth EPP Congress in Berlin on 11–13 January 2001.

in the EPP's ideological commitments. In the Christian democratic tradition, none of the particular societal classes is favoured; instead, the emphasis is put on individuals and their fundamental freedoms. Guarding fundamental values such as freedom, equality, justice and solidarity, Christian democracy sees individuals as being responsible for their actions towards both today's society and future generations.[261]

The process of enlargement put pressure on the EPP in organisational and ideological terms. Following the expansionist strategy to include conservative and other like-minded parties, the programmatic profile of the EPP became somewhat diluted. Nevertheless, in 1991, the EPP Secretary General Jansen noted that "we are not prepared to abandon either the Christian Democratic identity or the function of the EPP as a centrist people's party".[262] Furthermore, the Christian democratic Europarty was seen as "a people's party par excellence"[263], allowing the widening of political orientation.

A *federalist Europe* is an intrinsic element of the EPP's ideological profile, and this became a crucial distinction between the EPP and the AECR. The vision of a federalist Europe unites the EPP's other core values, such as subsidiarity, social market economy and personalism:

> The EPP considers that only a federal construction of the European Union can: — on the hand, guarantee unity within diversity and hence respect the national identities and cultural and regional diversities that characterize Europe and result from its history; — on the other hand, ensure a common approach to the solution of common problems.[264]

---

261 EPP Basic Programme, adopted by the Ninth EPP Congress in Athens on 12–14 November 1992.
262 Johansson, *Transnational Party Alliances*, 184.
263 Martens, *Europe: I Struggle, I Overcome*, 39.
264 EPP Basic Programme, adopted by the Ninth EPP Congress in Athens on 12–14 November 1992.

The principle of subsidiarity is the main mechanism of power distribution in a federalist Europe, where national, regional and local authorities retain their functions. "For us a federal structure is best adapted to give form to the principle of subsidiarity: only what we can deal with within the larger entity should be transferred to that entity. In this way the federalism is our 'personalism' in political form".[265]

A *social market economy* is the EPP's next ideological pillar, shaped by the Christian democratic understanding of economic and socio-political models. In this respect, it marries free market competition with social justice and responsibility. Based on the German economic model, the social market economy establishes an order that combines growth with sustainable economic, social and environmental development.[266] For example, "an active climate protection policy is an economic and moral obligation towards safeguarding the natural basis of existence for future generations".[267] In contrast to social democracy, Christian democracy supports personalism and aims to empower individuals to make their own decisions and to remain independent from permanent government support.[268] Finally, *family values* are the fundamental core of Christian democracy; families are treated as social units indispensable for societal cohesion, intergenerational solidarity and responsibility.[269]

The EPP and The People's Movement of Ukraine Rukh (Ukraine)

The ideological match between the EPP and *Rukh* is one of the closest within the EPP and across the Europarties cross-regionally. The party profiles proved to be highly compatible *prior* to *Rukh*'s engage-

---

265 Martens, *Europe: I Struggle, I Overcome*, 41.
266 Jansen and van Hecke, *At Europe's Service*, 241.
267 KAS, "Guidelines for Prosperity, Social Justice and Sustainable Economic Activity" (Sankt Augustin: Konrad-Adenauer-Stiftung, 2009), 4.
268 KAS, "Christian Democracy: Principles and Policy-Making," Handbook for European and International Cooperation (Sankt Augustin: Konrad-Adenauer-Stiftung, 2011), 26.
269 Ibid., 27.

ment in the EPP activities. Thus, although the ideological congruence is high, due to the lack of adaptational pressure, the EPP imposed little impact on *Rukh* in ideological terms. Within the EPP family, *Rukh* possesses close contacts with the German CDU.

The People's Movement of Ukraine *Rukh* was established in 1988 by dissidents of the Ukrainian Helsinki Group, civil activists and intellectuals. As a movement, *Rukh* triggered the emergence of different oppositional parties and civil groups. In 1991, after Ukraine's independence, the party strongly positioned itself against old Soviet *nomenklatura*. Led by Vyacheslav Chornovil, the party supported conservatism and nationalism. After the death of its party leader, *Rukh* was divided from within. One wing, led by the former foreign minister Hennadiy Udovenko, maintained good relations with the *nomenklatura*, whereas the other wing, headed by Yuriy Kostenko, stood radically against the oligarchic system and subsequently developed close relations with Tymoshenko's *Batkivshchyna* party. In 2002, together with other parties, *Rukh* coalesced into the "Our Ukraine" bloc. In 2013, the party underwent another split. One part merged with the Ukrainian People's Party (Vasyl Kuybida faction), while the other part, led by Borys Tarasiuk, joined the *Batkivshchyna* party.

Ideologically, *Rukh* showed the closest match to the EPP in terms of Christian democracy and conservatism under the leadership of Tarasiuk. The party's programme referred to "Christian, ideological and moral-ethical values" for state-building.[270] In line with the EPP, the party supported the idea of state guarantee of individual rights and family welfare. The programme underlined the importance of solidarity and development of local government. On the economic dimension, *Rukh* firmly stood for social market economy. The party supported free market principles and creation of a competitive environment. Yet, the state was given a role as an indirect regulator for the provision of common goods and welfare. Regarding foreign policy, the party strongly supported Ukraine's

---

270 The People's Movement of Ukraine *Rukh*'s website, http://www.nru.org.ua/pro-partiiu/prohrama-rukhu

Euro-Atlantic aspirations, with clear prefe-rences for EU and NATO memberships.

High congruence between party profiles was also acknowledged in the EPP membership report.[271] After the change in the party leadership, when Tarasiuk joined Bloc of Yulia Tymoshenko (BYuT) and Kuybida headed the party, the cooperation with the EPP and KAS became less pronounced. Having lost its relevance and credibility in the country, the EPP's and KAS's focus was shifted towards newly accepted Klitschko's UDAR party.[272] Currently, the party is suffering a sliding decrease in voter support. KAS has admitted to having largely only informal contacts with Tarasiuk and former members of the party's youth branch.[273]

Overall, among the non-EU parties, *Rukh's* match with the EPP is very congruent, favouring conservatism on cultural issues and liberalism on economic ones. Despite its minor position in Ukrainian politics, the party enjoyed the EPP's wide support. The personal factor seemed to predetermine and facilitate its close cooperation as well. Well-known and well-accepted by the Europeans, Tarasiuk, a career diplomat, embodied the party's active engagement in the EPP activities. As a proof of his high credibility, he was appointed as the chairman of the EPP's parliamentary initiative EURONEST. The party's viability and credibility became questionable for the EPP and KAS after Tarasiuk left the party.

The EPP and the People's Union "Our Ukraine" (Ukraine)

The next closest match after *Rukh* is between the EPP and "Our Ukraine". Strengthened during the Orange Revolution, the party shared democratic values and Ukraine's European future and was viewed by the EPP as its strong partner in country's democratic transformations. Over time, however, personal conflicts between Yushchenko and Tymoshenko, party leaders of the Orange forces, exacerbated and led " Our Ukraine" to abstain from participation in the EPP's activities. Although "Our Ukraine" enjoyed a

---

271   EPP Report (Brussels: EPP, January 2005).
272   Interview with the KAS representative, 5 December 2013.
273   Ibid.

longstanding observer status since 2005, it had barely any effect on the party's socialisation. Moreover, by 2010 the party became marginalised and shifted further to the right, showing less and less compatibility with the EPP. Among the EPP members, the party identified their closest parties as the German CDU and the French UMP.

"Our Ukraine" was accepted to the EPP while it was in the process of establishment and crystallisation. Lacking a solid ideological profile, the party was traditionally built top-down around the presidential candidacy of Yushchenko. Comprised of different factions from national democratic to centrist, the party lacked a unified programmatic platform and was overly populist. Nevertheless, the EPP's report on the party's application declared its compatibility and pro-European profile.[274] In fact, the EPP's programme was taken as a template by the party as it developed its own programme. Positioning itself on the centre-right, "Our Ukraine" claimed to be the first Ukrainian party to combine cultural traditionalism and economic liberalism.[275]

While forging its centre-rightist profile, the party campaigned on general slogans like combating corruption, the rule of law and European values. On social issues, "Our Ukraine" shared the EPP's view on cultural traditionalism and conservatism. The consolidation of the Ukrainian nation was announced as the national idea, which was to be achieved through social dialogue and collective historical memory. On the economic dimension, the party supported a liberal economic model based on harmonisation with the norms and rules of the WTO and the EU.[276] The party also favoured a transition to the European model of quality and protection in the agricultural sector.[277] The party referred to the European social standards as a guideline for poverty reduction and for implementation of the social welfare system. In terms of foreign policy, the party firmly supported Ukraine's European integration and stood

---

274 Timus, "Transnational Party Europeanization," 62.
275 Interview with the former "Our Ukraine" representative, 21 December 2013.
276 "Our Ukraine" Party Programme 2010, 11.
277 Ibid., 13.

in favour of EU and NATO memberships in the short term. Multi-vector foreign policy, which was practiced by the Kuchma regime, was completely abandoned, and the European vector became unquestionable. The party's document "European choice: unchangeability of a chosen path" underlined the importance of cooperation with the EPP as one of the prioritised activities during the process of European integration.

Overall, the ideological match between the EPP and the party was quite high on both the social and economic dimensions. Nevertheless, the acceptance of the party was highly politically motivated and was rather based on the decision to consolidate democratic forces after the Orange Revolution. Increasing disillusionment and disappointment with Yushchenko domestically and internationally significantly undermined the party's viability. By 2010, "Our Ukraine" became highly marginalised and shifted from moderate liberal conservatism towards strong conservatism with a nationalist slant. Together with its low credibility and high marginalisation, the party's drift to the right moved it further away from the EPP's profile. As a result, in 2013 the party was excluded from the EPP observer members.

The EPP and the Batkivshchyna party (Ukraine)

The cooperation between the EPP and the *Batkivshchyna* party demonstrates an interesting case of a domestic party that changed its party identity to be fully compatible with the Europarty and to increase its prospects for achieving a membership. Thus, blurry in ideological terms, the catch-all *Batkivshchyna* easily shifted from centre-left to centre-right to fit within the EPP profile. In contrast with *Rukh's* case, although the ideological congruence is low, the EPP's impact on *Batkivshchyna* is more profound.

The *Batkivshchyna* party originated from *Hromada*, a Dnipropetrovsk-based citizen association, in the 1990s. After Pavlo Lazarenko, a *Hromada* leader, was accused of embezzlement, Yulia Tymoshenko found the *Batkivshchyna* parliamentary group and officially registered the party. In the early 2000s, the party took an antipresidential position and participated in the "Ukraine without

Kuchma" campaign. Since 2002, the *Batkivshchyna* party has represented the core of BYuT. During the Orange Revolution, the party constituted one of the driving forces together with Yushchenko's "Our Ukraine". In 2005, Tymoshenko was elected prime-minister in the Orange coalition. In the 2007 parliamentary election, the Bloc won landslide support among the population, overtaking the regions with previously high support for "Our Ukraine". In 2007, Tymoshenko headed the second government; however, the Bloc moved in opposition due to political crisis among the Orange leaders. The 2010 presidential election were marked by Tymoshenko's defeat in favour of Yanukovych, the Party of Regions' leader. During his incumbency, Tymoshenko was sentenced to prison for power abuse and non-transparent gas contracts with Russia in 2009. Without its prominent leader, the Bloc underwent a series of transformations, absorbing the remnants of "Our Ukraine" and merging together with *Rukh* as well as Reforms and Order Party. In 2012, the party was chaired by Arseniy Yatsenyuk, the former leader of "Front for Changes". After the Euromaidan protests in 2013–2014 the party returned to government, however it moved to opposition already in 2016.

The BYuT is a motley of forces, including various ideological groups such as the Ukrainian Social Democratic party (Onopenko), a longstanding partner of *Batkivshchyna*, and the Socialist party (Vinsky), the third most influential group in the bloc then. Apart from a left wing, BYuT comprises the liberal Reforms and Order party and the centre-rightist Christian Democratic and Conservative Republican parties. A blurred ideological profile was also reflected in the affiliation with different groups in the Council of Europe—from socialist to liberal and centre-right. Similarly, it is reflected in its choice of close partners—the *Batkivshchyna* party identified the German CDU in the EPP and the Polish "Law and Justice" in the AECR as its like-minded partners.

In August 2007, *Batkivshchyna* applied for an observer membership, and in January 2008 it joined the EPP as the third Ukrainian party. The poor ideological match triggered many reactions from both the party leadership and the EPP to justify its affiliation. In response to the critical article on its ideological mismatch in *Ukrainska pravda*, a leading Ukrainian online newspaper, Nemyria explained the *Batkivshchyna's* choice as a new level of party development.[278] With acknowledgement of its charismatic style of leadership and vague ideological profile, the affiliation on the European level was perceived as a facilitator of the party's clear ideological positioning. In an attempt to draw ideological similarities, Nemyria underlined common positions on social market economy, justice and solidarity. The party's new positioning was supposed to combine centre-left and centre-right policies, resembling Tony Blair's "Third Way".[279] However, the *Batkivshchyna* party pragmatically emphasised a *social* component rather than a *market* one in its understanding of social market economy. Isolated from the context, appeals to justice and solidarity were used with a pronounced leftist meaning. In practice, Tymoshenko's government implemented a series of leftist policies that were hardly compatible with the centre-right position. During her term, the government introduced a moratorium on the sale of private agricultural land, a price ceiling for meat and petrol and a compensation programme of the Savings Bank's contributions. In an interview, Tymoshenko admitted that she shared centre-leftist orientations, but also referred to the left wing of the EPP, which includes agrarian and social democratic parties.[280]

The EPP itself tried not to emphasise ideological discrepancies but rather to highlight the common position on European values and principles.[281] The EPP representatives justified the party's affiliation via its process of self-identification and self-crystallisation.[282] The KAS representatives reiterated a similar position, pointing out the interest in a viable pro-European political force rather than in a highly compatible but marginal Christian democratic party.[283] In

---

278 "Тимошенко змінює орієнтацію," *Українська правда*, 7 серпня 2007. ["Tymoshenko changes her orientation," *Ukrainska Pravda*, 7 August 2007].

279 Taras Kuzio, "Populism in Ukraine in a Comparative European Context," *Problems of Post-Communism* 57:6 (November/December 2010): 7.

280 "Тимошенко змінює орієнтацію," *Українська правда*, 7 серпня 2007. ["Tymoshenko changes her orientation," *Ukrainska Pravda*, 7 August 2007].

281 EPP Press Release (Brussels: EPP, 18 December 2007).

282 Interview with the EPP representative, 15 October 2013.

283 Interview with the former KAS representative, 5 November 2013.

this respect, the *Batkivshchyna* party matched the EPP's search for a pro-European party quite well. Since 2006, Tymoshenko started actively advocating EU orientations as the only vector of Ukraine's foreign policy. Whereas in 2002 EU and NATO memberships were considered long-term goals, by 2008 the party's position shifted towards a strong Euro-Atlantic stance in a short-term period. In the same vein, Nemyria, who then became the Deputy Prime Minister for European and international integration, emphasised the importance of "the 'journey' to European integration as a means to forge political consensus, stability and lasting prosperity", whereas the timeframe was considered to be irrelevant."[284]

Comparing the compatibility of the EPP and the *Batkivshchyna* party's profiles, it is clear that the party was an outlier among the non-EU observer members. The match was largely based on the party's personal connections and its pro-European position rather than on its compatible socio-economic profile. As in the previous cases of "Our Ukraine", the *Batkivshchyna* party's recognition as a credible democratic force with European aspirations was sufficient for the EPP to accept the party

The EPP and the United National Movement (Georgia)
Similar to the cases of "Our Ukraine" and *Batkivshchyna*, the party's viability and credibility as the leading forces behind the Rose Revolution facilitated its application. Together with the party's pro-European stance, geopolitical factors determined the UNM's choice. As a result, the ideological match between the UNM and the EPP is rather ambiguous. The congruence of party profiles is time-dependent. Whereas until 2008 the match was quite compatible, despite its economic stances being too liberal for the EPP, after 2008 the UNM's authoritarian leaning and strong state regulation led to a profound misfit. Within the EPP, the party identified the Swedish Moderate Party and the Polish Civic Platform as the closest like-minded parties.[285]

---

284 Hryhoriy Nemyria, "EU integration: a healthy dose of realism," *Business Ukraine*, 8 August 2009.
285 Interview with the UNM representative, 18 April 2014.

Established in 2001, the UNM was formed as a result of the merger of Zurab Zhvania's United Democrats and Saakashvili's National Movement. The party grew as a protest movement that opposed Shevarnadze's authoritarian regime. After the Rose Revolution in 2003, the UNM won landslide support and became a new "party of power", aiming to represent the whole nation. The UNM and its party leader ruled the country unchallenged for almost nine years, implementing neoliberal reforms. In 2007–2008, the party reached its peak of unpopularity when mass demonstrations erupted in protest against power abuses, patronage and government corruption. During the 2012 parliamentary election, the party accepted its defeat and moved into opposition, making Georgia's first peaceful transfer of power possible.

Assessing the party's compatibility with the EPP, the UNM representatives identified an ideological match between the party and the EPP through shared positions on the state's role in the economy and on Georgia's Euro-Atlantic aspirations.[286] The limited role of government and the EPP's favourable position on Georgia's joining the EU and NATO were conducive factors that outweighed the UNM's other potential partners. As a matter of fact, at the beginning the UNM applied at the ALDE for an observer membership. Despite the party's obvious strategic considerations, the UNM representatives justified their choice on the ideological level through the party's process of ideological self-identification. In contrast to conventional cases when a party joins Europarty because it shares its identity, it was the affiliation with the EPP that contributed to the crystallisation of the UNM's identity.

On the economic dimension, the UNM can be identified as a libertarian party with strong appeal to American neo-conservative tradition. The UNM had close contacts with the US Republican Party and was actively engaged in the US-based Cato Institute's activities, which promoted small government and lower taxation. Until 2007, the party embarked on American-style libertarian reforms which were hardly comparable with the European style. The scope of the party's neoliberal approach did not correspond with the

---

286 Interview with the UNM representative, 18 April 2014.

EPP's principles of social market economy. The UNM paid less attention to a "solidarity" component. Most of the party's implemented reforms were purely libertarian: diminishing market barriers, introduction of unified tax rates, vast programmes for privatisation of the public sector, drastic cuts of public spending, and abolition of state control bodies such as the Anti-Monopoly Agency and the Food Quality and Control Service.

However, after 2008 the UNM turned to a state-oriented economy, favouring state regulation. Domestic dissatisfaction, the Russian-Georgian war and the financial crisis 2007–2008 put limits on the implementation of a neo-liberal model. The party could no longer rely on foreign direct investments, so the state intervened to boost economic growth. Labelled as "corporate political responsibility", the interventions into market mechanisms started with coerced investments into the energy, tourism, and agricultural sectors.[287] Georgian companies were forced to invest in projects the state and the ruling party supported. For instance, due to the Russian wine embargo in 2007, various companies were coerced into purchasing grapes and wine in vast amounts to prevent the collapse of the wine industry.[288] By 2010, active state interference in the economy became strongly evident. The establishment of 100% state-owned wine company Gruzvinprom, Georgian Agricultural Corporation and the Partnership Fund indicated the broken dogma of non-intervention policy. Welfare spending increased, whereas the governmental sector boosted due to an increasing number of staff in the district councils and administrations.[289] In this respect, the shift from a neoliberal paradigm towards bigger government and its role as the lender of last resort made the closeness with the EPP's economic style more compatible. Needless to say, the authoritarian elements the party was utilising in the reform implementa-

---

287 Christian Timm, "Economic Regulations and State Interventions. Georgia's Move from Neoliberalism to State Managed Capitalism," *Research Paper* 03 (2013): 16.
288 Timm, "Economic Regulations and State Interventions," 17.
289 Ibid., 17.

tion have nothing common with the European standards. Democratisation was sacrificed for modernisation, as decisions were made by the president and his inner circle of advisors.

On social issues, the match between the UNM and the EPP is partial. The party shared the EPP's position on the protection of individual liberal rights. The UNM protected ethnical, religious minorities and defended their equal treatment, which perfectly fitted into the EPP's profile. In contrast, the party's position on the role of the church in the state was quite radical for the EPP's understandings. The party was strongly in favour of the separation of church and state with no interference of religion in politics.[290] However, the strong position of the Georgian Orthodox Church is difficult to omit from any party's political agenda in Georgia — the Patriarch Ilia II gained the most support and trust as a public figure among the population.[291] In this situation, preserving the Christian cultural tradition and promote individual liberties became a challenging task for the UNM. Within the party, there have been tensions between libertarian and paternalistic groups on the subject of educational reforms and protection of sexual minority rights.[292]

The ideological match between the EPP and the UNM proved to be somewhat ambiguous. In the political spectrum, the UNM could be located somewhere in-between the EPP and the ALDE. Whereas, at first, the party was very prone to libertarianism, after 2008 the UNM preferred state regulation over free market instruments. On the social dimension, the UNM failed to match the EPP's cultural traditionalism, having a strong anti-clerical narrative. In this case, the party's governmental position played a double role. On the one hand, despite the UNM's divergence from the EPP's acceptable behaviour, the Europarty was particularly interested in preserving the UNM's membership. On the other hand, the UNM's economic and social policies were more visible and consequential when it was in power, and therefore, they were more exposed to clearer evaluation. In contrast with non-governmental parties,

---

290 Interview with the UNM representative, 15 April 2014.
291 Public opinion poll, Caucasus Research Resource Center, May 2013.
292 Nodia and Scholtbach, *The political landscape of Georgia*, 123.

which claim their policies on paper, the *realpolitik* of parties in power makes the ideological misfit more pronounced.

The EPP and the Liberal Democratic Party (Moldova)
Similar to the UNM's case, the ideological congruence between the EPP and the LDPM is rather ambiguous. Like the UNM, the LDPM's economic stance was too liberal for the EPP at the beginning, but it later descended to state regulations and corruption scandals. Moreover, the match was influenced by the LDPM's governmental position. The party's power position helped the LDPM to enjoy the EPP's strong backing even despite its obvious wrongdoings. On the other hand, in assessment of the party's impact, there is a strong overlap between the LDPM as the EPP observer member and the LDPM as a driving force behind Moldova's European integration process. Among the European counterparts, the LDPM singled out close relationships with the German CDU, the Romanian Democratic Liberal Party and the UK Conservatives.

The Liberal Democratic Party was founded in 2007 under the leadership of Vlad Filat. The party embraced disillusioned members from different political parties. Vlad Filat withdrew from the leftist Democratic Party, whereas other party members left the Christian Democratic People's Party and the Party of Communists to join the newly created liberal force. After the successful 2009 early parliamentary election, when the LDPM gained 16.5% voter support, the eight-year communist dominance ended. Together with other oppositional parties — the Democratic Party, the Liberal Party and Our Moldova Alliance — the LDPM formed the Alliance for European Integration as a leading force. The party unquestionably supported a European path of Moldova. In 2013, due to constitutional and coalition crisis, a new pro-European coalition was re-built under the leadership of Iurie Leancă (the LDPM). In 2015, the eruption of a bank scandal and disclosure of corruption allegations endangered the coalition setting one more time, as a result of which Leancă stepped aside and Victor Strelec was designated as prime-minister. Leaving the LDPM, Iurie Leancă accused the LDPM of departing from the European and democratic principles and registered his own party called "The European People's Party".[293] After the 2014 parliamentary elections, the party's position was significantly weakened which is exemplified by a short-lived minority coalition Political Alliance for a European Moldova together with the DPM in 2015 and its decision to move to opposition in 2016.

In its statute, the LDPM identifies itself as "a centre-right political party with conservative doctrine".[294] In the interviews, the party representatives admitted that at the time of application to the EPP, the party was in the process of self-identification. They were lacking any kind of policy platform and party-building. The vacuum was supposed to be filled through cooperation with established Western counterparts. As a newly established political force, the Liberal Democrats were interested in exchange of experience and information and actively engaged themselves in the educational process. From the party's point of view, the cooperation was very important for building trust and mutual understanding. By sharing the same values and approaches to party-building, the LDPM aimed to increase convergence and adjust their ideology and structure to those of the European partners.[295]

In the application process, the party changed its statute, adding a reference to conservative values.[296] In the party statute, the Liberal Democrats declared general democratic objectives for the party to fulfil: the rule of law, reconstruction and modernisation of the country, efficient market economy and decent standards of living.[297] The party advocated limited state interference in the economy, de-bureaucratisation, enhancement of investment climate and fostering development of SMEs, and lowering taxes.[298] The idea of European integration penetrated all party policies. The Association Agreement and Deep and Comprehensive Free Trade Agreement

---

293 "Filat reserved some names of parties; Leanca: Let him register "Moldova without PLDM," *Jurnal.md*, 18 March 2015.
294 LDPM Statute (Chisinau: LDPM, 11 December 2011).
295 Interview with the LDPM representative, 13 January 2014.
296 Interview with expert, European Union Institute for Security Studies, 14 February 2014.
297 LDPM Statute (Chisinau: LDPM, 11 December 2011).
298 Electoral platform of the LDPM, 2009.

(DCFTA), as its integral part, were taken as a blueprint for the country's modernisation. The LDPM frequently referred to the implementation of the European agricultural model and European transport standards as well as integration into the European energy system as guiding templates for reform implementation. In the social care, the state's role was essential in securing minimum pensions, creating monthly childcare allowances and providing social dwellings. In the sphere of education and healthcare, the government's role was again significant. The party promised to increase salaries in education and healthcare sectors. On the social dimension, the party firmly stood for the separation of state and church and, according to Filat, "since the state does not interfere in the activities of the church, the church should also stop interfering in the business of the state".[299] The LDPM leader also defended the government's initiative to recognise Islam as an official religion in Moldova despite some protest rallies. Equal treatment of all religions was explained as Moldova's drive on the path to the EU.

Apart from the reforms in public administration and the judicial system, the major achievements of Alliance for European Integration (AEI) led by the LDPM were accomplished in the foreign policy realm. Moldova became the "success story" of the Eastern Partnership. The coalition managed to achieve some successes: launching small border traffic with Romania and the "5+2" negotiations with Transnistria, achieving the visa free regime with the EU and signing the Association Agreement. As part of the visa liberalisation process, the coalition passed anti-discrimination law protecting sexual minorities despite fierce opposition from religious groups and the Communists.[300] However, by the end of 2014, the Moldovan "success story" started to fall apart. In March 2015, doomed by the corruption scandal when $1 billion disappeared

---

299 "Moldovan Premier Warns Church Against Political Meddling," *Radio Free Europe/Radio Liberty*, 25 September 2011.

300 David Rinnert, "The Republic of Moldova in the Eastern Partnership: from "Poster Child" to "Problem Child," *FES*, August 2013.

overnight from the country's three major banks, Moldova irreversibly lost its image of success. As a result, together with the IMF and the World Bank, the EU froze financial aid to Moldova until the formation of a new government.[301]

As in the other cases of EPP affiliation, the LDPM was in the process of self-identification, searching for European partners to win over European support. Similar to the UNM and *Batkivshchyna*, the preference towards the EPP was given due to its strong position in the EP and powerful European party elites. These factors were essential for the LDPM, which gained its support due to its pro-European aspirations. In terms of ideological match, the congruence between the EPP and the LDPM is ambiguous. Although the party formally included a "Christian democratic" component in its party statute, it was hardly reflected in the LDPM's policies. Similar to the UNM in terms of economic stance, the LDPM could be positioned between the EPP and the ALDE. Because the party tried to address different social groups, its policy stances were frequently vague and blurred, overshadowed by the strong pro-European foreign policy. In light of the last corruption scandal, it is clear, however, that the LDPM utilised the European support, including a strong backing from the EPP, for its rent-seeking goals. Built on business interests and driven by the desire to stay in power, the LDPM used the "European card" for its own purposes.

Overall, the ideological compatibility between the EPP and its Moldovan, Georgian and Ukrainian sister parties varies to a great deal (Table 6.1). Whereas *Rukh* shows a perfect ideological match, "Our Ukraine", the UNM and the LDPM are partially congruent, and the *Batkivshchyna* party is an obvious outlier.

---

301 "EU freezes funding for Moldova," *EurActiv*, 10 July 2015.

Table 6.1   Ideological congruence between the EPP and its Georgian, Moldovan, and Ukrainian sister parties

EPP core principles	"Our Ukraine"	Batkivshchyna	People's Party Rukh	UNM	LDPM
Christian democracy	+	-	+	-	-
Federalist Europe	0	0	0	0	0
Social market economy	+	-	+	A	+
Principle of subsidiarity	i	0	+	-	+
Personalism	+	+	+	+	+
Family values	+	+	+	+	+
European integration	+	+	+	+	+

Note[302]: (+) congruent with the EPP
(−) incongruent with the EPP
(0) not mentioned
(A) ambivalent position
(i) implicitly present

The Party of European Socialists (PES)

The PES's principles are defined in The Hague Declaration of November 1992. Two main initiatives shaped the ideological profile of the PES: a debate on the New Europe and an employment strategy. In fact, both elements are entangled and were used to coin the PES' strategy "Towards a Social Europe". Pledging to create an economically sustainable and competitive Europe, the PES announced a pan-European strategy of *full employment*.[303] Based on the Larsson Report, the Europarty introduced the European Employment Initiative, which sought to utilise the EU's institutional structures for stimulation and economic revival at the national level.[304] Through coordination and correction of national economic policies, the full employment strategy aimed to increase productivity through better

---

302   The measurement options are taken from Hloušek and Kopeček, *Origin, Ideology and Transformation of Political Parties*, 2010 and adjusted by the author.
303   Ania Skrzypek, *Europe – Our Common Future. Celebrating 20 Years of PES* (FEPS, 2013), 34.
304   "Put Europe to Work: The European Employment Initiative." The report (June 1994 revised version) adopted at the PES Summit in Corfu, December 1993.

coordination of human resources and skills, reduced working hours, flexible working arrangements, investment in social infrastructure, and education.[305] Subsequently, the full employment strategy was directed at achieving fair and sustainable growth, contributing to *economic and social cohesion*. Creating a coherent agenda of social and economic policies, the PES intended to ensure that "all citizens have a fair share of the fruits of our common policy".[306] In this respect, the protection of the vulnerable against the consequences of economic failure was an important part of the PES's profile. In times of economic crisis, "every person becoming unemployed should be offered a job, re-training or a socially useful activity, with a decent remuneration, in a reasonable time".[307]

As a part of balanced and sustainable growth, the PES supports *a carbon-free economy and green growth*. "Renewable energy, energy efficiency and recycling technologies need to receive increased support".[308] Guarding the principles of justice and solidarity, *equal opportunities for men and women* is another crucial value for the PES. The Europarty strongly favours gender-balanced representation in the working and family environments. The PES aims to tackle the gender pay gap to enhance women's economic independence and to ensure women's participation in decision-making levels.[309] Debating on the future of Europe, the PES stated its belief in the principles of democracy, pluralism, freedom and equal rights. Having adopted the declaration "For a modern, pluralistic and tolerant Europe", the Europarty reaffirmed its pledge for *fighting racism and extremist nationalism* and those concepts' incompatibility with European values.[310] Underlining the PES' beliefs in freedom and the

---

305 David J. Bailey, *The Political Economy of European Social Democracy: A Critical Realist Approach* (Abingdon: Routledge, 2009), 133.
306 Skrzypek, *Europe – Our Common Future*, 41.
307 "A European Employment and Social Progress Pact for fair growth," PES Policy Paper adopted by the PES Council in Warsaw on 2 December 2010.
308 PES General Resolution, adopted by the PES Council on 24 November 2011.
309 "Strategy for jobs, growth, inclusion, fairness and sustainability." Joint Declaration adopted by the PES Presidency and the S&D Group in the European Parliament on the Europe 2020 strategy.
310 "For a modern, pluralist, and tolerant Europe." The PES Declaration adopted by the 5th PES Congress on 7–8 May 2001 in Berlin.

equality of all people, the Europarty firmly opposes all kinds of discrimination. The PES strongly defends religious, ethnic and minority rights.

The PES and the Democratic Party (Moldova)

The only example of the affiliation between the PES and the Moldovan sister party is a strong indicator of the PES inability to find an appropriate partner in the region. Being in an obvious minority in contrast to the EPP representation in the region, the PES lowered its standards in finding a perfect match. Fully aware of the DPM problems, the PES nevertheless took on board this oligarchic and unreformed party, legitimising its position in the European and domestic arenas.

The DPM has its origins in the social democratic movement "For a Democratic and Prosperous Moldova" established in 1997. Later the movement was transformed into the party led by Dimitru Diacov. Under his leadership, the party decided to join the governing Alliance for Democracy and Reforms. In 2000, the party adopted its current name. Due to numerous mergers and transformations, the inner structure of the party is incoherent. Within the party, there are social democratic and liberal groupings. Since 2009, under the leadership of Marian Lupu, a former Communist, the Democratic Party has positioned itself as a centre-left force with European orientations. The party is targeting the moderate communist electorate, among which there are many Russian-speaking voters. This is pushing the party to find a balance between European aspirations and good relations with Moscow. In 2009–2014, the Democratic Party was a member of the ruling AEI. After the 2014 parliamentary elections, the party is consolidating power under the newly elected party leader Vlad Plahotniuc, the Moldovan oligarch.

In terms of ideological match, the party ambiguously fits into the grouping of European Socialists. Pleading for social justice and equality, structure-wise the party did not match with its promoted social democratic profile. The DPM is an oligarchic party financed by Plahotniuc. On the economic dimension, the party advocates a competitive market economy through the mechanisms of price liberalisation, privatisation and macroeconomic stability. To achieve the goals of poverty reduction and full employment, the Democrats stand for abolition of barriers to business development and support of SMEs. Interestingly, the middle class was identified as a potential for the party's future.[311] In this respect, a liberal approach prevailed in eradicating social problems, whereas the emphasis on redistribution was very weak.[312] The Ministry of Economy headed by Valeriu Lazar, a DPM member, acted in a liberal fashion. For instance, during Lazar's term, the Ministry passed the Chisinau International Airport for a 49-year concession to a foreign company and privatised the Savings Bank of Moldova (BEM).[313]

Regarding foreign policy, the party consistently remained a supporter of Moldova's EU and NATO memberships. Marian Lupu enjoyed good standing in Brussels as a thoroughly Western-oriented politician.[314] Nevertheless, Lupu frequently voiced his favoured stance on "strategic cooperation" with Russia. For the Democrats, there was no contradiction in signing the visa-free regime with the EU and in maintaining free travel with Russia and other CIS countries.[315] As Lupu explained:

> We need relations of cooperation, not confrontation with Russia. This is the message of the political agreement we signed. Second, Moldova cannot ignore and will not ignore the Russian Federation. Third, we have to be pragmatic and constructive if we want the best for the citizens of Moldova.[316]

---

311 Programme of the DPM, *E-democracy.md*.
312 Interview with expert, European Union Institute for Security Studies, 14 February 2014.
313 "Economy Minister Valeriu Lazar to Resign Soon, Democrats to Decide," *Infotag*, 1 July 2014.
314 Vladimir Socor, "Russia Accepts Pro-Western Candidate for Moldova's Presidency," *Eurasia Daily Monitor*, 4 November 2009.
315 "Marian Lupu's bifurcates: Moldova to have visa-free travel with the EU, Russia and CIS in the same time," *Moldova.org*, 6 January 2011.
316 Robert Coalson, "Kremlin's Ruling Party Boots Ties Across the Former Soviet Union," *Radio Free Europe/Radio Liberty*, 29 September 2009.

The ambiguity on the foreign dimension is also reflected in the party's range of partners. Among the European partners, the Moldovan Democrats identified intense cooperation with the Swedish Social Democratic Party and its affiliated Olof Palme Foundation, the Romanian Social Democratic Party and the Dutch Labour Party and its close Alfred Mozer Foundation.[317] Despite its European proneness, in 2010 the DPM also established cooperation with Putin's United Russia.

Overall, the ideological match is rather contradictory (Table 6.2). Despite defending the social democracy, the Democrats supported the implementation of liberal economic reforms. Social justice and equality are not reflected in the party's organisational structure either. Financially, the DPM is largely reliant on the Moldovan oligarch. Even in foreign policy, the match is somewhat ambiguous. Despite its pro-European orientations, the party still supports strategic relations with Russia.

Table 6.2   *Ideological congruence between the PES and its Moldovan sister party*

PES core principles	DPM
Full employment	A
Economic and social cohesion	+
Carbon-fee economy and green growth	0
Equal opportunities for men and women	+
Fight against racism and extremist nationalism	+
European integration	A

Note: (+) congruent with the EPP
(−) incongruent with the EPP
(0) not mentioned
(A) ambivalent position
(i) implicitly present

The Alliance of Liberals and Democrats for Europe (ALDE)

Similar to the PES case, due to weak and undeveloped liberal tradition in post-communist countries, it is difficult for the ALDE party to find genuinely liberal partners. However, the ALDE's liberal values are based on a meta-ideology comprising general democratic

---

317   Interview with the DPM representative, 22 January 2014.

values — individual freedoms and rights, market economy, and protection of minority and sexual rights — which are fundamental to democratic parties. However, in a weakly defined ideological space, post-communist parties often refer to those values in a populist manner.

Being less influential than the EPP and the PES, the ALDE fails to attract catch-all parties from the region. Sharing some of the EPP values, the ALDE position is weakened because stronger parties that are interested in the promotion of European integration would strategically prefer affiliation with the EPP. Nevertheless, the ALDE has managed to establish cooperation with Georgian and Moldovan parties. In both cases these are minor parties with small shares of the electorate.

The ELDR's liberal principles were defined in the Stuttgart Declaration.[318] In this declaration, the Europarty underlines the combination of human, civilian rights and free market demands as its core values. Liberals have perceived the guarantee of *human, civil and political rights* as their fundamental principle. The European Liberals' understanding of human rights is based on the European Charter of Fundamental Rights and on the idea that "societies should be based on freedom, justice and economic liberalisation where free democratic elections are kept, where political opinions can be expressed without imprisonment and the individual's privacy is respected".[319] As part of the protection of fundamental human rights, *equality and minority rights* is a top priority for the European Liberals, "whether the case has been people belonging to one ethnicity, linguistic minorities, sexual minorities or indigenous people".[320] On social policy, the same applies regarding LGBT rights and gender-equality issues. The European Liberals firmly stand for *freedom of expression* and fight against media censorship and the limitation of opinion expression.

---

318 Emil J. Kirchner, *Liberal Parties in Western Europe* (Cambridge: Cambridge University Press, 1988), 4.
319 ELDR Declaration (Stuttgart: ELDR, 1976).
320 Policies of the ELDR Party on Fundamental Freedoms and Human Rights, the ELDR Policy Center, 2010.

The next of ALDE's core beliefs is the *free market economy*, which is based on competitiveness and free trade. The ALDE strongly defends the EU Single Market's fundamental principles – free movement of people, services, capital and goods. The EU Single Market is seen as an instrument for stimulating and sustaining economic growth and prosperity. For this reason, further liberalisation of the market is promoted to protect against protectionism and nationalism. The Europarty supports the reduction of administrative and technical regulations as well as the creation of stable and predictable business environments for investment. In such environments, the SMEs play a crucial role in creating jobs and fostering economic growth. Emphasising balanced economic growth, further *progress towards environmental and energy policies*, including the development of the Common Agricultural Policy, should be achieved.[321]

The ALDE and the Republican Party (Georgia)

Together with the EPP and *Rukh*, the ideological match between the ALDE and the Republicans is one of the closest in the region. Similar to the Ukrainian case, the ALDE's impact on the Georgian Republicans was negligible, as the party profiles proved to be congruent *prior* to their cooperation. Although the pressure to adapt was low for the party, the Georgian Republicans utilised the affiliation mainly for enhancing their domestic legitimacy.

The Republican Party is one of the oldest parties in Georgia. Established in 1978, the party positioned itself as a longstanding fighter against Communism. The party was formed around dissident groups that aimed to restore political pluralism, democratic institutions and freedom of the press. The members of the party were prominent activists in the Georgian political life, such as David Berdzenishvili, Levan Berdzenishvili, Ivlihan Haindrava and Davit Usupashvili. Since that time, the party has created a strong liberal image within the country and remained consistent to their declared ideas throughout the years. Although the core of the party

---

321   ELDR Declaration (Stuttgart: ELDR, 1976).

is strongly liberal, the stances of individual party members may diverge to a centre-left position. One of the party founders admitted that once social democratic ideas were not alien to them, but the national movement forced them to the right.[322] Overall, the party can be described as a liberal one in German terms.[323]

The profiles between the ALDE and the Republicans are one of the most compatible among all the non-EU party affiliations. Clear commitments to liberal principles make the Republicans' profile the closest match with the ALDE within the region. Together with the European Liberals, the party shares such values as market economy, protection of minority rights, state decentralisation, and development of local self-government.[324] In terms of social policy match, the Republicans are well-known for safeguarding equality and human rights with an emphasis on minority rights. For instance, the party strongly condemned an anti-minaret demonstration and the subsequent removal of a minaret in the village of Chela of Adigeni. The party's anti-discrimination position was expressed in a critical statement by Usupashvili:

> Religious tolerance is more important and of greater public value than disassembling of any building, even if illegally [constructed]. For that reason the state should try to take such a decision, which would not insult believers' religious feelings and which at the same time would enforce requirements set by the law.[325]

Equally, the party has been a firm proponent of the Euro-Atlantic integration. Moreover, both stances are intertwined in the party's views. As one of the party representatives noted:

> Our current government needs most of all to make European ideals and values the way of life in Georgia… We need courage for ensuring equality for all and not for enforcing this equality by the means of law and police; we

---

322 Nodia and Scholtbach, *The Political Landscape of Georgia*, 132.
323 Ibid., 123.
324 Interview with the UNM representative, 18 April 2014.
325 "Republican Party Condemns Minaret Removal," *Civil Georgia*, 30 August 2013.

should turn equality into the way of life and only then we will become a European country.[326]

Similarly, in line with the Liberals, the Republicans advocated free market economy. In an interview, Khatuna Samnidze, the newly elected chairwoman, supported the establishment of free trade zones between the EU and Georgia:

> I believe that the competitiveness of the Georgian market has to be strengthened. We welcome the import and the production of any goods in a competitive and free environment, of course with consumer protection conditions. We hope that Georgian entrepreneurs and businessmen will be able to compete with EU and other goods by rightly targeted marketing and business strategies and activities.[327]

The party considers like-minded partners within the ALDE as a platform of expertise where the party can get consultancy on different policies. Thus, the party seeks to enhance agricultural policy in line with the European standards and they launched the project on free education with the UK Liberal Democrats.[328] Apart from the British partners, the Republicans identified the Dutch VVD as their like-minded party.

In contrast to catch-all parties, the minor Republican Party remained very consistent with their liberal policies. The close match with the ALDE is tracked on both the economic and social dimensions. Moreover, a strong pro-European position completed the party's profile in line with the European Liberals' position.

The ALDE and Our Georgia-Free Democrats (Georgia)

The ideological congruence between the ALDE and Free Democrats is less compatible than between the ALDE and the Georgian Republicans. Small deviations on economic and social dimensions as well as strong party leader position lower the match, but it is still fully in line with the European Liberals' values.

---

326   "Georgia Ratifies EU Association Agreement," *Civil Georgia*, 18 July 2014.
327   Khatuna Samnidze, "Georgia stays firm on its way to European integration," *Friedrich Naumann Foundation Georgia*, 13 November 2013.
328   Interview with the Republican Party representative, 14 April 2014.

Founded in 2009, "Our Georgia-Free Democrats" is a newly established party, cultivating liberal principles. The party was formed by former diplomats and politicians who were in opposition to Saakashvili's UNM. The party leader Irakli Alasania, the former United Nations ambassador, classified his party as "right-centrist".[329] Together with the Republican Party, they advocate fundamental individual rights and Euro-Atlantic aspirations. What separates the parties is the position on the form of government and the stronger party leadership. Whereas the Republicans support the parliamentary system, the Free Democrats favour presidentialism. In November 2014, the party withdrew from the ruling Georgian Dream coalition and moved to the opposition.

The Free Democrats' profile was built around fundamental human rights. After the winning 2012 election, party leader Irakli Alasania reiterated the party's goals:

> Individual freedoms are central in our ideology. Restoration of rule of law and general appreciation of justness, building democratic institutions that guarantee and secure the provision of basic human rights will be the primary goals for Our Georgia-Free Democrats.[330]

The role of the state was also subordinated to the protection of individual liberties. As a party representative claimed, the main goal of the state is to secure human liberties.[331] Similarly, religious and sexual minority rights should be equally protected. Despite its liberal position on social issues, the party favours the preservation of Georgian traditions. In their views, progress should not be associated with the abolition of traditions. The current position of the Georgian Orthodox Church, which has a constitutional agreement with the state, is perceived by the party members as the maximum point of interference into state affairs. On the foreign policy, the party firmly supports the promotion of European integration and NATO membership. Pro-Western orientations of the country are unquestionable for the party leadership. Within the Georgian Dream

---

329 "Alasania Sets Up Political Party," *Civil Georgia*, 16 July 2009.
330 "Individual Freedoms are central in our ideology," Exclusive Interview with Irakli Alasania, *Caucasus Elections Watch*, 20 September 2012.
331 Interview with the Our Georgia-Free Democrats representative, 17 April 2014.

coalition, Alex Petriashvili, then a member of the Free Democrats, was appointed as the State Minister of Georgia on European and Euro-Atlantic Integration.

On the economic dimension, the party shares the principles of small government and minimal state regulation. The primary goal of the party is the development of SMEs and the attraction of investment in industry, agriculture and education. Similarly, the Free Democrats look at the problems of poverty and unemployment through the lens of labour rights—"people are unable to protect their rights out of fear of losing their jobs".[332] In a socialist manner, the party stands for the protection of employees' and trade unions' rights, adoption of a new Labour Code compatible with the European standards and equal pay for equal work. Similarly, on agricultural policy, the party advocates the establishment of a fund that will provide farm enterprises and small holdings with fertile seeds, fertilizers and quality pesticides. Subsidies and aid will be provided at the local level. Spending on education and science will be increased from the state budget and directed towards lowering of student fees and free school textbooks.[333]

Due to the party's recent establishment and minor position in Georgia's party system, the ideological congruence is not as easily discernible as in the cases of longstanding Republicans or governmental UNM. However, the match between the ALDE and the Free Democrats can be assessed as slightly less congruent than in the case of the Republicans. Despite its liberal positioning, structure-wise it is a strongly leader-driven party, and the perso-nality of Irakli Alasania is central to the party's longevity. In 2016, the top party leadership, including Irakli Alasania and Alex Pertriashvili, ex-Minister for European and Euro-Altantic integration, left the party, putting in question the party's future prospects.[334]

---

332 "Individual Freedoms are central in our ideology," Exclusive Interview with Irakli Alasania, *Caucasus Elections Watch*, 20 September 2012.
333 Ibid.
334 "Irakli Alasania: Ex-official, Free Democrats leader quits politics," *Agenda.ge*, 10 October 2016.

The ALDE and the Liberal Party (Moldova)

The ideological match between the ALDE and the Moldovan Liberals is another outlier in the Europarties' affiliations in the region. Poor ideological congruence, based on the party's strong pro-European stances only, demonstrates both the ALDE's and the Moldovan Liberals' strategic choice in forging this cooperation. Although it uses a liberal label, the party in fact possesses a nationalist standing and shares intolerant views on minority rights.

Historically, the Liberal Party had its origin from the Party of Reforms established by Anatol Salaru in 1993. Under his leadership, the party's ideology was of Christian democratic nature, pleading for the support of traditional family values. During the elections in 1994, 1998 and 2001, the party failed to enter parliament, which led to a questioning of the party's strategic positioning. As it appealed to conservative values, the party could not compete with the then popular Christian Democratic People's Party in the same electoral field. At the party congress in 2005, the party statute and leadership had been changed. The party adopted a new name — the Liberal Party — and elected a new party leader, Mihai Ghimpu. Position-wise, the Liberal Party targeted anti-Communist, "unionist" votes, namely voters who supported the unification with Romania and favoured the constitutional changes to the language status (Romanian as an official language).[335] Until 2013, the Liberals formed the pro-European Alliance and possessed a large share of government positions, e.g. defence, transportation, environment ministries, the National Bank and Energy Regulatory Agency.[336] In April 2013, however, the party suffered an internal split that resulted in its withdrawal from the AEI coalition and the formation of the Liberal Reformist Party. With Ion Hadarca as a leader, the latter remained loyal to the AEI. With the collapse of the AEI in 2014, the party moved in the opposition. Among the European partners, the Moldovan Liberals named the Romanian National Liberal Party as the closest like-minded partner.

---

335 Vladimir Socor, "Moldova's Political Landscape on the Eve of General Elections: Part One," *Eurasia Daily Monitor* 6:53, 19 March 2009.
336 Vladimir Socor, "Sources of Moldova's Political Chaos: The Partition of State Institutions," *Eurasia Daily Monitor* 10:97, 22 May 2013.

Ideologically, the Moldovan Liberals strongly advocated the rule of law, anti-corruption measures and justice reforms. At first glance, the party's profile perfectly coincided with the agenda of the European Liberals. However, further analysis of the party's profile disproves the match. In fact, the Moldovan Liberals are far from being consistent with European liberal values. Striking incompatibility can be tracked in the party's hostile position on sexual minorities and in favouring specific relations to Romania. In 2008, the parliament was reviewing the amendments to anti-discrimination legislation. In its support, peaceful demonstrations were planned in the capital. Nevertheless, the Chisinau Mayor's office, headed by Chirtoaca, a vice-president of the party, did not approve the request and banned demonstrations. Furthermore, party leader Ghimpu, then also the interim president of Moldova, used intolerable language and stated, "we are liberals, but we are healthy and we want to have healthy families. Homosexuality is a deviation, nature is nature, but we don't have to put them in the frontline".[337] This statement had a detrimental impact on the party's international image and halted its application to the Liberal International.

On the foreign policy, the Liberal Party solidly positioned itself as a pro-Romanian force pledging for unification with Romania. This mismatch between the liberal image and the party's nationalist stances is an issue of concern for the European Liberals; however, the ALDE seems to ignore it and tries to emphasise the party's strong position on the rule of law and Euro-Atlantic aspirations.[338] Furthermore, internally, the decision-making within the party is far from being liberal. The party suffered from its dominant party leader, who was newly re-elected in September 2014. Ghimpu and his nephew Chirtoaca are overseeing the decision-making process within the party.

Overall, the match between the party profiles is weak. The liberal image of the Moldovan party is mainly drawn upon its Euro-Atlantic

---

337 Report on the use of homophobic language by politicians in Moldova, GenderDoc-M and ILGA Europe.
338 Interview with the FNS representative, 18 February 2014.

aspirations. Other party's policies are better in line with parties of nationalistic profiles, as the Liberal Party's support for unification with Romania and its intolerant position towards sexual minorities proved.

From a cross-national perspective, the ideological congruence between ALDE and its Moldovan and Georgian sister parties is particularly interesting (Table 6.3). The European Liberals have the perfect party profile match with the Georgian Republicans and slightly less perfect with the Georgian Free Democrats, whereas it shows the worst match with the Moldovan Liberals:

Table 6.3 *Ideological congruence between the ALDE and its Moldovan and Georgian sister parties*

ALDE core principles	The Liberal Party	The Republican Party	Free Democrats
Free market economy	+	+	+
Guarantee of human, civil and political rights	+	+	+
Ethnic and minority rights	-	+	+
Freedom of expression	A	+	+
Environmentalism	0	0	0
European integration	+	+	+

Note: (+) congruent with the EPP
(−) incongruent with the EPP
(0) not mentioned
(A) ambivalent position
(i) implicitly present

The European Left (EL)

For the EL the difficulties in finding like-minded partners in the region are manifold. As a marginal force in the EP, the EL is less attractive for leftist parties than the PES. In Western Europe, the Europarty comprises member parties that have undergone ideological transformations and stand for anti-neoliberal, anti-capitalist and anti-war policies. In contrast, in Eastern Europe, the Communist parties that were either banned and ceased to exist, transformed themselves into social/social democratic forces or remained untransformed, dwelling on their anti-Western narrative. In the first case, where communist parties were banned, the space on the extreme left remained unoccupied, which constrained the EL's room to manoeuvre. In the second case, ex-communist parties agreed to abandon Marxist-Stalinist ideology and transformed themselves into progressive pro-European political forces. In this case, the PES offered more attractive opportunities for them for European integration promotion and networking than the EL, again narrowing its options for finding a partner. Finally, the Communist parties that remained mainly untransformed continued campaigning on Soviet nostalgia and anti-Western rhetoric. Those parties are not interested in any affiliations on the European level. In this respect, the EL's affiliation with the Moldovan Communists is exceptional. On the post-Soviet terrain, the Moldovan Communists are the only Communists who remained in power for eight long years after the collapse of Soviet Union.

Although the ideological core values of the communist parties are rooted in the Marxist-Leninist doctrine, the EL party members have distanced themselves from the classical communist positions. In the 1970s, initiated by Western Communist parties in France, Italy and Spain, the Eurocommunism as a political movement rejected Soviet-style communism, which proclaimed the class struggle and the dictatorship of proletariat. The Communist Party was no longer seen as a major force responsible for the creation of a communist society. Strong hierarchy within the party, strict subordination and the absence of disobedience were condemned as anti-democratic practices. Democratic principles such as pluralism, the multiparty system, and individual and collective rights were adopted by the Eurocommunist parties.[339]

As an internationalist force, the EL underlines cross-national networking and *international solidarity*. Despite the internationalist nature of the communist parties' past, the EL was formed only in 2004 at the Party Congress in Rome. Until that time, the European left represented a heterogeneous group and comprised various

---

339 Hloušek and Kopeček, *Origin, Ideology and Transformation of Political Parties*, 43–45.

groupings—the communist parties, including Trotskyist and traditionalist and unreformed communist parties; the green and new politics parties; and the social populist parties.[340]

At the EL's Second Party Congress in Prague, the Political Theses "Building Alternatives" were developed. This document and the Europarty Statute laid down ideological principles and values. As a radical left force, the EL is *anti-capitalist* in its nature. The Europarty rejects "the underlying socio-economic structure of contemporary capitalism and its values and practices".[341] Justifying its radical element, the Europarty seeks to transform economic and power structures in Europe by discarding neoliberalism and globalisation and firmly standing against capitalist exploitation.[342] The EL's goal is "to break this [neoliberal] consensus through the convergence in action of the various political forces that exist in the European countries, struggling in the street and in the institutions, with an anti-capitalist perspective".[343] The EL's socio-economic and socio-ecological proposal includes full and qualified employment, a leading role for public financial interventions, the need to overcome overexploitation, guarantees of income, and pensions.[344]

Secondly, the EL firmly rejects war and stands for *pacifism* and *anti-militarism*. The Europarty opposes "political oppression and criminal wars", "fascism and dictatorship", "patriarchal domination" and "discrimination against 'others'".[345] In line with its anti-war narrative, the EL condemns the US strategy of solving conflicts through military interventions and describes the occupation of Iraq

---

340   Luke March and Cas Mudde, "What's Left of the Radical Left? The European Radical Left after 1989: Decline and Mutation," *Comparative European Politics* 3 (2005), 25.
341   March and Mudde, "What's Left of the Radical Left?" 25.
342   EL Statute (Rome: EL, 2004).
343   EL Congress Document "Unite for Left Alternative in Europe," adopted at 4th EL Congress (Madrid: EL, 2013).
344   EL Political Theses "Building Alternatives" (Prague: EL, 2007).
345   EL Statute (Rome: EL, 2004).

and Afghanistan as a new form of imperialism.[346] Opposing militarisation and armament, the Europarty denies NATO, the European Rapid Reaction Force and the European Arms Agency.[347] On the other hand, the Europarty is an anti-Stalinist leftist group which condemns the cult of personality, dictatorship, undemocratic practices and Stalinist crimes.

An environmental dimension also strongly shapes the EL's profile. The EL identifies capitalism as a factor that exacerbates the environmental crisis, and it defines its policies through the lenses of justice and equality. Pledging for *an ecological Europe*, the Europarty supports a series of environmental protection measures such as the promotion of energy saving and alternative energy sources, a carbon tax, the equality of emissions per capita, affordable energy prices and equal access to energy.[348]

The Europarty defines *feminism, gender mainstreaming and gender democracy* as basic principles for the EL's functioning and development.[349] Criticising the neoliberal model, the EL calls for equal pay for equal work and the same opportunities for women and men at work, for equal participation and representation of women in politics and for the possibility of combining work and family life.[350]

The European Left's forces do not question the existence of the EU, but they do criticise its functioning. The EL calls to revoke the European treaties from Maastricht onwards and pledges to create fundamental political and economic reforms in the EU. Claiming that it will re-found Europe, the Madrid party document proposes "a break in order to found a new European project, one which is based on the interest of the peoples and respect for their sovereignty".[351]

---

346 Kate Hudson, *The New European Left: A Socialism for the Twenty-First Century?* (Basingstoke: Palgrave Macmillan, 2012), 53.
347 EL Political Theses "Building Alternatives" (Prague: EL, 2007).
348 Ibid.
349 Ibid.
350 "8th March 2010: 100 Years of Struggles for Gender Equality," *EL News*, 8 March 2010.
351 Dick Nichols, "Party of the European Left's fourth Congress: Building Unity to Build Hope," *LINKS International Journal of Socialist Renewal*.

The EL and the Party of Communists (Moldova)

Similar to the PES case, the EL's only affiliation in the region says a lot about the Europarty's ability to find a matching partner in the region. Driven by its strategic desire to expand its network in the post-communist countries, the EL swiftly accepted the Moldovan Communists. As a result, the Communists enjoyed the prestige of being the only governmental party in the Europarty family. On the other hand, the opportunistic choice of the PCRM was driven by electoral politics. Shrinking pro-Russian public support and boosting support of European integration made the party change its standing on foreign policy. However, once the party was out of government, it changed its standing towards the pro-Russian electorate again.

In 1991, the Communist Party of Moldavia was outlawed as it had been elsewhere in the post-Soviet countries. Yet, in 1994 the former members of the *nomenklatura* re-grouped and registered the Party of Communists of the Republic of Moldova (PCRM) led by Vladimir Voronin. Under this name the PCRM claimed to be a "successor party" of the former Communist Party. In 1998, the party entered parliament and by 2001 the Communists managed to gain the majority of seats, a feat it repeated in 2005. Moldova was the only post-Soviet country where the Communists gained wide support among the population and ruled the country uncontested. Nevertheless, when it was in power, the party significantly mitigated its Marxist-Leninist agenda and foreign policy orientations. Whereas in 2001 the Communists won the election by appealing to the nostalgic Russian-speaking electorate, by 2005 the party was elected on a pro-European platform. As the circumstances stipulated, the Communists dropped the Russian vector due to the Moscow-backed Kozak memorandum and gravitated to the European orientation. Despite all the party's manoeuvres, the Communists lost voters' support and after the 2009 election the party moved into opposition. However, during the last 2014 parliamentary election the Communists managed to gain 17.48% vote shares, proving their relevance in the country.

The opportunistic choice in favour of the EL finds its evidence in the party's understandings of European integration. For the Moldovan Communists, European integration is a broad notion and does not necessarily imply integration to the EU. The party understands European integration rather as a process of national modernisation and harmonisation with European democratic standards.[352] The latter party associates with the Council of Europe rather than with the EU. In fact, the Council of Europe played a more crucial role in maintaining the party's links to Europe than the EU bodies. The Council encouraged the party leadership in its rapprochement towards European democratic values and granted it international recognition.[353] This interpretation of European integration, which is loose and non-binding to the EU, gave the party necessary room to manoeuvre. Depending on the domestic situation, the Communists interpreted European integration either solely as a modernisation tool or as a path to EU membership. In this respect, the Eurosceptic position of the EL and its alternative view on the EU allowed the Communists to instrumentalise it for their needs and to distinguish themselves from other pro-European Moldovan parties. Criticising both the Association Agreement with the EU and the Eurasian Customs Union, the party was balancing between a nostalgia-prone older electorate and European-friendly young voters.

Apart from the opportunistic rationale behind the cooperation, the links to the EL appeared to be of a prestigious matter as well. The privileged position within the EL was of an undisputable importance for inner-party consumption. In October 2007, the EL organised the conference "The EU New Neighbourhood Policy — challenges for the political left in Europe: correlations between the Party of the European Left and Eastern European left parties", where the Moldovan Communists had a leading role as the governmental party.[354] The party shared its unique experience being in government for a long-time period. It was a rare situation when a

---

352 Interview with the Party of Communists representative, 23 January 2014.
353 March, "From Moldovanism to Europeanization?" 616.
354 EL Press Release (Brussels: EL, 27–28 October 2007).

non-EU party's experience was delivered to its European counterparts. High positions within the EL (back then Grigorii Petrenko was appointed as a vice-president of the EL) bolstered the party's self-credibility and image internally. However, domestically, the Communists were rather cautious in making loud public statements on their affiliation to the EL.

The compatibility of party profiles is rather full of contradictions and varies depending on the time period. At the Congress in 2004, the Communists announced transformations of their ideology and party structure. The party claimed to become a European left-wing party. The PCRM officially abandoned authoritarian elements by rejecting "dogmatism", "totalitarianism", "ideological monopoly" and the Stalinist "cult of personality".[355] However, cosmetic reforms did not change the nature of the party significantly. The PCRM remained a "socialist populist party", addressing the broader electorate rather than the proletariat.[356]

Economic and foreign policies appeared to be tightly entangled and contradictory. Starting as a supporter of the Russian-Belarusian Union, the party shifted from anti-Western rhetoric towards European orientations. During the PCRM's term, Moldova adopted the EU Action Plan. The Communists announced European integration as the party's blueprint for the country's economic revival. European integration was considered as a tool for modernisation and renovation of the system. European integration was espoused with new types of reforms which aimed to stimulate "social growth" and "economic effectiveness".[357] In the communist interpretation, the reforms aimed to combine state social guarantees and expanded economic liberties. Furthermore, the Communists

---

355 Luke March, "The Moldovan Communists: from Leninism to Democracy?" *Eurojournal.org*, September 2005, 1.
356 March, "The Moldovan Communists," 2.
357 "Материалы третьего «круглого стола» из серии «ПКРМ во власти и в оппозиции»," *Ava.md*, 23 февраля 2011. ["Documents of the third round table from a series «PCRM in power and in opposition»," *Ava.md*, 23 February 2011].

seemed to support the principle of the market economy and developed clientelistic relationships with business through privatisation in the wine and tobacco sectors.[358] As a result, the Communists were accused of departure from their roots and utilisation of the communist brand for mobilisation of the nostalgic electorate.

Despite the allegations, domestically the Communists enjoyed broad support, which prevented them from making real transformations. Only after the defeat at the local election in 2007 the party embarked on tangible internal reforms. At the Congress in 2008, the party adopted a new programme with cardinal ideological changes and included references to the EL. Party representatives claimed that some elements of the programme were borrowed from the EL's programme.[359] The party managed to re-brand its communist image to position itself as a modern, pro-Western force. Despite previous Soviet-nostalgic appeals, the party aimed to build "a European Moldova". For the first time in Moldova's history, the party congress was broadcast online to a wider public. It was attended by Lothar Bisky, the former president of the EL, and Constantin Rotaru, the chairman of the Romanian Socialist Alternative Party.

The Communists claimed to build "democratic centralism" and reiterated their commitments towards European integration, which aimed to be achieved through a process of gradual modernisation towards a post-industrial society.[360] Nevertheless, the "liberal revolution" announced in 2007 in the economic sphere contradicted the EL's negative attitude towards neoliberal policies. The country's investment climate was enhanced solely by liberal measures — zero interest rate on income tax, tax amnesties etc. Later, at the Congress in 2012, Vladimir Voronin reiterated the party's position on its liberal approach: "we are going to build a real market economy, but not a market society".[361]

---

358   March, "The Moldovan Communists: from Leninism to Democracy?" 3.
359   Interview with the PCRM representative, 22 January 2014.
360   Igor Botan, 6th Congress and its first consequences, *E-democracy.md*, 31 March 2008.
361   "Доклад председателя ПКРМ Владимира Воронина: почему ПКРМ не признала президента, куда ушел Мишин и что будет дальше,"

Consistently, the Communists advocated the neutral status of Moldova, echoing the EL's anti-NATO rhetoric. Another part of rebranding concerned rejuvenation of the party by including younger party members in the Executive Political Committee. In line with the EL's gender-mainstreaming, a successful strategic move was made by the appointment of Zinaida Greceanii as the head of the government. By the promotion of women in high-ranking positions, the party showed its capability of innovative decisions congruent with the EL.[362] Nevertheless, little changed in the internal party structure, in particular in terms of women's promotion and decision-making. All the authority remained in the hands of the party's founder and strong, charismatic leader, Voronin. Likewise, the party refused to abandon its name and symbols despite the implicit preferences of some European parties.[363] However, the overwhelming dominance of the permanent party leader and lack of internal party democracy seemed to be tolerated by the Europeans. They considered it a natural process of the trend of party transition and transformation in the post-communist countries.[364]

To a large extent, the affiliation of the Moldovan Communists with the EL was an opportunistic decision. Deteriorated relations with Russia and favourable public opinion on the European integration forced the party to change its orientations. At first glance the seemingly perfect match of the Moldovan Communists with the European Communists failed on the economic and social dimensions. The congruence is rather eclectic and contradictory (Table 6.4).

Комсомольская правда, 9 июня 2012. ["Report of PCRM party leader Vladimir Voronin: why PCRM did not recognise the president, where did Mishin go and what is next?" *Komsomolskaya Pravda*, 9 June 2012].
362 Botan, 6th Congress and its first consequences, *E-democracy.md*, 31 March 2008.
363 Interview with the PCRM representative, 22 January 2014.
364 Interview with the *transform! europe* representative, 3 February 2014.

Table 6.4   Ideological congruence between the EL and its Moldovan sister party

EL core principles	The Party of Communists
International solidarity	+
Anti-capitalism	–
Pacifism and anti-militarism	i
Environmentalism	0
Gender equality and gender-mainstreaming	+
Fundamental and political reforms in the EU	0
European integration	A

Note: (+) congruent with the EPP
(–) incongruent with the EPP
(0) not mentioned
(A) ambivalent position
(i) implicitly present

The Alliance of European Conservatives and Reformists (AECR)

Founded in October 2009 after a split from the EPP, the AECR pledges to create broader conservative and economically liberal principles. Led by the UK's Conservatives, the Europarty comprises various Eurosceptic parties, including the Civic Democrats (Czech Republic), the Independence Party (Iceland), the Law and Justice Party (Poland) and the Justice and Development Party (Turkey). The AECR shares key positions with the EPP, but it criticises the current EU structure and strongly defends the federalist views. Marginal position in the EP and its Eurosceptic views made the Europarty less attractive for the non-EU parties that are looking for support in their European aspirations. Nevertheless, the AECR managed to integrate a Georgian party from the region.

The AECR's core principles and values are defined in the Prague Declaration[365] and the Reykjavik Declaration.[366] One of these core principles is *the promotion of inter-governmentalism*. Indeed, the opposition to supranationalism and to the idea of "a federalist Europe" were among the factors that caused the AECR's separation

---

365   AECR Declaration (Prague: AECR, 2009).
366   AECR Declaration (Rejkjavik: AECR, 2011).

from the EPP. Describing the process of unification between the EPP and the European Democrats in the early stages, Johansson noted that "the British Conservatives have objected to a formal alliance with Christian Democrats on the grounds that the latter were seen as Euro-federalists. In terms of credibility and identity, a formal link to the Christian Democrat EPP, committed to a 'United States of Europe', has remained sensitive for the British Conservatives".[367] Following a Eurosceptic line, the Europarty declares that it stands for "the sovereign integrity of the nation state, opposition to EU federalism and a renewed respect for true subsidiarity".[368] The AECR supports the exercise of power at the lowest practicable level in preference to supranational bodies.[369] Criticising the EU's design, the Europarty condemns the EU's excessive bureaucracy and supports *greater transparency and integrity in EU institutions*.[370] The European Conservatives favour a new equilibrium of power and competence between the EU level and the national level. Apart from this institutional redesign, the AECR promotes new controls on immigration, rejecting a European quota system for immigrants. The other ideological pillar of the AECR is *broader economic liberal values*. The Europarty supports "free enterprise, free and fair trade and competition, minimal regulation, lower taxation, and small government".[371] On the social dimension, the AECR's policy is grounded in three principles: the value of *personal liberty* with inherent responsibility, the family as the bedrock of society, and civic communities. Similar to other Europarties, the AECR favours the individual's rights and liberties, such as "freedom of religion and worship, freedom of speech and expression, freedom of movement and association, freedom of contract and employment, and freedom from oppressive, arbitrary or punitive taxation".[372] The AECR

---

367 Johansson, *Transnational Party Alliances*, 185.
368 AECR Declaration (Prague: AECR, 2009).
369 AECR Declaration (Rejkjavik: AECR, 2011).
370 AECR Declaration (Prague: AECR, 2009).
371 Ibid.
372 AECR Declaration (Rejkjavik: AECR, 2011).

shares the principle of "equality of all citizens before the law, regardless of ethnicity, sex or social class".[373] The Europarty opposes intolerance and extremism in all forms of its expression. Like the EPP, the AECR firmly stands for the *traditional model of society*. The AECR sees civil communities and their activities at the local level sees as a guarantee of social cohesiveness and collective action.

The AECR and the Christian Democratic Movement (Georgia)

The affiliation between the AECR and the CDM is a particularly interesting case, as it represents an example of how a party changed its preferences and shifted to a less desirable choice. Due to the UNM's blocking of the party's entry and the EPP's waiting strategy, the Georgian Christian Democrats expressed their protest by moving to another Europarty. Despite the CDM's strong pro-European stances, the party was satisfied with the Eurosceptic AECR.

In 2008, the Christian Democratic Movement was founded by the former Imedi TV journalist Georgi Targamadze. During his political career, Targamadze also served as Aslan Abashidze's spokesman and as a member of his Revival bloc in parliament. The party positioned itself as being centre-right and defended Orthodox Christianity as Georgia's official religion. During the 2008 parliamentary election, the CDM gained 8.7% of votes, becoming de facto the largest oppositional force. In 2009, the party obtained membership in the IDU and the ECPM. In August 2012, the Christian Democrats joined the AECR. Despite tenuous relationships with the UNM, there have been some allegations that the party was controlled by the UNM. As the former ruling party was strongly against the church's involvement in politics, the CDM was supposed to accumulate a conservative and religious electorate and counterbalance the UNM's anti-church narrative and play the UNM's opposition.[374]

As a CDM representative openly admitted, the affiliation with the AECR was not necessarily based on shared values. Value-wise,

---

373 AECR Declaration (Rejkjavik: AECR, 2011).
374 Interview with expert, 20 February 2014.

they were more in line with the ECPM's principles.³⁷⁵ Nevertheless, in its application letter to the European Conservatives, the CDM highlighted similar policies the party shares, such as free trade, market economy, conservative family values and Western orientation. The party underlined the supportive position of the UK Conservative and the Czech Civic Democratic Platform, who endorsed their application to the AECR.³⁷⁶

Nonetheless, the ideological match between the CDM and the AECR is rather shallow. KAS expressed its concerns about the party's congruence with the EPP as the CDM was becoming deeply conservative. Some of the observers accused the party of being engaged with nationalistic groupings.³⁷⁷ On the social dimension, the Christian Democrats took a strong conservative stance, defending traditional family values through strengthening the position of the Georgian Orthodox Church. As Targamadze explained:

> We want to raise [...] the status of the Orthodox Church to strengthen the church's role in the development of social [programs] and the development of education programs.³⁷⁸

Additionally, the party advocated a constitutional amendment to recognise Orthodox Christianity as Georgia's official religion, as the church has always played a decisive role in the country's national interests. In the same vein, in March 2013 the party leader condemned a rally of sexual minorities in Tbilisi and suggested the constitutional ban of gay marriages in the future.³⁷⁹ On economic issues, the party also referred to the Georgian Orthodox Church. In its program, the party quoted the Patriarch Ilia II, saying that "Georgia's future economic development should probably be linked to water resources".³⁸⁰ Although the CDM advocated the

---

375　Interview with expert, 29 April 2014.
376　CDM Application to Join AECR (Tbilisi: CDM, August 2012).
377　Molly Corso, "Georgia: party promotes church as defender," *EurasiaNet*, 15 March 2008.
378　Ibid.
379　"Christian-Democratic leader quits politics," *Agenda.ge*, 15 March 2014.
380　"Christian-Democratic Movement," *Civil Georgia*, 22 May 2008.

country's integration into the Euro-Atlantic structures, the party's Western orientations are rather unclear. In his media interviews, Targamadze mentioned several times that NATO membership is not "a goal in itself".[381] In contrast, European integration was perceived as significant both for the party and for the country.

However, the fact that they were affiliated with the Eurosceptics seemed to be irrelevant for the party members. In its argumentation, the party referred to minor differences between the AECR and the EPP concerning the views on the EU's internal structure. In the party's views, as Georgia's chances of joining the EU in the near future are quite slim, the affiliation with the Eurosceptic party makes no difference for the CDM. Being a non-EU member, the party considered the EU's institutional design not necessarily to be an important issue.[382] This short-sighted position and engagement with the pro-Russian party the Democratic Movement — United Georgia, led by Nino Burjanadze, questions the party's European aspirations in general.[383]

Overall, the ideological congruence between the AECR and the CDM is rather shallow (Table 6.5). The party openly admitted that its move was triggered by blocking the UNM's behaviour and the EPP's unwelcoming attitude. Having an affiliation with a marginal ECPM, the CDM's strategic move was driven by the idea of finding a more powerful Europarty, neglecting a perfect ideological match. The match is congruent only in terms of personal and family values, whereas other AECR core principals either were not mentioned or were absent. Despite the party's official strong pro-European stance, the CDM was ready to join the Eurosceptic AECR.

---

381 "Christian-Democratic leader quits politics," *Agenda.ge*, 15 March 2014.
382 Interview with CDM representative, 29 April 2014.
383 "Christian-Democrat leader quits politics," *Agenda.ge*, 15 March 2014.

Table 6.5   Ideological congruence between the AECR and its Georgian sister party

AECR core principles	Christian Democratic Movement
Promotion of intergovernmentalism	0
Transparency and integrity of EU institutions	0
Broader economic liberal values	-
Personal liberty	+
Family values	+
European integration	-

Note: (+) congruent with the EPP
(−) incongruent with the EPP
(0) not mentioned
(A) ambivalent position
(i) implicitly present

6.2   Analysing the Ideological Match

Across all the cases, the closest ideological match can be identified between the EPP and the Ukrainian *Rukh* as well as the ALDE and the Georgian Republicans, whereas the ideological fit between the Moldova Liberals and the European Liberals is one of the worst among the Europarties. In the cases of the PES and the EL, the "goodness of fit" is rather ambiguous, showing a patchy match on economic and social issues.

To a large extent, the cooperation with the Europarties did not affect the ideological profiles of the non-EU parties but made them a bargaining chip in the application process. In contrast to Western and Central European parties, which joined the Europarties based on their ideological profile, in Eastern Europe the affiliation with the Europarties helped the non-EU parties to identify their party identity first. In this situation, strategic calculations prevailed, whereas ideological congruence was of secondary importance, which in the end impeded the establishment of a perfect match.

Overall, the "goodness of fit" proved to be better where domestic parties were already well established and ideologically crystalised. In those cases, the non-EU parties, following the logic of Central European parties, joined the Europarties based on their ideological proximity and sense of "like-mindedness". In turn, whereas the ideological match in these cases proved to be more congruent, the Europarties' impact on their ideological profile was less significant. In contrast, in those cases where domestic parties poorly matched with their preferred Europarties, the impact was more pronounced. As a result of strong adaptational pressure to comply, these non-EU parties changed their party identity and incorporated necessary provisions in their party programmes to be compatible with the Europarties.

It is interesting to note that the duration of the contact does not seem to be relevant on the ideological dimension, as it shows no effect on the parties' socialisation process (H1). The assumption that over time parties will be programmatically socialised in line with the European norms and values failed. There was no proof to be found that the longstanding observer members adjusted their programmes by borrowing the Europarties' norms and values due to their convictions. As examples of "Our Ukraine" and the Moldovan Christian Democrats showed, despite being the longstanding EPP's observer members, the parties failed to incorporate the EPP's core values. In contrast, the intensity of the contact proved to be crucial in incorporation of the Europarties' norms and values. Frequent and intense contacts between ALDE and the Republicans, EPP and People's Party *Rukh* led to a more involved process of socialisation, resulting in cognitive and reflective borrowing of ideological issues.

Moreover, the pattern shows different timing; the observer parties either had the ideological match with the Europarties *prior to the cooperation* or were compelled to adjust their identity *in the process of application*. In the first case, the profiles of the Ukrainian *Rukh* and the Georgian Republicans were already congruent with the EPP and the ALDE respectively, even prior to their observer membership. As a result, the affiliation had little impact on parties' ideological profiles because the adaptational pressure was low. In the second case, observer parties adjusted their ideological profiles during the application process to fit into respective Europarties. For instance, *Batkivshchyna*, the LDPM and the UNM swiftly adjusted their ideological foundations by shifting to centre-right from centre-left and liberal positions, respectively. Having low "goodness of fit" prior to the cooperation, *Batkivshchyna*, the LDPM and the UNM were compelled to adjust their party profiles to the EPP requirements.

The party position of applicant parties had a substantial effect on the Europarties' admission process (H2). In this respect, the EPP case was the most conspicuous. The Liberal Democratic Party of Moldova, the United National Movement and the *Batkivshchyna* party—all the governmental forces—managed to obtain membership with the EPP. Their strong party position in terms of governmental status increased their leverage vis-à-vis the Europarties. The parties were in a position to mitigate or diminish the Europarties' requirements during the application process, knowing the Europarties' interest in influential parties. On the other hand, due to awareness of the weak ideological profiles of Eastern European parties, ideological congruence was not a crucial factor for the Europarties themselves to grant an observer membership. In contrast, democratic credentials and pro-European orientation of a viable political force were seen as minimal requirements to be accepted.

The motivation structure of observer parties proved to be a strong predictable factor in the ideological congruence (H3). Those political parties which were driven by prestigious affiliation and strategic considerations showed less ideological match as they were less interested in ideological adjustments and transformations from the beginning. In contrast, those observer parties that were looking for like-minded party families and genuinely shared the Europarties' principles showed a better ideological match.

7. Impact on Organisational Structure

Lacking substantial experience in building sustainable party structures, parties from the non-EU countries consider the structure of their European partners as templates to follow. During their cooperation with Europarties, domestic parties are exposed to various types of impacts on the organisational dimension. During the application, the Europarties apply criteria of political conditionality with regard to internal democratic principles and procedures. Applicants must provide evidence of internal democratic mechanisms and decentralised party structure. In this situation, post-communist parties that are willing to join the Europarties comply with rules and regulations defined by the Europarties. On the other hand, domestic parties are socialised through numerous meetings and mutual activities in line with standard norms and practices of European party-building. In particular, the non-EU parties access expertise and knowledge on organisational matters through training programmes of the Europarties' members and their party foundations. The absorption of European experience in party-building may help them to review their functioning, improve their daily work and thus increase their organisational compatibility with European parties.

The first section of the chapter focuses on organisational changes mother parties have implemented after establishing cooperation. The organisational changes in mother parties are measured in terms of (1) introduction of changes to the party statutes, including references to the affiliation with a respective Europarty; (2) introduction of changes to the internal selection process, such as primaries or internal referenda; (3) the import of European techniques for electoral campaigning.

The second section analyses the cooperation between the Europarty's youth and women's associations and domestic party's youth and women's branches. On the youth branch level youth branch, it explores organisational changes in terms of (1) amendments to youth branches' party statutes; (2) institutional changes in relationships between the mother party and the youth branch, by looking at the involvement of youth in the internal decision-making process; and (3) the promotion of youth to the mother party. On the women's branch level, it explores whether the organisational changes were implemented after cooperation in terms of (1) the introduction of gender quotas on the candidate lists and/or party boards; (2) strengthening of the organisational capacity of women's branches; and (3) gender mainstreaming.

Since the Europarties' activities in institutional strengthening usually address general democratic standards of party-building, they often overlap with party aid assistance that international actors provide for domestic parties. In order to disentangle the impact caused solely by cooperation with the Europarties, each section is supplemented by the analysis of international donors' activities in the field of capacity-building.

Looking at the various factors that might impact organisational compa-tibility, the time factor is expected to positively influence the non-EU party structures. The longer the observer members are affiliated with the Europarties' associations, the more "borrowing" in terms of structural adjustments is expected to be observed (H4). Secondly, depending on the party position, strong parties are expected to be more compatible with the European parties. Having better developed party structures, strong parties have more structural opportunities for cooperation with Europarties' associations and more resources to implement the changes (H5). Ideational motives of cooperation — as opposed to rational motives — are expected to contribute to a better structural match. Genuine motivations are likely to lead to more borrowing from their European partners in the party-building process (H6).

7.1 Organisational Changes in Mother Parties, Youth and Women's Branches

The EPP and the Liberal Democratic Party (Moldova)

Apart from the introduction of formal references to its party statutes, underlining its centre-right position and conservative doctrine,[384] the EPP impact on the LDPM's organisational structure was negligible. The internal decision-making remained unchanged, while the party placed its emphasis on electoral campaigning skills. The LDPM mainly used the EPP as opportunity structure for networking and participating in trainings on electoral campaigning. For example, having established cooperation with the Austrian People's Party, the LDPM delegation participated in the seminar on the online election campaigning organised together with the Robert Schuman Institute and the Austrian People's Party.[385]

With the aim of strengthening the party's electoral campaigning, the UK Conservatives assisted the LDPM in creating a database of citizens' voting intentions and local issues. Working with its grassroots, the LDPM conducted an analysis of voters' partisan preferences and local problems on the micro-level. In addition, during the party's visit to the UK, the LDPM representatives experienced door-to-door campaigning together with Boris Johnson, the ex-mayor of London, and subsequently employed that experience domestically.[386]

Following its mother party, the Liberal Democratic Youth of Moldova (LDYM), a youth branch, established a full scope of cooperation with various European youth organisations on national and international levels. The cooperation between the LDYM and the Youth of the EPP, YEPP started through its contacts with European

---

[384] The Party Statute of the Liberal Democratic Party of Moldova, Article 3, paragraph 1.
[385] LDPM Press Release, "PLDM Secretary General, Victor Rosca paid a working visit to Austria," 19 September 2013.
[386] Interview with the LDPM representatives, 13 January 2014.

Democrat Students (EDS). Following experience of its closest partner *Junge Union*, a youth branch of the CDU, in November 2013 in Germany, the LDPM changed its statute stating that the president of a youth organisation would be automatically included in the party's local bureau, which would provide a chance for youth to take part in decision-making at the local level.[387] Applying Western practices of information dissemination, the LDYM launched "The School of European Studies", which aimed at the promotion of European values and knowledge of functioning mechanisms in the EU.[388]

Although the relationships between the LDPM and its youth wing remain highly subordinated, it indicates a shift in relationships. The mother party became more open and welcomed the career promotion of youth members to its structure. Thus, Gheorghe Mocanu, the former LDYM president, was invited to the party board and in 2010 became a member of the Moldovan parliament. Nevertheless, the youth branch remains hardly involved in the mother party's decision-making process.

Despite the numerous affiliations with the EPP, officially, the only member organisation of the EPP Women is the LDPM Women, a women's branch of the LDPM. However, considering the infrequency of the EPP Women gatherings—General Board meetings twice a year and Summer Academy once a year, the role of EPP Women is constrained. The main actors that conduct seminars and trainings on behalf of the EPP Women are KAS and the Robert Schuman Institute.

In 2009, the party adjusted its party charters, introducing a provision on gender equality. In Article 1.9 of the LDPM Statute, the party supported equal representation of both men and women and strives to increase the percentage of women in decision-making bodies and on the candidate lists by at least 30%.[389] In 2010, Liliana Palihovici, then the president of the LDPM Women, presented a

---

387 Interview with the LDYM representative, 14 January 2014.
388 LDPM Press Release "YLDM launched the School of European Studies" (Chisinau: LDPM, 2012).
389 Iurie Munteanu, *Political Parties Legislation in Moldova: Review and Recommendations for Reform*, (Chisinau: IDIS "Viitorul," 2010), 172.

legislative initiative to amend the Electoral Code and to introduce a 30% quota on the candidate lists for elections. According to the party's view, this amendment would increase the representation of women in the parliament and would have a positive impact on social, political, and economic development.[390] However, the organisational strength of the LDPM Women is likely to be caused by achievements in the framework of European integration, where the LDPM as a leading force in this process was committed to conducting reforms, including gender equality. An overlap of governmental and partisan positions led to a synergy effect. The position of Liliana Palihovici as deputy speaker of the Moldova Parliament and as president of the LDPM Women provided her with another level of protocol and gave her an opportunity to meet other women party leaders during her state visits.

Despite the commitment to gender equality, in 2009, the LDPM had the lowest proportion of women on the candidate lists. Among the top ten candidates, there was only one female candidate.[391] During the 2014 parliamentary elections, the situation changed slightly in favour of equal representation. The party placed 35 female candidates out of 101 candidates, and three female candidates were among the top ten.[392]

The EPP and the United National Movement (Georgia)

Similarly to the LDPM's case, the UNM used the EPP's framework to forge bilateral cooperation with the Europarty's well-established party, whereas the EPP's impact was rather negligible.

Prior to 2012, the UNM had only cooperated with the core of the EPP without having any affiliation with youth or women's associations. The reason for this was the underdeveloped structure of

---

390 LDPM Press Release, "The LDPM proposes a compulsory quota of women representation on the candidate lists for elections," (Chisinau: LDPM, 21 September 2010).

391 Iurie Munteanu, *Political Parties Legislation in Moldova: Review and Recommendations for Reform* (Chisinau: IDIS "Viitorul", 2010): 172.

392 "Lista candidaților la funcția de deputat în Parlamentul Republicii Moldova pentrualegerile parlamentare din 30 noiembrie 2014 din partea Partidului Liberal Democrat din Moldova," *E-democracy.md*, November 2014.

the UNM, where youth and women's branches simply did not exist. In 2013, after its election defeat, the UNM started a transformation process of re-building the party. During this process, a new strategy for the party's development was elaborated, youth and women's units were created, and more decentralisation was envisaged. In this situation, international actors, including IRI and NIMD, as well as sister parties contributed to the UNM's organisational development. Within the EPP, the UNM established close contacts with the EPP's sister party — the Swedish Moderate Party — which assisted the UNM in its party-building. In particular, the Moderate Party was a valuable source of information for the UNM on how to build grassroots within the party.[393] NIMD helped to build the youth wing of the party and provided training on party management and budgeting for the party candidates.[394]

In order to enhance intra-party democracy, the UNM introduced primaries for candidate selection. Thus, in 2014 the candidates for the Tbilisi mayoral position were selected through internal primaries.[395] According to the IRI representative, the UNM's primaries resembled debates rather than primiries where party members from different regions gathered to discuss the nomination.[396]

Although there is no official connection between the EPP Women and the UNM's women's branch, the Swedish Christian Democratic International Center (KIC), affiliated with the Swedish Moderate Party, and the Robert Schuman Institute, the EPP partner, helped in the planning process of the further development of newly created UNM's women's branch. The organised workshop was focused on political planning and effective activities for engaging the

---

393   Interview with the UNM representative, 18 April 2014.
394   Interview with the NIMD representative, 17 April 2014.
395   "United National Movement announce Tbilisi Mayoral Candidates," *Agenda.ge*, 1 March 2014.
396   Interview with the IRI representative, 24 April 2014.

public, recruiting new members and activating volunteer supporters.[397] Nevertheless, the implementation of gender quotas was not an issue which was discussed, as the party leadership shares a negative view of this mechanism for promoting women.[398]

The EPP and the Batkivshchyna party (Ukraine)

Similar to its Moldovan and Georgian sister parties, *Batkivshchyna* did not change its internal party mechanisms while being the EPP observer member. Although the party altered its party statute[399], an amendment remained on paper, whereas the main interest was in electoral campaigning and trainings on leadership skills. Being a highly centralised and personalised party, *Batkivshchyna* did not introduce any changes to its internal decision-making process. To a large extent, the impact from trainings remained on the individual level without any further penetration to mother party structures.

The *Batkivshchyna* party participated in NDI and IRI trainings on party management, campaign management, and voter mobilisation. The party's activists reported that the party adapted interactive approaches to internal party trainings on campaign management, and practices of internal communication were borrowed by the party to revise centre-oblast communication processes.[400]

The impact of cooperation between *Batkivshchyna moloda*, the party's youth branch, and the YEPP on organisational structure is rather negligible. *Batkivshchyna moloda's* emphasis on the fact that it is the largest youth organisation in Ukraine and that the YEPP is the most influential youth organisation in Europe indicates that power relations shaped the youth wing's choice much more than

---

397 "Women and Political Influence Follow-up: strategic development of the UNM's women organisation," *Robert Schuman Institute*, 26–27 April, Tbilisi, Georgia.
398 Interview with the UNM representative, 18 April 2014.
399 Article 1 of Batkivshchyna's party statute: "being an observer member of the European People's Party, the grouping of centre-right and Christian Democratic parties, the party entirely shares the ideological foundations declared in the key programme documents of the EPP."
400 Andrew T. Green, Sarah Birch and Sean Roberts, *Evaluation of USAID Political Party Program: Ukraine* (Pittsburgh: University of Pittsburgh Press 2010), 11–12.

the YEPP's ideological commitments. On the organisational level, the relationships between the youth wing and its mother party did not change. *Batkivshchyna moloda* remained highly subordinated to the mother party. The only indirect impact is the launch of the unification process, bringing such youth organisations as Young *Rukh*, Front of Changes, and Reforms and Order under one roof. The initiative emanated from the YEPP during *Batkivshchyna moloda's* application process. Due to personal ambitions this initiative failed, however, by 2012, *Batkivshchyna moloda* suffered a loss in membership, and up to 80% of members left the organisation. In this situation, due to pressure from the KAS and the YEPP's endorsement, the process of unification with other youth organisations commenced.[401]

In terms of youth promotion, the tendency is similar across the region—only the leadership of the youth organisation experiences career lift to the mother party. Thus, Ivan Krulko as the president of *Batkivshchyna moloda* was promoted to the *Batkivshchyna* party and became a member of parliament.

Batkivshchyna moloda utilised the YEPP's structure for disseminating its messages and gaining international support, by bringing additional attention to Ukraine's situation via the YEPP. *Batkivshchyna moloda* reinforced the mother party's voice in the EPP and drew a lot of attention to such problems as deterioration of the level of democracy in Ukraine, political prosecution and imprisonment of Tymoshenko.

The PES and the Democratic Party (Moldova)

Being an oligarchic party, the DPM was not interested in the introduction of organisational changes what would weaken its status quo. As a result, no changes to internal party democracy were implemented. The Moldovan Democratic Party did not introduce any reference to its affiliation with the PES to the party statute. The party mainly benefited from bilateral cooperation in terms of electoral campaigning techniques. Thus, through the Westminster Foundation for Democracy, the UK Labour Party organised training on

---

401 Interview with the KAS Ukraine representative, 5 December 2013.

electoral campaigning for the Moldovan Democrats. As a result, the party increased its support by 20% in Chisinau. The successful result was partly credited to the Labour Party's training on door-to-door campaigning skills. After the training, the party recognised the importance of face-to-face contact and started developing a database of citizens' voting intentions.[402]

Although its mother party is a member of the PES, its youth branch the Democratic Youth, is not affiliated with YES PES, the Europarty's youth association. However, through the mother party's network, the youth branch established cooperation with party foundations and international associations via its engagement in the International Union of Socialist Youth (IUSY) and the mother party, having trainings for campaigning techniques and leadership skills. Similarly to other youth branches, the top leadership of the youth organisation was promoted to the mother party. Thus, the former president of the youth organisation, Oleg Tulea, moved to the mother party and became a member of parliament.

With regard to the women's branch, there is no officially established cooperation with the PES Women network. However, gender equality was the main focus of the programme "In EU's waiting room" launched by the the Social Democratic Party of Sweden and its affiliated Olof Palme International Center. The programme aimed at increasing the number of women in decision-making bodies on different levels, raising awareness of gender issues within the parties and strengthening the capacity of women's organisations in the party structure.[403] After the cooperation with Swedish counterparts, there has been a significant increase in women's participation on the local level. In some localdistricts, the percentage of female candidates on the electoral lists was 50%. Considering its previous institutional development, the increase of

---

402 The Labour Party's International Democracy Programme, *Annual Review*, 2014-15, 12.
403 Olof Palme International Center, Report on Gender Evaluation, 2014.

women's participation locally has been perceived as tangible progress.[404] However, despite this moderate progress in gender balance, the placement of women on the party lists has a clear tendency towards the bottom.

The strong position of Valentina Buliga, chairwomen and the former Minister of Labour, Social Protection and Family in the Filat government set a good example for women's branches: once there is a strong female candidate within the party and especially in the government, discouragement and indecision are supplanted by a renewed sense of purpose.[405]

The ALDE and the Liberal Party (Moldova)

For the Moldovan Liberals, the main partner within the ALDE is the Dutch VVD International. The engagement with VVD International did not change the status quo of internal party democracy within the Liberal Party though. The main activities did not even target this aspect and focused mainly on electoral campaigning skills. In the wake of the 2011 local elections, the VVD experts conducted training on party strategy and "know-how" knowledge in the election campaign, such as how to deliver a message and how to create a poster.[406] In terms of capacity-building, the VVD International organised training for newly elected politicians on how to attract investments and support small and medium-sized businesses in the rural regions. After the training, a liberal network of entrepreneurs was launched.[407]

Within the youth branch, there is no tangible impact on the organisational changes of Young Liberals. The mother party is still protective and reluctant to give the youth organisation space for initiatives. "We still have quite a bit of persuading to do", admitted Mihai Pascovschi, Secretary General of the Moldovan Young Liberals. For example, the young liberals lobbied for the introduction of

---

404   Interview with expert, Olof Palme International Center, 2 January 2015.
405   Ibid.
406   VVD International Report 2011, 34.
407   Ibid., 36.

membership fees in the youth organisation, but this effort was not supported by the mother party. Since the Liberal Party does not have its own membership fees, deviations and experiments in the youth organisation that contradict the functioning of the mother party were not welcome.[408]

In the same way, the mother party is protective of its seats and positions. Although there are a couple of examples of youth promotion to the mother party, it is still difficult for young party members to get a position in the mother party. As usual, only the leaders of the youth organisation get promoted to the mother party. For instance, Sergiu Boghean, the former president of the Young Liberals, is currently Chief of Staff at the Ministry of Education of Moldova.

Within the ALDE party family, the women's branch of the Liberal Party of Moldova is the only women's organisation that is officially affiliated with the ALDE Gender Network. The relationship between the Liberal Party and the ALDE Gender Network can be described as rather intense. In 2013, Corina Fusu was elected as a member of Congress representing the ALDE Gender Network. Together with the ALDE party, Fusu organised several events on gender issues, including conferences on domestic violence and economic empowerment of women.[409]

Similar to the LDPM case, the women's branch of the Liberal Party is stronger than other female organisations across the region due to its governmental and partisan synergy. Acting as vice-president in the party, Corina Fusu possessed better access for establishing contacts and more power for implementing reforms and enjoys more media attention. Despite active participation in events dedicated to gender equality, the situation within the party remains unsatisfactory. To a large extent, the women's organisation is subservient to the mother party and fails to make independent decisions and initiatives.

---

408 Interview with the Youth of Liberal Party representative, 23 January 2014.
409 Interview with the Liberal Party representative, 21 January 2014.

The ALDE and the Republican Party (Georgia)

The Georgian Republicans are considered to be the most democratic party cross-regionally in terms of intra-party democracy.[410] Although the Georgian Republicans show the highest organisational compatibility with European liberal parties, the ALDE's impact in this respect was negligible. The organisational changes were either triggered by the party leadership itself or due to the cooperation with other international actors.

On the mother party level, the internal democracy mechanisms are quite developed. Prior to the affiliation with ALDE, the Republicans organised party congresses twice a year, at which the National Committee was elected. The Republicans claim to be the only party in Georgia in which the party leadership has ever changed.[411] In fact, at the Party Congress in November 2013, Khatuna Samnidze was elected as chairwoman.

With NIMD, the party participated in the NIMD's Political Party Assistance Programme focusing on SWOT analysis and strategic planning. As a result, in March 2013 representatives of the Republicans, including members of the Secretariat, National Committee, Regional Organisation and Administration, renewed their strategic planning document.[412] Via the Westminster Foundation for Democracy the UK Liberal Democratic Party conducted seminars on improving their capacity of communicating policies to the electorate and developing a clear campaigning and communication strategy while part of the coalition government.[413] The VVD International conducted a seminar on inner-communication and intra-party dialogue to involve regional representatives in the party's institutional development.[414]

The Young Republicans party is organisationally more compatible with its European youth wings than other youth branches in

---

410 Interview with the IRI representative, 24 April 2014.
411 Interview with the Republican Party representative, 14 April 2014.
412 The Republican party of Georgia Finalized the Strategic Plan Review, NIMD Archive.
413 Mary Reid, "LibDems International Office: strengthening liberal democracies," *Liberal Democrat Voice*, 29 January 2013.
414 VVD International Report 2011, 17.

the region. The degree of its involvement in decision-making and its relationship with the mother party are akin to those of the European parties. The relationships between the mother party and the youth branch are more independent in comparison with other cases cross-regionally. The reason for this is a higher level of intra-party democracy within the mother party itself, which is interested in encouraging the youth to become "a critical element of the party".[415] As a result, the impact of cooperation with ALDE is rather low, as it is the mother party that triggers changes.

Although the Republican Party of Georgia is an active ALDE member, its connection with the ALDE Gender Network is weak. In the same vein as other liberal parties, the Republicans do not support the introduction of gender quotas. Nevertheless, the party was described as potentially the most "women-friendly party".[416] For example, in 2010, women made up 44% of the party membership in central parts of Georgia and 40% in the regions. In the party's decision-making body – the Committee – there were 10 women out of 35 representatives. On the local level, women constituted 20% of the party representation in the local governments.[417] In November 2013, Khatuna Samnizde was elected as the party chairwoman. In May 2015, Tinatin Khidasheli, the former director of the Georgian Young Lawyers Association, a legal watchdog and until now the chairperson of parliament's European Integration Committee, was appointed as the first female Defence Minister.[418]

The EL and the Party of Communists (Moldova)

As can be expected, the Moldovan Communists inherited the organisational model of the Soviet Communist Party. Following democratic centralism as its core principle, the PCRM's decision-making is highly centralised, and rank-and-file members are excluded from the process. At the Party Congress in 2012, the Communists

---

415 IFLRY strengthens Young Republicans in Georgia, 27 February 2014.
416 Nodia and Scholtbach, *The political landscape of Georgia*, 173.
417 Čáslavská, *Increasing Women's Representation*, 18.
418 "Georgia Nominates Its First Female Defence Minister," *Gender Information Network of South Caucasus*, 5 April 2015.

conducted several reforms to re-brand the party's image. For example, younger party members were included in the Executive Political Committee to rejuvenate the party. In line with the EL's gender-mainstreaming, the appointment of Zinaida Greceanii as the head of the government was a successful strategic move. By promoting women to high-ranking positions, the party showed its capability to make innovative decisions congruent with the EL.[419] Nevertheless, little changed in the internal party structure, in particular in terms of women's promotion and decision-making. All authority remained in the hands of the party founder and strong charismatic leader, Voronin. However, the overwhelming dominance of the permanent party leader and lack of internal party democracy seemed to be tolerated by the Europeans. They considered it part of the natural process of party transition and trend of transformation in the post-communist countries.[420]

Through the EL's network, the Moldovan Communists established close relationships with the German *Die Linke*. As a result of the Summer University in 2010, the PCRM's members were invited for an exchange stay with *Die Linke* to get a better understanding how the German Left functions and share the insights at home.[421] Apart from that, no trainings on capacity-building have been conducted. Similar to the EL, the *transform!* network assisted in organising summer universities where the participants only debated on different topics and no seminars on organisational strengthening were provided.

The cooperation between the Youth Union of Communists in Moldova and ENDYL, the EL's youth association, is very weak. Despite the fact that ENDYL's Secretary General, Alexander Roshko, was the Komsomol's longstanding youth activist[422], the range of mutual activities is constrained to the EL's Summer Universities.

---

419 Igor Botan, "6th Congress and its first consequences," *E-democracy.md*, 31 March 2008.
420 Interview with the *transform!* europe representative, 3 February 2014.
421 Kathrin Voss, "Hammer, Sichel, heiss. Die 5. Sommeruniversität der Europäischen Linken in der Republik Moldawien," *Die Linke's website*, 1 August 2010.
422 Due to the party's internal conflict, Alexandr Roshko was excluded from the PCRM in March 2012.

The marginal cooperation between the two parties is stipulated by their mutual weaknesses. On the one hand, the Moldovan Communists' youth wing is hardly a viable organisation, while, on the other hand, ENDYL is an underdeveloped organisation itself.

Considering the mother party's ad hoc affiliation with the EL, stipulated by rational geostrategic considerations, the weak connection between ENDYL and the "Komsomol" is less surprising. Situational affiliation with the EL did not presuppose encompassing affiliation with the EL's youth association. After the fatigue with European integration among the Moldovan population, the Moldovan Communists returned to its turf and started exploiting orientation towards Russia again.

With regard to the women´s branch, there is no affiliation with the EL FEM. Apart from the EL FEM, formally, the PCRM's women's branch is affi-liated with international women's organisations, but the cooperation is of low profile and sporadic nature. Despite having a strong female representative, Zinaida Greceanii's strong position within the party and government, it did not trigger any strengthening of the Communists' women's branch. In Greceanii's opinion, Moldovan women are hard-working in politics, business and other areas, but due to patriarchal mentality and societal stereotypes, the political empowerment of women is still lagging behind.[423]

7.2   Analysing the Organisational Changes

Evaluation of the cooperation with the Europarties and their youth and women's associations reveals very little impact on the organisational dimension. Beyond political conditionality on internal party democracy, the Europarties' ability to impact on organisational matters is very low during the application process. The factors behind this low impact are anchored both in the nature of the Europarties and their associations and in the nature of East European parties. As umbrella organisations, the Europarties and their

---

423   (Interview) Zinaida Greceanii: "There was an agreement between the Dodon group and some of the AEI parties," *Tribuna.md*, 25 November 2011.

associations operate rather as a platform for the facilitation of contact establishment. Mutual events are scarce and often limited to congresses and board meetings twice a year. Moreover, the Europarties, their sister parties and partner institutes rarely target the party's internal mechanisms: the problematic candidate selection process, intransparent party funding, and non-participatory and highly personalised internal decision-making remain untouched. The Europarties are not interested in challenging the status quo and interfering in the party's internal affairs. International party aid donors follow a similar logic. Dependent on external funding, they have to deliver fast positive results. In this case, trainings on election campaigning give prompt and tangible results to report about.

On the other hand, the range of the Europarties' and international actors' activities is partly demand-driven. In this situation, domestic mother parties and their youth and women's branches ask specifically for trainings mainly on electoral campaigning and leadership skills. As a result of the focus on external party activities, internal mechanisms remain untargeted in the trainings and workshops. Domestic parties were not interested in implementing ground-breaking reforms that would change the logic of party functioning in the region and thus endanger their existence. To target internal candidate selection, party funding or decision-making would require a complete redesign of the institutional and legal setup of the party system. In this situation, leadership and campaigning skills is a low-risk area for trainings which, as a result, only solidifies the party's status quo. Equipped with better techniques, parties increase their efficiency as electoral machines.

The time factor remains irrelevant in the organisational dimension, as parties with longstanding affiliation with the Europarties have not succeeded in learning more from the experience of their European counterparts (H4). Secondly, the party position has an ambiguous impact on the structural match. On the one hand, strong parties indeed have more structural opportunities for cooperation with the Europarties' associations. Moreover, being part of a strong party gives youth and women's branches a more pronounced voice in the Europarties' associations. On the other hand, it has no straightforward impact on their structural compatibility.

Strong parties such as *Batkivshchyna* and the UNM have failed to implement organisational changes in their party structures. In contrast, despite its weak party position, the Georgian Republicans party has succeeded the most in learning from European experiences of party-building and structural entanglement (H5). In turn, this was the set of motivations which guided the non-EU mother parties and their youth and women's branches to establish cooperation that predetermined their capacity to implement organisational changes domestically. In contrast to prestige and/or geopolitical considerations, a genuine desire to borrow experience in party-building opens the way for implementation of organisational changes. As the cases of the Moldovan Liberal Democrats and the Georgian Republicans proved, the impact on the organisational dimension was higher because the parties possessed genuine interest in transferring expertise knowledge (H6).

Impact on the mother parties

The Europarties provide the non-EU parties with opportunity structure through which domestic parties can establish bilateral cooperation with the Europarties' sister parties. It is sister parties who are mainly involved in its capacity-building. Due to their efforts in organising workshops and seminars, domestic parties are trained in various aspects of organisational strengthening. Since most trainings are demand-driven, the focus lies on leadership skills and electoral campaigning. In parallel with the sister parties' work, the Europarties' partner institutions and think tanks are also involved in organisational strengthening.

Overall, the impact on capacity-building in the mother parties is very low (Table 7.1). Among eight analysed cases, only three parties amended their party statutes and mentioned the affiliation on the European level in their internal documents. Of those three, only the *Batkivshchyna* party referred to EPP affiliation as its ideological foundation, whereas the Ukrainian *Rukh* and the Moldovan Christian Democrats only mentioned EPP affiliation as their type of activity.

With regard to intra-party democracy, no impact can be detected. The parties' internal selection mechanisms remain untouched, whereas the decision-making is deeply rooted in the top leadership. The introduction of primaries or nomination is often perceived as a danger to the status quo of the party leadership. The only exception among all of the cases is the Georgian Republican party, which has a long-standing tradition of democratic selection mechanisms. However, there is no link between the party's affiliation with ALDE and democratic internal mechanisms, as the Republicans implemented them prior to the cooperation.

Table 7.1   Organisational changes in mother parties

Organisational changes	Changes to the party statutes/Reference to the affiliation	Changes to internal decision-making	Electoral campaigning techniques
EPP family			
LDPM	+	−	+
The *Batkivshchyna*	+	−	+
UNM	−	A	+
PES family			
DPM	−	−	+
ALDE family			
The Liberal Party	−	−	+
The Republican Party	−	−	+
EL family			
PCRM	−	−	+

Note: (+) present
(−) absent
(A) ambivalent change
(i) implicitly present

The recently introduced primaries in the UNM need further observation to determine whether they will be truly implemented within the party and whether the Swedish Moderate party's experience has impacted the UNM.

Most impacts on the organisational dimension can be tracked in terms of the import of campaigning skills. Many parties have willingly employed Western techniques of electoral campaigning, such as door-to-door campaigning, targeted message development and databases of citizens' voting intentions. As all domestic parties are strongly election-orientated, there is no difference between the Europarties' affiliation and the party position. From liberals to communists and from strong to weak parties, they are interested in enhancing their campaigning techniques in order to stay in power.

The impact on youth branches

Through establishing affiliation with the Europarties' youth associations, unfledged youth branches of Georgian, Moldovan, and Ukrainian parties have received an opportunity to socialise in line with European norms and practices of youth activism. The youth wings of non-EU parties could compare the functioning of youth organisations in Western parties and apply this European experience in their party-building domestically. However, as umbrella organisations, the Europarties' youth associations did not impose any direct impact on the organisational structure of domestic youth branches (Table 7.2). None of the youth branches have introduced changes to their party statutes after establishing cooperation with the Europarty's youth associations.

Table 7.2   Organisational changes in youth branches

Organisational changes	Changes to the party stautes/ references to the affiliation	Changes in relationships between mother party and youth branch	Promotion of the youth
YEPP			
LDYM	+	A	+
Batkivshchyna moloda	-	-	+
YES PES			
Democratic Youth	-	-	+
LYMEC			
Young Liberals	-	-	+
Young Republicans	-	-	+
ENDYL			
„Komsomol"	I	-	A

Note: (+) present
(−) absent
(A) ambivalent change
(i) implicitly present

The introduction of organisational changes was often blocked by the principal organisation. As a result, the autonomy of youth branches vis-à-vis mother parties remained unchanged. However, trainings and workshops have triggered some organisational changes. For instance, mother parties have started to include youth activists in the local party boards or organise training activities for their youth. Nevertheless, this has hardly altered the relationships between mother parties and their youth branches. On the one hand, involvement of youth in local boards is a "low-cost" reform for the mother parties and is harmless in terms of preserving the status quo. On the other hand, the effect of trainings and workshops clearly remains on the individual level. Due to resistance from the mother party, youth branches do not obtain enough autonomy and space to undertake initiatives and implement new experience. Youth branches are still mostly used during election periods. The cases of promotion of youth to the mother party have proved to follow a pattern: only the top leadership of the youth branches gets a career lift to the mother party.

The impact on women's branches

With regard to the women's branches, in that handful of cases where affiliation with women's associations is present, the impact is barely measurable (Table 7.3). Across all the Europarties, only the Moldovan LDPM's and Liberal Party's women's organisations have officially established affiliation with the EPP Women and ALDE Gender Network, respectively.

Table 7.3   Organisational changes in women's branches

Organisational changes	Gender quotas on the candidate lists	Strengthening of organisational capacity	Gender mainstreaming
EPP Women			
LDPM Women	+	+	-
UNM's women's branch	+	+	-
Batkivshchyna's women's branch	+	+	-

PES Women			
DPM's women's branch	+	+	−
ALDE Gender Network			
Liberal party's women's branch	+	+	+
Republican party's women's branch	−	+	−
EL FEM			
PCRM's women's branch	+	−	−

Note: (+) present
(−) absent
(A) ambivalent change
(i) implicitly present

Within the party case, it is difficult to separate the effects in a situation when state-to-state relations are entangled with party-to-party relations. Women's branches seem to significantly profit from the synergy of governmental and partisan tracks. A high position in the party hierarchy and/or go-vernment gives women leaders an additional channel to promote women's issues and implement reforms. In the cases of the LDPM, Liberal Party, and the DPM, due to the convergence of their high positions in the party hierarchy and in the government, Liliana Palihovici, Corina Fusu, and Valentina Buliga have managed to gain significant media attraction, to establish wide partisan contacts, and to initiate reforms in gender equality. In those cases, successful examples of women in the top leadership have provided women's branches with strong role models for their female colleagues to aspire to.

The reasons for the limited impact again stem from both the European and domestic sides. In contrast to the Europarties' youth associations, the activities of the Europarties' women's associations are even more limited in range and are constrained to networking and discussion meetings. The activities of the Europarties' women's associations can hardly influence organisational changes on the subject of gender equality within the party because they are dedicated to broader topics and organised only once or twice a year. Moreover, it seems not to be on their agenda at all. The Europarties' women's associations are not interested in imposing gender mechanisms within the party. Considering societal stereotypes and resistance within the party, women's associations are ready to compromise and prefer to work on a long-term perspective by changing the attitude in the society. From the domestic perspective, women's organisations mirror the mother parties in their unfledged organisational structure. Rigid mother party structures hinder the institutional development of women's branches and prevent the penetration of any potential impact.

8. Impact on Inter-Party Behaviour

Apart from ideological and organisational changes, the cooperation with the Europarties has an impact on inter-party behaviour that is, on the relationships between sister parties. In their press releases and official statements, the Europarties endorse and actively support the cooperation between like-minded parties. Interested in viable and sustainable political forces, the Europarties have a strong interest in endorsing cooperation between like-minded parties. The main objective is to consolidate democratic and pro-European forces – either via domestic inter-party cooperation or through party fusions – and thus to contribute to the strengthening of democratic institutions in transition countries. Cooperation can have different faces such as government formation, coalition-building, the formation of an electoral block, the nomination of a presidential/parliamentary candidate in single-member constituencies, or party mergers between sister parties.

On the behavioural dimension, factors such as length of cooperation, party position, and motivation are expected to have the following impact. The time factor is likely to have a positive impact on parties' readiness to cooperate with each other. The longer and the more intense they cooperate with the Europarties, the more they are socialised in line with the European values and practices. In turn, due to this effect of socialisation, sister parties are expected to cooperate with each other more willingly in comparison with those parties that only recently joined the Europarties (H7). With regard to the party position, the cooperation is more likely to happen between strong and weak parties than between two strong parties. In cooperation between strong and weak parties, both parties profit by supporting each other. Forging cooperation with weak parties, strong parties can profit from staying in power, whereas weak parties can benefit domestically from international recognition. In contrast, cooperation between strong parties is likely to lead to rivalry, as both strong parties, which usually target the same electoral field, will compete for unique relationships with the Europarty (H8). Finally, the motivation factor is expected to have a positive effect on the inter-party relationships in the cases where the party's motives for affiliation were ideational and based on a genuine wish to borrow the European experience (H9).

To assess the impact on the inter-party relationships, this chapter is structured in the following way. Firstly, the relationships within the EPP and the ALDE families are investigated, considering their numerous affiliations with the non-EU parties. The sister party's support during the application process and their relationship after being accepted to the European family is analysed. Secondly, the chapter proceeds with the analysis of inter-party relationships across the Europarties. Of particular interest is the cooperation within the Moldovan "Alliance for European Integration", whose three coalition partners were all affiliated with the Europarties. Another example from Georgia sheds light on inter-party conflict resulting from the Europarties' support of their sister parties. Finally, the chapter moves to the analysis of sister party cooperation and explores whether the Europarties' affiliation triggered any effect.

8.1 Inter-Party Relationships between Sister Parties

The ALDE: the Republican Party and
Our Georgia–Free Democrats (Georgia)

The ALDE party's representatives openly supported the participation of their Georgian sister parties in government formation and coalition-building. After the 2012 parliamentary election, the European Liberals welcomed the official results and congratulated the Republican Party and Free Democrats on entering the governing Georgian Dream coalition. Guy Verhofstadt, ALDE Leader in the EP, praised the strengthened position of the liberal forces in the Georgian parliament and expressed his hopes that confrontation and animosity would be put aside to "pursue a national consensus on key projects like justice and jobs, Euro-Atlantic integration and territorial integrity".[424] In the same vein, Sir Graham Watson, ALDE Party Leader, welcomed a peaceful transition in the country and Mr. Ivanishvili's appointment of Alexi Petriashvili[425] as European Affairs minister. In his view, it was a clear sign of the government's European intentions. "Georgian democracy was on a slippery slope, but now with our liberal friends so strong, we trust Georgia will remain committed to its long-term European and NATO ambitions, and its new leaders initiate new efforts towards great prosperity for their country and their citizens", assured Sir Graham Watson.[426]

Within the ALDE family, cooperation between the Republicans and Free Democrats represents a positive example. The cooperation between the parties became very productive, especially after entering the Georgian Dream coalition. The Republicans publically acknowledged the Free Democrats as "long-term partners"[427] based on their ideological common base. Within the Georgian Dream coalition, they supported each other on issues of educational and anti-discrimination reforms.[428]

The party relationships remained friendly even after the Free Democrats' withdrawal from the Georgian Dream coalition in October 2014. During the meeting of the Georgian Dream coalition' leadership, Khatuna Samnidze, chairwomen of the Republican Party, described the withdrawal as "a great loss" for the coalition. Samnidze maintained that the Free Democrats remain their long-term partners and that their cooperation will continue in the future.[429] Furthermore, as a result of the coalition's weakening, the Republicans called for refinements in the coalition system and for

---

424 ALDE Press Release, "Liberals in the Driving Seat in Peaceful Transition of Power in Georgia" (Brussels: ALDE, 2 October 2012).
425 A former member of the party Our Georgia–Free Democrats.
426 ALDE Press Release, "Peaceful Transition of Power in Georgia" (Brussels: ALDE, 26 October 2012).
427 "Alasania's Free Democrats Quit GD Coalition," *Civil Georgia*, 5 November 2014.
428 Interview with the Republican Party representative, 18 April 2014.
429 "Alasania's Free Democrats Quit GD Coalition," *Civil Georgia*, 5 November 2014.

building a truly "European-style coalition".[430] To achieve this goal, the Republicans considered two options:

> either it can make the currently assembled coalition—which was created with the aim of unseating the previous authorities—into a European-style coalition, which would form the basis of a coalition agreement completely redistributing responsibilities and clearly and practically uniting them on a shared political platform, or alternatively to make it the kind of coalition in which the component parities are guaranteed the freedom to position themselves according to their own ideologies and to make clear their differing positions within the framework of agreements reached within the coalition.[431]

The positive example of Georgian sister party relationships was possible due to a long and intensive socialisation period, the weak positions of both parties, and their ideational motivations. Considering the length and intensity of the affiliation, the Republicans are a long-standing partner of ALDE, which joined the Europarty in 2007, whereas the Free Democrats became an ALDE member only in 2011. The affiliation between ALDE and the Republicans is marked by active participation and close cooperation. As an example, in January 2015, Tinatin Khidasheli, the Republican International Secretary, was elected vice-president of the ALDE faction of the Parliamentary Assembly of the Council of Europe. At the same time, she became a member of the ALDE Bureau. In contrast, the cooperation with the Free Democrats was just recently settled.

With regard to party position, both the Republicans and Free Democrats are minor parties with small vote shares. Despite being the oldest Georgian party, the Republicans were not represented in the Georgian parliament until recently. In 2008, the party obtained only 3.78% of voter support and failed to enter parliament. Similarly, the Free Democrats are a recently established minor party that managed to enter parliament as a part of the Georgian Dream coalition, obtaining 8 seats. Being a minor party, the Republicans wel-

---

[430] "Republicans Want GD to Turn into 'European Style Coalition'," *Civil Georgia*, 29 October 2014.
[431] Statement by the Republican Party on "The Political Agenda of the Next Two Years," Tbilisi, 26 October 2014.

comed the Free Democrats' application to ALDE and greatly supported the joining of another Georgian liberal party to the Europarty. Although both parties are weak parties in terms of electoral performance, the Republicans have a dominant position in this relationship. Being the oldest Georgian party, the Republican Party considered itself an authority on liberalism. In their "student-teacher" relationship, the Republicans shared the experience with the Free Democrats and showed them "the path of being a liberal party".[432]

The decision to join the ALDE family was driven by ideational motives and was perceived by the Republican Party as an obvious choice. As an ideologically consolidated party, the Republicans knew where they belonged from the very beginning.[433] Through the affiliation with the ALDE, the party wanted to show their voters and their sceptics "where we belong" and "the commitment we have made"[434] as well as to share their values and practices by co-operating with international parties.[435]

Nevertheless, despite sharing a liberal identity and competing for political survival, both parties refused to merge their party structure. During the application process, there were some attempts from the ALDE party to endorse a party merger between the two like-minded parties. Sharing the same core liberal values, it was difficult for ALDE to comprehend the difference between the parties. Moreover, it was difficult for the Republican Party's representatives themselves to name the main difference. The major distinction between the parties appears to be a view on the constitutional form of government. Whereas the Republicans are strongly in favour of the parliamentary form, the Free Democrats support the presidential form. However, there are personal and electoral factors that hindered a party merger and kept the party structures apart. On the one hand, the Free Democrats, led by Alasania until 2016, is

---

432 Interview with the Republican Party representative, 18 April 2014.
433 Interview the Republican Party representative, 14 April 2014.
434 Ibid., 14 April 2014.
435 Interview with the Republican Party representative, 18 April 2014.

a leader-driven party that preferred to stay independent. Due to personal conflicts among the UNM, the Republicans, and the Georgian Dream, the independent position of the Free Democrats was expected to give them more room for manoeuvre.[436] On the other hand, the Republicans opposed any attempts to change their well-recognised brand. For them, the process of merging and amending their name would conceal certain disadvantages. In their view, a party merger would confuse their core voters and harm their image as a traditional liberal party. In this respect, the Republicans considered only two options — either the Free Democrats should join their party without any changes in the party's name or both parties should consolidate more supporters individually and unite their strengths within the coalition.[437]

Overall, cooperation between the Republicans and Free Democrats represents a positive case when two parties supported each other. The fraternal relationships were, however, established prior to the affiliation with the ALDE. The limited impact of the Europarty is further shown in the ALDE's failed attempts to merge both parties. In this situation, domestic factors prevailed over the Europarty's calls for a party merger. Due to the high personalisation of the Georgian parties, neither the Republicans nor the Free Democrats were ready to unite their party structures.

The EPP: the Batkivshchyna party, the People's Movement of Ukraine Rukh, and UDAR (Ukraine)

Another positive example of inter-party cooperation is between *Batkivshchyna*, *Rukh*, and UDAR. Although the parties showed mutual support, their cooperation was driven by strategic factors, in particular by electoral gains.

In the 2007 early parliamentary election, facing the power consolidation of the Party of Regions, Yulia Tymoshenko, party leader of the *Batkivshchyna* party, called on all democratic forces for unification. However, having already been affiliated with the EPP since 2006, *Rukh's* party leader, Tarasiuk, denied his party's intentions to

---

436 Interview with expert, Zentrum für Demokratie Aarau, 27 March 2014.
437 Interview with the Republican Party representative, 18 April 2014.

unite under BYuT's umbrella, arguing that any potential unification should be based on ideological foundations. Whereas Tymoshenko's bloc had a leftist leaning, *Rukh* positioned itself on the right side of the spectrum. "We are ready for cooperation and coordination, but not for merging", stressed Tarasiuk.[438] In fact, for *Rukh*, the oldest and the most ideological political force in Ukraine, a party merger with BYuT, an amorphous bloc, did not promise any political or electoral dividends and would be perceived as a betrayal by its voters.

In the wake of the 2012 parliamentary election, however, *Rukh* altered its position as the political situation in the country radically changed. In 2010, Viktor Yanukovych, the candidate of the Party of Regions, won the presidential election. Tymoshenko's second government was dismissed, and later on, in October 2011, she faced criminal charges and was convicted of embezzlement and abuse of power. In this situation, the imprisonment of Tymoshenko and the gripping authoritarian regime of Yanukovych mobilised the pro-democratic forces. Tymoshenko's second appeal to all the democratic forces to unite and to form a united candidate list in order to prevent the Party of Regions' win in the upcoming 2012 parliamentary election was heard. As a reaction to this appeal, Tarasiuk expressed *Rukh's* full solidarity with regard to the unification of oppositional forces. In the party's opinion, this would increase the chances for the democratic forces to oppose the "anti-Ukrainian and anti-democratic activities of Yanukovych' regime".[439] Tarasiuk called to put aside personal interests and ambitions and unite the opposition on the basis of BYuT, whose party leader was "a real

---

438 "Тарасюк не збирається об'єднуватись з Тимошенко," *Корреспондент*, 16 лютого 2007. ["Tarasuik is not going to unite with Tymoshenko," *Korrespondent*, 16 February 2007].

439 "Борис Тарасюк вважає, що опозиції треба об'єднуватися навколо Тимошенко, бо вона найбільш популярна серед громадян," *Політична думка*, 26 січня 2011. ["Borys Tarasuik thinks that opposition should unite around Tymoshenko because she is the most popular among the population," *Politychna dumka*, 26 January 2011].

oppositional leader".[440] As a result, the announced party merger triggered a split within *Rukh*, and Tarasiuk moved to BYuT.

Both sister parties seemed to benefit from the cooperation. The marginal *Rukh* gained an opportunity to enter parliament, while Tarasiuk was appointed as the co-chairman of the parliamentary assembly of EURONEST in 2011. Being the leader of a driving oppositional force, Tymoshenko strengthened her numerical advantage in parliament and obtained strong support and solidarity in Europe via *Rukh* during her imprisonment. This case illustrates how, once again, domestic factors overruled the Europarties' calls for the consolidation of sister parties. Only after being threatened by the Party of Regions' power accumulation, both parties reconsidered their interests and united their efforts in an attempt to win the parliamentary elections.

The relationships between the *Batkivshchyna* party and UDAR, another Ukrainian sister party in the EPP, provides another example where electoral benefits predetermined parties' cooperation. In September 2013, the EPP granted an observer status for Klitchko's party, UDAR. In reaction to UDAR's affiliation with the EPP, the *Batkivshchyna* party welcomed the Europarty's decision. The party representative Nemyrya expressed his opinion that it will unquestionably strengthen cooperation both within the country as well as outside for the sake of Ukraine's European perspective. He added that the first test of this strengthened cooperation will be the upcoming 2013 parliamentary election and the parties' decision to unite their candidate lists in a single-member constituency.[441] In the wake of the 2013 parliamentary election, the *Batkivshchyna* party and UDAR

---

440 "Борис Тарасюк вважає, що опозиції треба об'єднуватися навколо Тимошенко, бо вона найбільш популярна серед громадян," *Політична думка*, 26 січня 2011. ["Borys Tarasuik thinks that opposi-tion should unite around Tymo shenko because she is the most popular among the population," *Politychna dumka*, 26 January 2011].

441 Віталій Єреміца, "У Європі «поміняли» «Нашу Україну» на УДАР і критикують Кремль," *Радіо Свобода*, 6 вересня 2013. ["Vitaliy Eremiza, 'Europe changed Our Ukraine on UDAR and critisises Kremlin'," *Radio Svoboda*, 6 September 2013].

agreed to unite their forces against the Party of Regions and coordinate their candidates in single-member districts. After a long round of discussions, 26 of UDAR's candidates withdrew their nomination in favour of the *Batkivshchyna* party members. Although the EPP's calls for unification were acknowledged by sister parties, *Batkivshchyna* and UDAR had purely rational reasons for their cooperation. Their strategy was based less on ideological closeness and more on political survival and electoral advantage. By nominating one candidate, the parties expected to have a better chance of winning against the Party of Regions.

Nevertheless, the parties' fraternal relationship did not last for long. Already during the 2014 early presidential election, UDAR, adapting itself to the country's new political constellation, began to cooperate with Poroshenko's bloc "Solidarnist".[442] Refusing to support Tymoshenko's presidential candidacy, Vitaly Klitchko favoured Poroshenko as the future president. Later in 2015, Klitchko's UDAR and Poroshenko's Solidarnist announced the unification of their party structures. By this time, Solidarnist had submitted its application to the EPP. "The EPP welcomes the merger of our partners, Solidarnist and UDAR, and further supports the unification of the center-right democratic forces in Ukraine… The creation of such a strong pro-European political force will help to continue the reform process in the country," said EPP President Joseph Daul.[443] In contrast, Tymoshenko's presidential running was not very well received in the EPP, and particularly in Germany. Angela Merkel non-publicly called for the withdrawal of her candidacy

---

442 Petro Poroshenko's block "Solidarnist" was established in 2014 in the wake of the 2014 early presidential election, resulting from the 2013–2014 protests on the Maidan in Kyiv.

443 "EPP supports unification of Ukraine's UDAR, BPP and PF parties," *UNIAN*, 3 September 2015.

and for the dedication of her political career to preserving the country's unity.[444]

Although formally the Ukrainian parties complied with the EPP's endorsements for cooperation, the rationale of supportive inter-party behaviour can be explained through electoral politics. On the one hand, Poroshenko's Solidarnist profited from the UDAR party's well-developed organisational structure, its numerous activists, and its strong position in the western regions of Ukraine. On the other hand, despite weak popularity, through a party fusion, Klitchko obtained Solidarnist's support at the local election during his campaign for the mayor's office.[445]

The EPP: the People's Union "Our Ukraine"
and the Batkivshchyna party (Ukraine)

In contrast to the previous cases, the inter-party relationships between "Our Ukraine" and the *Batkivshchyna* party were marred by personal conflicts and confrontation. By 2005, when "Our Ukraine" joined the Europarty, the EPP provided full support to Yushchenko, the then newly elected president and former party leader, by praising the country's democratic achievements in the Orange Revolution. The contact between the EPP and "Our Ukraine" intensified through numerous mutual visits and activities, including Yushchenko's speech at the EP, which received a standing ovation. In 2007, however, the EPP started to support other forces of the Orange Revolution openly and favoured the formation of the Orange government.[446] Later in 2008, the EPP welcomed the creation of a

---

[444] "Меркель призвала Тимошенко «работать на единство» и предложила Лечение," *Українська правда*, 23 лютого 2014. ["Merkel called on Tymoshenko to work for the unity and offered treatment," *Ukrainska Pravda*, 23 February 2014].

[445] Oleksandr Holubov, "Ukraine's New Party of Power," *Carnegie Endowment for International Peace*, 31 August 2015.

[446] EPP Press Release, "Elections in Ukraine. Martens and Daul congratulate Yushchenko and Tymoshenko — support orange government coalition" (Brussels: EPP, 1 October 2007).

coalition between the People's Union "Our Ukraine" and the *Batkivshchyna* party and expressed full confidence in its partners. Mr. Lopez-Isturiz congratulated the parties on behalf of the EPP: "I think it is very good news for Europe and for Ukraine that President Yushchenko and Prime-Minister Tymoshenko decided to join their efforts and to work together for the better future of the country, especially at the difficult moment of economic and political crisis in Ukraine".[447]

In 2006, after Yulia Tymoshenko was appointed as prime minister, the political crisis erupted and the relationship between the Orange democratic forces significantly deteriorated. The numerous EPP statements on consolidation and stabilisation remained unnoticed. Critiques of Yushchenko's unwillingness to build a coalition with Tymoshenko have led to more tense relations. Since 2008, as the EPP's support shifted to Tymoshenko and her party, "Our Ukraine" ceased its cooperation with the EPP, avoiding any participation in the Europarty's events. During the EPP delegation in Kyiv, Yushchenko cancelled his meeting at short notice due to his busy schedule. The EPP Summit in Brussels was similarly disregarded. Altogether it led to the EPP's disillusionment with Yushchenko as a trustworthy partner; it also weakened his relationship with Angela Merkel.[448] Both the EPP and KAS viewed the situation with the party with deep frustration and disappointment. They indicated having difficulty identifying an appropriate person to resume contact.[449] The long-lasting internal crisis put the party on the brink of "political death". Being completely marginalised, "Our Ukraine" lost its representation and credibility within the country. Unsurprisingly, in September 2013, the party was officially excluded from the EPP due to its unpaid membership fees. However, the feeling of bitter disappointment with Yushchenko as the party leader predetermined the expulsion.

---

447   EPP Press Release, "EPP congratulates Yushchenko and Tymoshenko for creation of coalition and believes in their joint cooperation for better future of Ukraine" (Brussels: EPP, 10 December 2008).
448   Taras Kuzio, "Big in Brussels," *Business Ukraine*, June 30–July 6, 2008.
449   Interviews with the former and current KAS representatives, 5 December 2013 and 5 November 2013.

The cooperation between both parties was doomed from the very beginning. Back then, both "Our Ukraine" and the *Batkivshchyna* party had just recently joined the EPP, without having undergone an intensive socialisation process. Personal confrontation between party leaders handicapped any potential cooperation between them. Moreover, being the drivers behind the Orange Revolution, both parties held a strong position domestically and were in fact competing in the same electoral field and fighting for the EPP's recognition and acknowledgement. In addition, both parties had rational considerations in mind for joining of the EPP — to buttress their domestic legitimacy and lobby the EU integration.

*The EPP: the Liberal Democratic Party
and the Christian Democratic People's Party (Moldova)*

The relationships between the LDPM and the CDPP can also hardly be called cooperative. During the application process, the Moldovan Christian Democrats blocked the LDPM's application to join the EPP. Being a small party, the CDPP enjoyed privileged attention from the EPP. At the beginning, the cooperation was marked by the Christian Democrats' active participation in the activities of the EPP, the Robert Schumann Institute, and KAS. Due to the EPP's efforts, and in particular those of Martens, the party's functioning was rescued from the politically motivated pressure of the judiciary. In 2002, being under the control of the Communists, the judiciary made efforts to announce the Christian Democrats' functioning as illegal and tried to outlaw the party from Moldova's political life. At the EPP Summit in Warsaw in 2009, party leader Rosca expressed his gratitude for the Europarty's support and pride in being part of the largest European political family.[450]

The mass protests of 7 April 2009, in the wake of which the LDPM came to power, were perceived by the CDPP as being staged by "radical liberal parties" and leading to a deep political crisis and

---

[450] "Iurie Roşca: Admiterea în PPE a partidului condus de Vladimir Filat poate aduce grave prejudicii de imagine creştin-democraţilor europeni," *Flux*, 19 November 2010.

destabilisation.⁴⁵¹ In the meantime, the domestic support for the CDPP was vanishing. During the 2009 parliamentary election, the CDPP gathered only 3% support, whereas the LDPM obtained 12.4%. In this situation, the EPP became interested in affiliation with the Liberal Democrats, who were a driving force behind the formation of the pro-European coalition. In the wake of the 2010 parliamentary election, the EPP president actively supported the LDPM, indicating that the LDPM was the only strong political force in Moldova. The CDPP was not willing to share the prestigious affiliation with other domestic parties. In response to this, Rosca questioned the EPP's objectivity, calling on the Europarty to refrain from campaigning on behalf of Filat and warning against potential damage to the EPP's image. In a video statement in 2011, the EPP president called for cooperation between the CDPP and the LDPM to foster fundamental reforms and modernisation in Moldova. Martens assured that the CDPP's support of the LDPM was in the interests of Moldova's European future and represented no risk for the party in terms of losing its Christian-democratic identity.⁴⁵²

Despite the EPP's efforts to reconcile both sister parties via internal talks with Iurie Rosca, the CDPP decided unilaterally to withdraw its membership. The Christian Democrats accused the LDPM of having undemocratic credentials and of being a misfit within the EPP party family.⁴⁵³ Moreover, the CDPP blamed the EPP for loosening its ideological criteria for newcomers and rebuked the Europarty for its support of anti-democratic and corrupt regimes. In the CDPP's views, the EPP became an ideologically eclectic Europarty

---

451 Cuvântarea lui Iurie Roşca, Moldova, PPCD, la Congresul PPE, 30 April 2009.
452 "Материалы XIII съезда Христианско-демократической народной партии," Ava.md, 24 лютого 2011. ["Document of XIII Christian-Democratic people's party conference," Ava.md, 24 February 2011].
453 In fact, since 2010, the Moldovan Christian Democrats' ideology has drifted to the far right, augmenting the crucial role of the Orthodox Church and neo-Eurasianism in Moldova's postmodern development. Referring to the works of Alexander Dugin, a Russian thinker known for his extreme right views, the Moldovan Christian Democrats criticised the dogmatism of liberal ideology dominant in Western Europe and the idolisation of European integration and European values.

driven by geopolitical interests and an unscrupulous expansion strategy through the admission of post-Soviet parties with dubious and corrupt party leaders. The party linked the deterioration of its relationship with the EPP with the CDPP's failure to enter the parliament in 2009. In the party's view, the EPP was keen on cooperation with governmental parties in order to influence domestic politics.[454] In contrast, the EPP claimed that the non-cooperative behaviour of Rosca's party and its subsequent deal with the Communists in parliament made the affiliation between the Europarty and the CDPP incompatible.[455]

Despite the claimed centre-right positioning, both parties failed to support each other. In this case, the long-standing affiliation with the EPP did not produce tangible effects for the Christian Democrats. The party reacted to the acceptance of another Moldovan party in a hostile and non-supportive manner. Due to the high personalisation of Moldovan party politics, the CDPP's party leader Rosca, attempted to preserve the prestigious status of being the only Moldovan party affiliated with the EPP. Having a weak position, the party did not have enough leverage to block the entry of the LDPM, so as a result, the Christian Democrats decided to withdraw their membership from the Europarty.

The EPP: the United National Movement, the New Rights Party, and the Christian Democratic Movement (Georgia)

Similarly, the relationships among the UNM, the New Rights Party, and the Christian Democratic Movement have proven to be complicated. Once Saakashvili's UNM party obtained an observer membership, the access for the New Rights Party and the CDM to the EPP was blocked. Since 2003, the New Rights Party applied for EPP observer membership. Despite the fulfilment of the EPP's general requirements, the New Rights Party's application was postponed until the official results of the 2008 parliamentary election. In the New Rights Party's opinion, the application was not reviewed because the party criticised the UNM's authoritarian policy.

---

454 Interview with the CDPP representative, 23 January 2014.
455 Interview with the EPP representative, 10 October 2013.

Additionally, the party argued that the EPP tried to avoid the inclusion of two opposing parties under one umbrella and promised to review the application if the party managed to enter parliament after the 2008 election. Having failed to enter parliament, the New Rights Party's membership remained pending, while the EPP favoured the UNM as a governmental party.[456]

In a similar way, the UNM opposed the EPP's affiliation with the CDM. The party applied for an observer membership in 2009; however, the review process was officially stopped due to the CDM's double affiliation. At the time, the CDM was already a member of the European Christian Political Movement, a marginal Europarty. However, it was allegedly the UNM that blocked the CDM's application in order to remain the only Georgian party in the EPP's family.

In 2012, aspiring to join a more powerful Europarty, the CDM applied for AECR membership and obtained it within the same year.[457] Surprisingly enough, it was the relationships between the CDM, the EPP, and KAS that deteriorated substantially rather than the relationships between the sister parties. From the CDM's point of view, the EPP treated them "badly and unfairly in the Georgian political landscape",[458] pointing out the EPP's unconditional support for the UNM. The CDM's representative described the relationships with the EPP as unequal, where the Europarty was demanding a lot but remained inattentive to the CDM's needs. The party representative claimed that the EPP expected them to drop their ECPM membership without offering a clear EPP observer membership.[459] From the EPP's perspective though, the Europarty was waiting for the election results before making its final decision on the application. A fact-finding mission to Tbilisi was already planned when the EPP and KAS were informed that the CDM had obtained membership with AECR. As a result, the application to

---

456 Interview with the New Rights Party representative, 14 April 2014.
457 Interview with the CDM representative, 29 April 2014.
458 Ibid.
459 Interview with the CDM representative, 29 April 2014.

the EPP was suspended and all events with local KAS were cancelled.[460]

The cooperation between Georgian sister parties failed for two reasons. On the one hand, the UNM did not support the applications from other Georgian rightist parties because the party perceived the EPP affiliation as an exclusive and prestigious membership and treated other potential sister parties as its rivals. On the other hand, the EPP's lack of encouragement towards small non-governmental parties fuelled discontent in the ranks of the New Rights Party and the CDM. Their high aspirations to join the EPP were met with a reserved attitude. The EPP was not interested in granting membership to parties with weak position, when they had an opportunity to incorporate the governing UNM. Keeping the parties in a long waiting process, the EPP and its ambiguous behaviour damaged the relationships with the New Rights Party and the CDM.

8.2 Inter-Party Cooperation across the Europarties

The EPP, PES, and ALDE: Alliance for European Integration (Moldova)

The three-party AEI was formed by the Liberal Democratic Party, the Democratic Party, and the Liberal Party after the so-called Twitter Revolution in 2009, and it marked a power change from the Communists to democratic forces. All three parties supported Moldova's pro-European course and secured their affiliations with the Europarties. Throughout the period 2009–2015, the AEI coalition experienced three political crises and the reshuffling of the coalition's composition. In each case, the Europarties – in particular, the EPP and the ALDE – encouraged the party members to preserve the pro-European coalition in order to secure Moldova's "success story" and prevent the Communists from returning to power.

In 2010, in a statement the EPP Group welcomed Moldova's achieved political reforms and its progress in the negotiations of the Association Agreement. The EPP Group chairman, Joseph Daul,

---

460 Interview with the KAS representative, 23 April 2014.

linked these successes to the AEI and its driving force, the Liberal Democratic Party. After the 2010 election, Daul congratulated Filat's government for achieving progress in the fields of democracy, the rule of law, and human rights. "This was possible with the support of all parties involved in the Alliance for European Integration, the current ruling coalition. I wish Mr. Filat's party, the LDPM, success in the forthcoming elections and I hope that under his leadership the cooperation of the pro-European Alliance will continue", said Daul.[461]

Later in 2010, the AEI II coalition agreement was signed, outlining a new distribution of power among the parties. Partly, thanks to the EU's insistence on preserving the coalition, the Alliance was kept alive; however, its internal dysfunctionality and conflict was neglected.[462] Behind the AEI's façade, Vlad Plahotniuc, financer of the Democratic Party, and Mihai Ghimpu, the Liberal Party's leader, opposed Filat-Leancă's ministerial team in an attempt to increase their power.[463]

On 5 March 2013, due to an unofficial deal between the Communists and the Democratic Party, a no-confidence vote against Filat was brought to parliament, again putting the AEI II coalition in jeopardy. In Moldova's crisis over Filat's renomination as prime minister, the Europarties expressed their strong support for the Alliance and warned about the rise of the Communists. Commenting on the political situation in Moldova, Sir Graham Watson pointed out the roots of political crisis: "this is what happens when political

---

461   EPP Group Press Release, "Moldova Reforms Supported by the European Parliament," Joseph Daul MEP, Chairman of the EPP Group and Monica Macovei MEP (Brussels: EPP, 21 October 2010).
462   Vladimir Socor, "Sources of Moldova's Political Chaos: The Partition of State Institutions," *Eurasia Daily Monitor* 10:97, 22 May 2013.
463   In 2012, the secret annex to the AEI II coalition agreement was leaked to the media. It described the division of state institutions among the three parties. Following the intra-coalition renegotiations, the Democratic Party expanded its influence by gaining some key law enforcement positions.

leaders fight for individual economic influence rather than concentrating on the interests of society as a whole".[464] In this situation, the EPP clearly backed the LDPM's leader. "Needless to say, the European choice is linked to a government formed by the AEI and led by the President of the strongest political party: Vlad Filat, President of the PLDM. I am confident that under the continued leadership of Vlad Filat, the country will be able to complete the negotiations of the Association Agreement by the end of this year", underlined Martens.[465] Both EPP and ALDE warned against early elections as being a path to political instability that would jeopardise Moldova's European future. In the EPP's statement, Martens urged the AEI party members to re-launch a dialogue as soon as possible and to put an end to the political crisis, in order not to undermine the country's European integration path:

> I also call on the leaders of the other European political families to relay the same message of responsibility and moderation to their partners in Moldova. Thanks to Vlad Filat and his government, a number of important reforms—such as the fight against corruption in public affairs—are being implemented and are helping to pave the way of the country's European path. Clearly, this commitment and determination of Vlad Filat is creating turbulence among some political circles in Moldova. But the future of the country lies in the hands of its politicians and the choice they have to make is clear: a European Moldova or not. The EPP firmly believes in a European future for Moldova and will, therefore, remain committed to make the Eastern Partnership Summit in Vilnius in November a success.[466]

Sir Graham Watson called on "all the leaders of the parties to the AEI—particularly the Liberal Democrats and the Democratic

---

464 "European Liberals Call on Moldova to Continue Reform Programme," ALDE News, 6 March 2013.
465 EPP Press Release, "Moldova: European Future in Jeopardy; EPP President Calls on AIE Members to Resume Dialogue" (Brussels: EPP, 7 March 2013).
466 Ibid.

Party—to make a new effort to relaunch their coalition government"[467] and warned that "if they fail, three years of work will be wasted".[468]

In May 2013, after a long-standing coalition crisis, Iurie Leancă, the LDPM member, was appointed as prime minister. Despite their adamant support of Filat's renomination, the EPP welcomed the news and expressed their hopes that "Prime Minister Leancă and his government can move forward with many crucial reforms—such as the fight against corruption—which are needed in order to guarantee the EU integration of Moldova".[469] Sir Graham Watson welcomed the new government, "provided it continues the successful and progressive reforms seen under the broad three-party AEI of previous years",[470] and called on the LDPM and the DPM to ensure Moldova's uninterrupted progress towards the EU.[471] In his views, under the new coalition, the Liberal Party will be "the Liberal conscience of Moldova as a constructive and pro-European party of opposition".[472]

After the 2014 parliamentary election, the AEI again went through the process of negotiating the coalition's format. In January 2015, at the invitation of the Moldovan party leaders, the EPP, PES, and ALDE representatives visited Chisinau and discussed the political situation. Regretting the Liberal Party's withdrawal, the EPP

---

467   "European Liberals Call on Moldova to Continue Reform Programme," ALDE News, 6 March 2013.
468   Ibid.
469   EPP Press Release, "Moldova: New Pro-European Parliamentary Majority Formed Led by PM Iurie Leanca" (Brussels: EPP, 31 May 2014).
470   "New Government in Moldova: Liberals Urge Reform Programme to be Continued," ALDE News, 3 June 2013.
471   During the reformation of the coalition, the Liberal Party split where the newly formed Liberal Reformist Party joined the AEI coalition, whereas Ghimpu's Liberal Party officially went in opposition. Despite the Liberal Party's withdrawal, ALDE also warmly welcomed the end of the political crisis and expressed its support for Leancă's government.
472   "New Government in Moldova Liberals Urge Reform Programme to be Continued," ALDE News, 3 June 2013.

expressed its support of forming a minority government. Acknowledging that this is not the best scenario possible, a minority government was preferred to an early election that could cause a greater political crisis.[473] "All three parties recommitted themselves to the EU integration process. On the basis of the formula proposed by the EPP, PES and ALDE they should be able to agree a coalition", reassured Sir Graham Watson. The PES President Stanishev expressed his "thanks to the Democratic Party, Moldova is on the right track towards EU integration, and the PES family stands by them and offers all our support and experience to facilitate the EU accession process. I am convinced that, with the Democratic Party as part of the new government, this process will have a successful conclusion for Moldovans and Europeans alike".[474]

Despite "the AEI's democratic-looking, European-sounding brand"[475], and its members' affiliation with the Europarties, the Alliance's composition and functionality remained far removed from that of a European-style coalition. Prone to intra-partisan rivalry and internal contradictions from the outset, the AEI was driven by non-ideological factors—a fear of the Communists' revenge and a wish to remain in power. Interested in expanding their powers against Filat's authority, Plahotniuc and Ghimpu utilised Brussels' pressure to preserve the coalition. In this situation, the EU prolonged the AEI's internal animosity at the cost of rampant corruption and internal dysfunction. Despite the Europarties' calls for cooperation among the coalition members for the sake of Moldova's European future, the parties' behaviour remained rooted in individual economic interests.

---

473 "EPP and PES Welcome Formation of Governing Coalition in Moldova," *Infotag*, 25 January 2015.
474 Ibid.
475 Vladimir Socor, "Sources of Moldova's Political Chaos: The Parliamentary System," *Eurasia Daily Monitor* 10:94, 17 May 2013.

The EPP, PES, and ALDE: the United National Movement and the Georgian Dream – War of Letters (Georgia)

In the Georgian case, the Europarty's affiliation was instrumentalised by domestic parties as a tool for mutual accusation and contestation. Whereas the Europarties' engagement in the case of the Moldovan AEI coalition remained on the domestic level, partisan rivalry between mainstream Georgian parties spilled over to the European level. The so-called "War of Letters" between the UNM and the Georgian Dream showed an example of intra-party rivalry that utilised the Europarties as an opportunity structure for tackling domestic issues.

On 6 March 2013, in an open letter to Bidzina Ivanishvili, the Georgian prime minister, 23 MEPs, 19 of them from the EPP, accused Ivanishvili of democratic backsliding and warned that Georgia's European prospects were diminishing. The open letter listed a series of grievances that accused the new government of putting public pressure on MPs and local legislators, putting ongoing pressure on judiciary and the Georgian media, and using inflammatory rhetoric and hate speech towards minorities. The MEPs shamed the new Ivanishvili government for blackmailing and threatening the UNM as an oppositional force and warned that such behaviour contradicts European values.

The European parliamentarians' remarks towards the country's worrying democratic state were met with harsh criticism in Tbilisi. Even prior to the open letter, then Georgian foreign minister, Maja Panjikidze, accused Western politicians, including Martens, of being biased towards the Georgian Dream and of being receptive to Saakashvili's messages spread though "a big network of lobbyists".[476]

As a direct reaction to the MEPs' open criticisms, Davit Usupashvili, then the chairman of the Georgian parliament, urged the European parliamentarians to refrain from statements based on

---

[476] "Georgian Foreign Minister Lashes Out at EU Centre-right Party," *EurActiv*, 21 December 2012.

"unsubstantiated claims" and asked them "not to set President Saakashvili and his former regime as a standard as it would be an insult to Europe".[477] In turn, Usupashvili named a few wrongdoings committed by Saakashvili's regime that did not correspond with European values, such as unprecedented constitutional provisions in 2004 and the victimisation of former MPs. In his response, Usupashvili said:

> If these are your standards of democracy, and if you are discussing a Europe built upon these standards, then we do not know such a Europe as you see it. Your letter once again confirmed that merely residing in Europe does not guarantee commitment to European values. You reside in Europe and yet you distance yourselves from Europe by supporting Saakashvili's former police regime. This way, you probably will not hurt Europe itself, yet my small country may become yet another victim, falling prey to such Europeans.[478]

Echoing the tone of Usupashvili's letter, in his open letter to the EPP Ivanishvili called the previous regime a façade democracy and listed plenty of wrongdoings by the former government such as power fusion and power consolidation through numerous constitutional amendments, politically motivated decisions by the Georgian courts, alarming media freedom, the intimidation of Georgian Dream's supporters, rampant corruption on the elite level, and appalling human right situations, especially in penitentiaries. "Before making far-reaching assertions about 'closing European doors', I urge you also to delegate long-term observers to Georgia and see for yourselves that the will of the Georgian government to ensure democratic governance is unwavering and that our mission implies unequivocal commitment to democratic values, the rule of law, and human rights, while the demand and desire of the Georgian people is to live by true Western values", underlined Ivanishvili.[479] He connected "groundless allegations" with blind support for the UNM as

---

477 "Parliament Speaker Responds to MEPs' Letter to PM," *Civil Georgia*, 12 March 2013.
478 Ibid.
479 "Georgian PM Bidzina Ivanishvili's Open Letter to European People's Party," *Civil Georgia*, 14 March 2013.

the EPP's sister party and asserted that "Saakashvili's allies in the European Parliament, as it seems, choose confrontational tactics".[480] In his views, such an approach "means that the European People's Party is not capable of articulating its own political conclusions about situation in Georgia".[481]

To support the new government, the Swiss Ambassador to Georgia, Günther Bächler, wrote an open letter to Ivanishvili. Having coined the debate a "War of Letters", the Swiss Ambassador described the EPP's tactics as "Soviet-style propagandistic methods"[482] and criticised the Europarty's arrogant lesson-teaching. Praising the first steps of Ivanishvili's government, Bächler noted the remarkable performance of the parliament and the ministries, welcomed progress in the elimination of elite corruption, and improved the relationship with Russia.[483]

In June 2013, following the presidential election, the ad hoc delegation of MEPs from different EP groups, including the EPP, S&D, ALDE, AECR, and Greens/European Free Alliance, was sent to Tbilisi to observe the political situation. MEP Rouček (S&D) called for more dialogue and cooperation among the parties and urged them to cool down their rhetoric. He asserted that it was a strong change for Georgia to ratify the Association Agreement regardless of political group in parliament.[484] Nevertheless, the members of the delegation remained rather critical towards Georgia's new government. Drawing a parallel with Ukraine, serious concerns about the imprisonment of former political leaders were expressed by Ms. Neyts (ALDE), Ms. Gomes (S&D), and Mr. Vajgl (ALDE). As a reaction to this, Usupashvili accused the EPP of pro-

---

480 "Georgian PM Bidzina Ivanishvili's Open Letter to European People's Party," *Civil Georgia*, 14 March 2013.
481 "Ivanishvili Addresses EPP in Open Letter," *Civil Georgia*, 14 March 2013.
482 "Georgia is Much Freer than it Ever Used to Be in the Past," *Georgian Journal*, 28 March 2013.
483 Ibid.
484 "MEPs Sum Up Georgia Visit," *Civil Georgia*, 4 June 2013.

ducing a biased assessment and described them as "European Kandelakis": "They are as loyal to Saakashvili and his party, as Mr. Giorgi Kandelaki is in Georgia."[485]

The debates continued through the public media. In his letter "Progress Through Pragmatism in Georgia", published in *The Wall Street Journal*, Ivanishvili called for the ending of Cold War rhetoric and enumerated the reforms his government had achieved over the last year, including the restoration of trade with Russia, Georgia's rapprochement to NATO and its active involvement in Afghanistan, the launch of a process to investigate human rights violations, the liberalisation of the criminal justice system, and the revitalisation of the agricultural sector.[486] In reaction to his letter, MEP Hökmark (EPP) questioned Ivanishvili's "progress through pragmatism". In the EPP's fashion, he praised Saakashvili for "a peaceful and orderly transition of power", which enabled the Georgian Dream coalition to have a decisive victory. "This would not have been possible without the progress made under Mr. Saakashvili's leadership. Yet now the Georgian Dream-led government is using legal institutions to threaten, harass and jail representative of the opposition, putting this progress at stake," added Hökmark.[487]

The so-called "War of Letters" shaped several outcomes in both the domestic and European arenas. Domestically, the strong reaction to the EPP's criticisms showed that both parties attributed importance to international actors' perception of Georgia. In the derailed cohabitation process between Saakashvili and Ivanishvili, their image as a democratic force was wishful for both the Western-oriented UNM and the Russia-friendly Georgian Dream. However, the official relationshipsbetween the EU and Georgia remained unaffected. On 16 March 2013, the EU declaration on how to restore the process of Georgia's Euro-Atlantic integration was adopted. "The

---

485 "European Liberals and Socialists Criticize Georgian PM," *Tabula.ge*, 24 June 2013.
486 "Bidzina Ivanishvili: Progress through Pragmatism in Georgia," *The Wall Street Journal*, 6 August 2013.
487 "Georgia's Fragile Democratic Process," *The Wall Street Journal*, 20 August 2013.

European People's Party reaffirms its support to the Euro-Atlantic integration process of Georgia, underlines with a high degree of satisfaction the progresses made during the last years in the fields of rule of law and democratic standards and encourages the current administration to implement the remaining necessary reforms", concluded the declaration.[488]

Secondly, this incident has partly triggered the Georgian Dream's aspirations to establish its own contacts with the Europarties. Having experienced the EPP's adamant support for Saakashvili's party, Ivanishvili and his party were motivated to find their own influential supporters on the EU level. After the "War of Letters", the Georgian Dream announced its plans to seek an affiliation with the PES. In the Georgian Dream's view, the Europarty membership would secure better chances for the promotion of European integration and would serve as an indirect lobby to defend its own position on the EU level.[489] After the EU's Vilnius Summit, a joint delegation from PES, S&D, and the European Forum for Democracy and Solidarity met with progressive parties such as the Georgian Dream and the Socialist Democrats to explore further ways to cooperate.[490] In June 2015, the Georgian Dream was officially accepted as an observer member to the PES.

On the European level, the "War of Letters" has revealed fierce competition between the EPP, PES, and ALDE in defending the interests of their sister parties. What started as the EPP's warning against democratic backsliding to the current Georgian government has turned into an intense debate in the EP about internal Georgian politics and into a battlefield for the Europarties themselves. Supporting the UNM, Martens called "on the other European political parties to condemn Ivanishvili and especially the ALDE party and its leader Graham Watson, who enthusiastically endorsed—even via paid adverts—Ivanishvili and the Georgian

---

488 "EPP Adopts Conditional Roadmap for Concluding Association Agreement," *Georgian Journal*, 16 March 2013.
489 Interview with the Georgian Dream representative, 18 April 2013.
490 "PES Meets Prime Minister of Georgia," *PES News*, 17 December 2013.

Dream".⁴⁹¹ The enormous provision of support for the UNM by the EPP triggered a reaction from other Europarties, in particular from the PES and the ALDE. The ALDE party leader warned the EPP that it was on a slippery slope with Saakashvili: "The European People's Party, keen to boost its majority position has welcomed into its fold people such as Berlusconi, Borisov and Basescu playing fast and loose with the rule of law. They are on the same slippery slope with Mr. Saakashvili as the elections campaign on 1 October has been mired with difficulties".⁴⁹² Sir Graham Watson stressed that "Georgian President Mikheil Saakashvili will not save Georgia's democracy. The EPP will not save Georgia's democracy. Only Georgian peoples' free and democratic choice can make Georgian dreams come true".⁴⁹³

The Georgian case of "War of Letters" illustrated how the Europarty's unconditional support of its sister party could further exacerbate the process of domestic cohabitation and cause tensions among the Europarties themselves.

8.3 Analysing the Inter-Party Behaviour

If in theory like-minded parties were expected to support each other, in reality they often tend to compete with each other. Although in terms of cooperation and support between sister parties the positive impact is very limited, the inter-party relationships in Eastern Europe showed rich dynamics and different faces of the Europarties' impact on their behaviour. Despite the Europarties' strong endorsement of cooperation among sister parties, there are only two cases of inter-party support: between the Georgian Republican Party and the Free Democrats in the ALDE family and between the Ukrainian *Batkivshchyna*, *Rukh*, and UDAR in the EPP family.

---

491 "Georgian Foreign Minister Lashes Out at EU centre-right party," *EurActiv*, 21 December 2012.
492 ALDE Press Release, "Peaceful Transition of Power in Georgia" (Brussels: ALDE, 26 October 2012).
493 Ibid.

Analysing the cases of cooperation and non-cooperation, it is worth noting that the length of the party's affiliation has no effect on its behaviour. Due to the longer and more active cooperation with the Europarties, sister parties were expected to follow the Europarties' calls for cooperation and change their behavioural patterns. However, the length of affiliation with the Europarties turned out to play no role in the analysed cases. Despite the fact that "Our Ukraine" and the Christian Democratic People's Party joined the EPP in 2005, both parties obstructed the cooperation with other sister parties. As the cases of the Republican Party and the People's Party *Rukh* showed, it is the intensity of the contact that had a positive impact on the inter-party relationships (H7).

In all analysed cases, the party position did not affect the admission process. There is evidence for cases where both strong and weak parties blocked another candidate party from the country. In this situation, timing was more important than party position. In all the negative cases, the first observer parties often acted as "gatekeepers", impeding newcomers' efforts to join the European party family (H8). With regard to the likelihood of cooperation between strong and weak parties, there is a mixed effect. On the one hand, there are positive cases when strong and weak parties supported each other—for instance, between the *Batkivshchyna* party, *Rukh*, and UDAR. On the other hand, there are negative cases where support was completely absent, as in cases between the strong LDPM and the weak Christian Democrats and between the strong Georgian UNM, the New Rights Party, and the Christian Democratic Movement (H9).

The motivation structure also had an ambiguous effect on the willingness of sister parties to cooperate with each other. Several cases of cooperation and non-cooperation showed that like-minded parties can support each other regardless of whether they are driven by rational or normative considerations. Whereas in case of strategic motives cooperation was triggered by prestige, status, and domestic and international credibility, in the case of ideational motives, cooperation occurred due to parties' convictions and beliefs.

However, in cases of ideational motives, the inter-party cooperation proved to be more sustainable than in cases of rational considerations (H10).

In those positive cases of inter-party cooperation among sister parties, the Europarties' endorsement had a rather limited impact on the behavioural pattern of like-minded parties. Although the Europarties publically supported the cooperation among sister parties, it is rather the motives of electoral politics that triggered the cooperation among them. As the positive cases showed, the cooperation between sister parties usually happens when parties either want to stay in power or lack voter support. In all the cases, the unification of party strengths favoured their rational interests. Thus, for example, despite the EPP's warm welcoming of the cooperation between the Ukrainian parties, it was the electoral win at several electoral campaigns that triggered the cooperation between the *Batkivshchyna* party, *Rukh*, and UDAR. Similarly, although the EPP explicitly encouraged the AEI parties to preserve the pro-European coalition, the Moldovan coalition remained united due to the parties' fear of the Communists' return to power.

Aimed at the consolidation of democratic forces, the Europarties' endorsement triggered more negative developments in inter-party relationships than positive ones. On many occasions, sister parties demonstrated a non-cooperative and even hostile attitude towards newcomers by blocking their affiliation or withdrawing from the European party family in protest.

The reasons for non-compliance are manifold. Firstly, the affiliation with the Europarties is perceived as being a prestigious opportunity for cooperation with the top European politicians. Lacking maturity in terms of institutionalisation, the East European parties desire to maximise their status, honour, and prestige. Therefore, the parties prefer to have a unique affiliation with the Europarties and avoid sharing it with other parties. Subsequently, the Europarties' cooperation becomes grounds for rivalry rather than for cooperation. For instance, the parties from the Orange coalition were competing with each other to be named the most genuine supporter of European integration. Secondly, sister parties belonging to the same European party family usually share the same electorate. In this situation, the Europarties' calls for party mergers do not match with the interests of the sister parties. Operating in a competitive environment, the sister parties utilise the Europarty's affiliation as proof of their legitimacy and credibility in the domestic arena and portray it as their achievement on the way to European integration. In the process of a potential merger, like-minded parties are afraid of losing their self-identity and their core voters. Despite the positive cases of sister party relationships, the Republican Party, for example, abstained from a party fusion with the Free Democrats, as it could have damaged the Republicans' image and led to the loss of its core voters. Finally, the loose ideological commitments and strong hierarchical party structures of post-communist parties impede cooperation between sister parties. While political parties in Eastern Europe are built around personalities and not around ideological alignments, the expected supportive behaviour of sister parties does not have any basis in reality; it is often substituted by obstructive behaviour instead. As domestic parties' like-mindedness refers more to their wish to stay in power than to their ideological closeness, sister parties compete with each other more often than they cooperate.

As an implication on the domestic level, the Europarties' endorsement of cooperation between like-minded parties has led to constrained options for coalition-building. Sending informal signals to their sister parties to cooperate with ideological allies and/or democratic forces, the Europarties have limited the pool of coalition partners. For example, during the Moldovan political crisis in 2010, the EPP discouraged the LDPM from cooperating with the Communists to build a parliamentary majority. Similarly, in Ukraine, the EPP warned the democratic forces against cooperating with the extreme right *Svoboda* party.

As a second implication, the Europarties' extensive political support for a party leader within the coalition might have a negative outcome for the coalition's sustainability. Expressing its encouragement for one party, the Europarties overemphasize their support for one party leader and neglect the other. For instance, being very sensitive to the EPP's support to Tymoshenko, the coalition government between Yushchenko and Tymoshenko proved to be short-lived. Similarly, the extensive and often biased support for Saakhashvili and Filat unleashed more partisan rivalry, revealing the sensitivity and vulnerability of party leaders to Europarty criticism and support.

Comparison across the Europarties finds no differences in behavioural patterns between sister parties in the EPP and ALDE families. Due to few affiliations within ALDE, it is difficult to draw any far-reaching conclusions from the sole case of sister party cooperation in Georgia. In the EPP family, however, the ratio between supportive and non-supportive cases is predominantly negative. This is explained by the fact that the EPP is the largest and the most influential Europarty in the EP, and an affiliation with it is considered by domestic parties to be a prestigious achievement, so that the willingness for cooperation between sister parties is very low. Although the positive impact of cooperation and support between sister parties is very limited, the domestic inter-party relationships show rich dynamics and different faces of the Europarties' impact on the behavioural dimension.

9. Conclusions

9.1 Key Empirical Findings

This thesis has approached the task of examining the cooperation between the Europarties and non-EU parties and its impact on party development in Georgia, Moldova, and Ukraine. The study was driven by answering two research questions: (1) what are the incentives for the Europarties and non-EU parties to cooperate with each other? and (2) what impact does cooperation have on the party development in Georgia, Moldova, and Ukraine?

Investigating the "why" question, the incentive structures of both actors were revealed. Each analysed case showed a combination of strategic and constructivist logics in its motives. For the Europarties, cooperation with non-EU parties was equally driven by the ideational motive of promoting their norms and values as well as by rational motives of having direct channels of access and influence on domestic policy-making and of expanding their networks.

From a strategic point of view, the Europarties sought to have channels of influence on the national policy-making in the EU neighbouring countries in order to reduce political risks and instability on the EU borders. To secure the democratic regimes, and thus to increase political predictability in the region, the Europarties, in particular the EPP and the PES, were looking for government or promising government parties. To have better leverage in the country, the Europarties were interested in parties with real political weight or looked for stable and viable partners to ensure the steady promotion of their norms and values. In fact, the desire to reduce transaction costs in the region sometimes prevailed over ideational norm promotion.

Finally, the competition between the Europarties themselves in expanding their networks became a factor that triggered the cooperation with non-EU parties. After the enlargement process, the balance of power among the Europarties changed in favour of the EPP. To compete with the EPP, other Europarties applied the same widening approach, while mitigating their selection criteria or introducing different membership types. As a result, the rivalry among the Europarties led to imperfect matches, resulting in patchy affiliations between the Europarty and its sister parties. The Europarties' readiness for such imperfect matches highlighted the predominance of strategic motivations in their selection process. On the other hand, it demonstrated the prestigious nature of cooperation of the Europarties' themselves. Having broad networks outside of Europe, the Europarties could buttress their role as Europeanists and democracy promoters beyond the EU.

In the same vein, this research suggests that the incentive structure of non-EU parties combined rational and ideational motivations. It included domestic legitimacy and international recognition, electoral and political support, geopolitical factors, lobbying of EU integration, and knowledge and expertise. A factor of prestige and external recognition played an enormous role for non-EU parties in the process of establishment of cooperation. Being immature and underdeveloped, post-communist parties used the affiliation with the Europarties as an external validation of their trustworthiness and credibility.

Deeply rooted in the need for external validation, non-EU parties often emphasised their affiliation during the electoral campaigning. It served as proof of parties' seriousness, credibility and a genuinely pro-European position. Addressing voters, non-EU parties underlined their *European* affiliation, while, in the inter-party debates, they emphasised their affiliation with *major* Europarties. It was very prestigious among the non-EU parties to be affiliated with the EPP or the PES. In this situation, power politics dominated the non-EU parties' preferences for ideological proximity.

As it is argued in this thesis, the next powerful incentive for non-EU parties was an opportunity to advance the country's European aspirations. In addition to governmental channels, the Europarties provided non-EU parties with a structural network wherein European integration could be propelled informally and tacitly. On the other hand, as part of ideational motives, the cooperation was understood by non-EU parties as a natural and inevitable move in the process of European integration.

In other cases, the cooperation with the Europarties was utilised in geopolitical conflicts. In the clash between pro-European and pro-Russian forces, the affiliated parties appealed to the European political elites to provide them with international support. Using the Europarties' opportunity structure, non-EU parties aimed to exert their influence in geopolitical conflicts.

Last but not least, one of the key findings is that knowledge and expertise equally motivated the unexperienced post-communist parties to establish cooperation with well-developed Europarties. Looking for a model of party-building, pro-European parties logically turned to the European experience. Seeking sustainable party structures, non-EU parties were attracted by the Europarties' provision of seminars and workshops on programmatic and organisational development as well as electoral campaigning.

The incentive structures of both the Europarties and non-EU parties impacted the selection and application processes. Driven by the motive to accept more viable/government parties, the Europarties could give a preference to a certain party and accelerate or decelerate its application process despite its poor ideological match or organisational incompatibility. On the other hand, knowing the Europarties' preference for viable/government forces, non-EU parties with a strong position could employ their leverage in the selection process and accelerate their own admission or obstruct another party's affiliation.

The study reveals that the selection criteria were very loosely defined and it was the informal criteria that played a significant role in the selection process. Established mutual trust was an important factor in political communication, which fostered the application process. Knowing party leaders personally created transparent and loyal settings which helped the Europarties to assess an applicant party's credibility. A trustworthy environment with the Europarties could be established either via strong bilateral contacts with major members of the Europarty or via good relationships with the Europarties' local partners. In this process, in particular the German party foundations, could accelerate the admission process. Operating as interlockers and mediators, the German party foundations acted as the Europarties' local informants who advised the Europarties on domestic affairs. On the other hand, the foundations created informal channels of communication between the Europarties and their potential applicants by organisating mutual events.

Another facilitating factor in the application process was election results. It is evident that viability was of significant importance in the selection process, as the Europarties were interested in dealing with sustainable political parties. Having negative experiences with fluid post-communist parties, the Europarties wanted to ensure that accepted parties would not disappear after a couple of years. For this purpose, the Europarties frequently used election results as a proxy for a party's viability before making any final decisions on acceptance.

Finally, the decision of acceptance could be influenced by other sister parties from the same country. After a certain negative experience with the past, the Europarties started obtaining informal approval from already affiliated sister parties regarding new applicants.

In an attempt to analyse the "how" question, this thesis concludes that overall, the Europarties' impact on the ideological, organisational, and behavioural dimensions is rather limited. Political elites poorly conformed to the Europarties' norms and principles. In the situation where admission conditionality over party ideology, internal organisational mechanisms and democratic credentials of the party leadership was loose, non-EU parties used the affiliation to buttress their domestic legitimacy and international recognition. Corroborating the findings from CEE countries of the non-impact of Europeanisation, this research also found little evidence of a genuine transformation but rather shallow or absent internalisation.[494] In a way, this study confirms Bil's and Szczerbiak's conclusion that "if one looks hard enough for 'EU impacts' then one will certainly find them".[495] However, this study also finds faces of

---

494 Szczerbiak and Bil, "When in doubt"; Haughton, "Driver, Conductor or Fellow Passenger?"; Holmes and Lightfoot, "Limited Influence?".
495 Szczerbiak and Bil, "When in doubt," 463.

Europeanisation similar to the CEE countries such as standardisation of party system, moderation of political spectrum, introduction of gender quotas and changes in parties' names and labels. Finally, this thesis corroborates with the previous CEE studies that the party foundations played a pivotal role in establishing channels for negotiations and admission[496] and that the causes for transformational changes lay primarily in domestic politics.[497]

Although the key findings indicate insignificant impact of the Europarties on party development, cooperation triggered a lot of dynamics in the domestic arena, showing many faces of Europeanisation in the non-EU countries. The affiliation demonstrated how sensitive and susceptive to the European level domestic party elites are. The way domestic parties reacted to the Europarties' praises or shaming tells us a lot about the nature of East European parties. They are still in the need of external validation of their actions and choices, as they do not feel credible enough and need a more prestigious institution to give them social proof and justify their actions.

The failure of the Europarties to have a profound impact on the party development in Georgia, Moldova, and Ukraine was stipulated by both European and domestic factors. From the European perspective, the Europarties are historically and institutionally weak in comparison with other EU institutions. As umbrella organisations, the Europarties are best described as "network facilitators" which provide opportunity structures for non-EU parties to gain access to the European party elites. As a result, the relatively weak position of the Europarties limited their normative power in dissemination and promotion of their principles and values. On the other hand, the particularities of post-communist party development have prevented the Europarties from having the desired effect. Fluid party politics, together with high personalisation, failed linkage with society, rampant political corruption, and oligarchic influence have proved to be rather resilient towards a socialising effect. Poor institutionalisation of the party system and parties'

---

496 Dakowska, "Beyond Conditionality," 287.
497 Szczerbiak and Bil, "When in doubt"; Pridham, Patterns of Europeanization and Transnational Party Cooperation."

weak position within the (semi-)presidentialist system has impeded any sustainable impact on party development.

On the *ideological* dimension, two factors in particular prevented a deeper penetration of the socialising effect. Firstly, due to the expansionist strategy employed, the Europarties diluted their core principles by embracing different ideological profiles. In turn, this affected the Europarties' internal cohesion and weakened their socialising power as consolidated ideological actors. The widening of the Europarties' profiles has become practical for post-communist parties that are poorly defined in ideological terms. Embracing eclectic positions, post-communist parties could place themselves within the European party families regardless of their patchy or contradictory matches. Secondly, the irrelevance of party ideology for post-communist parties made swift ideological adjustments possible. Since for vote- and office-oriented parties, ideological development is of less importance, the adjustment of ideological profiles.

On the *organisational* dimension, due to the Europarties' unwillingness to challenge the status quo, and, on the other hand, due to the personalistic and clientelistic nature of post-communist parties, the impact of cooperation on organisational structure was negligible. As umbrella organisations, the Europarties are supranational organisations with scarce mutual events which are often limited to congresses and board meetings twice a year. In this situation, the Europarties provided rather a platform for establishing contacts with national parties whose party structures were easier to imitate. It was rather bilateral relations than the Europarties themselves that triggered some effect on organisational matters. Furthermore, the Europarties were not interested in challenging the status quo. The Europarties were not deeply involved in parties' internal affairs and preferred to be engaged in trainings and workshops which provided short- or middle-term positive results. Therefore, flaws of post-communist parties such as public funding, internal party democracy, and intertwining of business and politics were hardly targeted. In contrast, the Europarties directed their activities rather towards areas such as electoral campaigning which could provide fast, harmless positive results without demolishing the whole party system. On the other hand, as a result of excessive personalisation and structural rigidity, these workshops and trainings sessions remained on the personal level, preserving the status quo of the relationships between the mother party and its youth and women's branches and solidifing the hierarchical party structure even further.

On the *behavioural* dimension, the endorsement of inter-party cooperation was affected by two factors: post-communist parties' weak ideological underpinnings and the Europarties' failure to understand the prestigious nature of affiliation. Deprived of any deep ideological commitments, post-communist parties usually forged ad hoc coalitions and partnerships which pro-mised short-term benefits. Guided by a pragmatic approach, post-communist parties did not search for like-minded partners but for winning situational constellations. Moreover, the prestigious affiliation has been a subject for rivalry among the parties rather than grounds for inter-party cooperation. Because of the Europarties' failure to acknowledge this, their constant endorsements for sister party cooperation have only led to further kindling of animosities among the parties.

9.2 Comparative Analysis

Cross-Dimensional Comparison

Across the dimensions, the behavioural dimension proved to be the most dynamic, showing various reactions in response to sister party cooperation. The range of reactions varied from positive faces in terms of coalition-building, formation of the electoral block, or nomination of a presidential/parliamentary candidate in single-member constituencies to negative ones such as blocking the affiliation of newcomers or withdrawing from the European party family in protest. On the ideological dimension, cooperation triggered fewer reactions — parties either were already compatible with the Europarties' norms and values prior to the affiliation or adjusted their ideological stances only on paper. In the last case, adjustments of ideological profiles were superficial, resulting in a shallow internalisation. The organisational dimension showed the least dynamics. Interested in preserving the status quo, non-EU parties did not implement any radical internal reforms but rather concentrated on the implementation of electoral techniques and improvement of leadership skills.

Within-Dimensional Comparison

The evaluation of ideological match showed various cases ranging from the perfectly congruent (e.g. the EPP and Ukrainian *Rukh*, and the ALDE and the Georgian Republicans) to the poorly compatible (e.g. the ALDE and the Moldovan Liberals, the PES and the Moldovan Democrats, and the AECR and the CDM). Generally speaking, the ideological match between the Europarties and their sister parties was patchy and incongruent. In all analysed cases, no genuine ideological transformation occurred. Driven by strategic considerations, parties changed their ideological stances in order to be accepted to the influential Europarties and profit from this prestigious affiliation. In contrast to Central Europe where the process of self-crystalisation was accomplished and where parties joined the Europarties based on their shared ideological commitments, non-EU parties identified their ideological positions through their affiliation with the Europarties. In this situation, the process of affiliation was reversed. Lacking ideological orientation, non-EU parties claimed to define their positions *after* joining the Europarties. The perfect ideological match was only detected in those cases where observer parties successfully finished their process of self-identification. In those cases, the perfect ideological compatibility and "goodness of fit" can be established, but the impact from the Europarties was absent.

This thesis revealed very little impact on the organisational dimension. Among eight analysed cases, only three parties mentioned the affiliation on the European level in their party statutes. Most impact on the organisational dimension was detected in the import of campaigning skills. This study found that many parties have willingly borrowed Western techniques of electoral campaigning, such as door-to-door campaigning, targeted message development, and databases of citizens' voting intentions. In the case of youth branches, the key findings is that the impact of cooperation remained on the personal level, while the organisational changes were often blocked by their principal organisations. Nevertheless, trainings and workshops have triggered some "low-cost" organisational changes. For instance, mother parties have started to include youth activists in the local party boards or organise training activities for their youth. With regard to the women's branches, in that handful of cases where affiliation with women's associations was present, the impact was barely measurable. The activities of the Europarties' women's associations have hardly influenced the introduction of organisational changes on the subject of gender equality within the party. None of the parties considered the introduction of a gender quota in the party boards, and gender mainstreaming was not on the parties' agendas. In turn, the Europarties' women's associations seemed not to be interested in imposing gender mechanisms within their parties. On the other hand, rigid mother party structures hindered the institutional development of women's branches and prevented the penetration of any potential impact.

On the behavioural dimension, although the evidence of support between sister parties proved to be limited, the inter-party relationships in Eastern Europe showed rich dynamics and different faces of Europeanisation. Surprisingly enough, the Europarties' strong endorsement of cooperation among sister parties, in fact, triggered more negative developments than positive ones. On many occasions, sister parties demonstrated a non-cooperative and even hostile attitude towards newcomers by blocking their affiliation or withdrawing from the European party family in protest.

Cross-Partisan Comparison

Overall, parties with powerful positions enjoyed more freedom in finding their own partners. While more powerful Europarties were more selective in finding a suitable partner, weaker Europarties were more restricted in their choice. On the other hand, domestic parties with a strong position possessed better leverage in the application process than non-government or weak parties. In terms of the impact, parties with a strong position proved to be more resilient vis-à-vis the Europarties' impact than parties with a weak position.

Across the observer parties, the empirical evidence showed that major or catch-all parties usually preferred to establish affiliations with the major Europarties—either the EPP or the PES. By a wide margin, the EPP is most desirable party family for the non-EU parties; 6 out of 11 affiliations belonged to the centre-right force. In this process, the prestige and political weight of the Europarty mattered a great deal. The EPP's strategic importance in the process of European integration and its influential position in the EP bestowed the Europarty with prestige, power, and attraction.

In the selection process, influential actors attracted each other; whereas the major Europarties were interested in viable and powerful political forces, the major/catch-all observer parties preferred cooperation with powerful Europarties. In this case, the incentive structures of the Europarties coincided with the motives of major/catch-all parties, reinforcing cooperation between them. As this thesis showed, the EPP managed to gather all the main government parties under its umbrella—the UNM, *Batkivshchyna*, and the LDPM. Proving its pragmatic motives, all three parties changed the European family of their first choice, which had a better ideological match, and switched to the EPP. In contrast, minor parties tended to end up with minor Europarties—the ALDE, the EL, or the AECR, as they were less attractive for the major Europarties and possessed less leverage to influence the Europarty's decision in the application process.

The affiliation with the Europarties proved to be equally important for parties in government and in opposition. Whereas government parties could buttress their domestic legitimacy by getting recognition from the Europarties, opposition parties could gather political support, in particular in the case of increasing authoritarian regimes, and as an alternative to governmental channels, they could obtain access to the European elites to promote the EU membership perspective.

Cross-National Comparison

Cross-nationally, the Moldovan parties covered the whole political spectrum, establishing cooperation with all four main Europarties. Due to the equally strong right and left forces, the Moldovan parties found their own niches on the European level. In contrast, in the Ukrainian case, cooperation was established only with the EPP, which shows a distortion of the Ukrainian political spectrum to the centre-right. In Georgia, cooperation was somewhat more diverse and was represented by affiliation with three European party families—the EPP, the ALDE, and the AECR.

Across the region, the best ideological congruence was exemplified by the match between the Ukrainian *Rukh* and the EPP as well as between the Georgian Republicans and the ALDE. Both non-EU parties proved high compatibility with their chosen European party families, which resulted in an almost perfect ideological match—no position on "federalist Europe" was found in *Rukh's* profile, while no stance on environmentalism was detected in the Republican Party's profile. The worst ideological match was established between the Moldovan Liberals and the ALDE, contradicting on the main lines of liberalism—ethnic and minority rights and freedom of expression and between the Georgian CDM and the AECR, which failed to match the AECR's main principles, such as the promotion of intergovernmentalism, transparency and integrity of EU institutions, and broader economic liberal values. Overall, across all the affiliations, the Moldovan parties showed the most contradictory ideological matches in comparison with the Ukrainian and Georgian parties—patchy congruence between the DPM and the PES, between the PCRM and the EL, and between the CDPP and the EPP.

With regard to the organisational changes, across the region, across the European party families, and across the left-right political spectrum, all the affiliated parties implemented Western techniques of electoral campaigning. Across the region, the Moldovan Liberal Democratic Youth and the Ukrainian *Batkivshchyna moloda* utilised the Europarties' opportunity structure the most. Due to the strong position of their mother parties, LDYM's and *Batkivshchyna moloda's* international cooperation was well-anchored in the European arena, and their voices were strongly represented in the European youth structures. Cross-nationally, all women's branches introduced gender quotas into their party lists (with the exception of the Republicans) and strengthened their organisational structures (with the exception of the PCRM's women's branch), whereas, apart from the Moldovan Liberals, none of the women's branches put gender mainstreaming on their agenda. Looking at the women's branches, the LDPM women's branch had the best organisational development in the region. However, the good standing of the LDPM women's branch should be understood in the context of Moldova's rapprochement to the EU.

Regarding the inter-party cooperation, the closest relationship proved to be between the Georgian Republicans and Free Democrats, both parties that were driven by their genuine interest in mutual support. In all three countries, the affiliation with the Europarty triggered hostile reactions from their sister parties. As a result, lacking the experience of multiparty dialogue and cooperation, post-communist parties reacted in a non-fraternal way by blocking the newcomers or withdrawing in protest.

9.3   Impact on the Party System

For this study the main implication of the Europarties' impact on the party system was expected to be in terms of standardisation, consolidation, and democratisation. The standardisation of the ideological spectrum, strengthening of organisational capacity, and stabilisation of inter-party relationships were expected to lay out the favourable conditions for the consolidation, stabilisation, and democratisation of the party system.

The failure to exert a profound enough impact on each dimension subsequently led to the failure to have an impact on the party system level. Paradoxically, the Europarties' engagement on the domestic level unleashed rather ambiguous effects. On the one hand, the Europarties contributed to the standardisation of political spectrum in the post-communist countries. Being still in the process of self-crystallisation, the post-communist parties used the affiliation with the Europarties as an identification of their ideological stances. Moreover, the Europarties' unequivocal support of pro-democratic and pro-European forces indirectly led to the constrained choice of coalition partners.

On the other hand, this study detects that the cooperation with the Europarties hardly contributed to the process of consolidation. On the contrary, treating the affiliation with great prestige, the Europarties' endorsement of cooperation with the sister party fuelled rather more rivalry than mutual support. As numerous cases illustrated, the Europarties' exaggerated support in favour of one party led to further exacerbation of inter-party relationships domestically. Since the affiliation with the Europarties was utilised by parties as a badge of approval and recognition, the Europarties' preference for a particular sister party was met with hostility and distrust.

With regard to democratisation, the Europarties failed to transform the party system and paradoxically contributed to its ossification in various ways. During the selection process, due to the Europarties' keen interest in viable and/or government forces, the status quo was solidified and legitimised. Relying to a great extent on trustworthy personal relations with the party leaders in the selection process, the Europarties contributed to further legitimisation of non-EU party structures. In this way, the Europarties de facto acquiesced to personality-oriented party politics that are embedded in clientelistic relationships and oligarchic business circles. During the cooperation, the Europarties chose not to interfere in the parties' internal affairs and directed their activities towards the external side of party-building. Selecting a low, short-term target, the Europarties did not aim to change the way the post-communist parties operated, but rather concentrated on the fine-tuning and window-dressing of their mechanisms. This attitude turned out to be detrimental to the Europarties' image itself when the affiliation was misused by non-EU parties to buttress their domestic legitimacy.

Moreover, the Europarties' established policy of showing public support but hiding public shaming proved to be counterproductive for consolidation and democratisation of the party system.

Desperately searching for "success stories", the Europarties tried to avoid negative storylines of sister parties that they had already approved. By revealing the undemocratic turn of their sister parties and publically shunning them, the Europarties would question their own ability to assess their like-minded partners correctly, which, in turn, would undermine their credibility and their role as democracy promoters. However, by avoiding public criticism of their like-minded partners, the Europarties created an illusion for the domestic population that all deeds of their partners were rightful and flawless. By practicing "teaching" of their sister parties behind closed doors the Europarties in fact did a disservice to the fragile democratic regimes. Due to the lack of public shaming, the party leaders often used the affiliation with the Europarties as a shield for their wrongdoings. In turn, the Europarties´ failure or unwillingness to acknowledge parties' wrongdoings damaged its reputation and that of the EU in the region.

9.4   Impact on the Europarties

As the Europeanisation is a two-way process, cooperation with non-EU parties affected the Europarties' behaviour as well. Adapting itself to the challenges of competition, some Europarties introduced an appealing full membership to the non-EU parties. Due to the weakly structured ideological space and a partial overlap between the EPP and the ALDE profiles as well as between the PES and the EL, minor Europarties tended to lose potential partners to the more prestigious EPP and PES. The offered equality between EU and non-EU parties was supposed to attract more members to the less "popular" ALDE, AECR, and EL.

Secondly, by interacting with non-EU parties, the Europarties gradually adapted their selection requirements. Aware of the risk of dealing with immature and unfledged political parties in the non-EU countries, the Europarties employed a different approach. Instead of heavily relying on formal criteria to find a perfect match, the Europarties gave the preference to informal factors which guided their selection and application procedures. As a result, the strictness of their formal requirements was diminished, and instead of searching for classical conservative or socialist or liberal parties, the Europarties became more interested in parties' sustainability, viability, and electoral results. Moreover, learning from the negative past experience, the Europarties tried to avoid future internal conflicts between the sister parties and started obtaining informal approval from already accepted sister parties to affiliate with potentially new parties.

Thirdly, domestic dynamics affected the nature of the Europarties' calls for cooperation. The Europarties' encouragement of cooperation appealed to democratic forces rather than to ideological allies. Considering the subtleties of the post-communist party development, the cleavage for cooperation was based on "democratic/non-democratic forces", in contrast to the European practices in which cooperation is based on ideological foundations.

9.5 Limitations

Among the limitations of this study are time and resource constrains, and unanticipated local events. First, this thesis has suffered from the problems of time and resources. In an ideal situation, more time could have been spent in the field; in particular, the second round of interviews could have been conducted with additional interviewees. However, as the research evolved, the amount of information gathered for sixteen cases extended enormously. Due to the multifaceted and multilayered research design, the collection of additional data could have undermined the manageability and clarity of the thesis. Since the nature of the thesis was mainly explorative and focused on the identification of faces of Europeanisation, the information gathered from the first round of interviews sufficed to find rich evidence and draw convincing conclusions.

Secondly, due to the turbulent event in Ukraine in November 2013, which coincided with the researcher's fieldtrip, the data collection for the Ukrainian parties was interrupted. To make up for the lack of information, the researcher conducted interviews with youth party members, academics, and experts. The rest of the information was substituted through media content analysis. Due to the researcher's linguistic competence in Ukrainian and Russian, the missing information was quickly restored. Nevertheless, interviews with the Ukrainian mother parties would have provided more accurate information on the parties' motivations to join the Europarties and their experience in borrowing the practices of European party-building.

Thirdly, as socialisation is a long-term process which does not occur overnight, in some cases a longer time period would have been needed to observe potential changes. Since a few parties only recently joined the Europarties, the empirical materials in those cases covered only a three- to five-year period. This may not have been enough time to detect any measurable signs of Europeanisation. Moreover, in some cases, implemented changes might be discarded once the incentive structure changes, while in others, new behaviour might be adopted where no incentives have existed before.[498] In order to evaluate the sustainability and degree of internalisation, further observation would be necessary.

Despite its limitations, this study is a first one to examine the dynamics of Europeanisaiton of political parties in the EU neighbouring countries with a systematic and comparative approach. On a basis of studying a large number of parties on various dimensions, it makes an original, theory-informed contribution. Not only it sheds light on the processes of Europeanisation and norm diffusion, but also provides an extensive analysis of the party development in Eastern Europe.

9.6 Future Research Trajectories

The results of this thesis demonstrated the first explorative findings, which can be further enhanced. There are a number of avenues along which the research can be further improved. Firstly, the analytical part of the thesis could be further enhanced by the application of a mixed-method research design. Considering the research design of the thesis, the application of Qualitative Comparative Analysis (QCA) would provide a better assessment of necessary and sufficient conditions for non-EU parties to embark on

---

498   Checkel, "International Institutions," 813.

transformations. In particular, the application of fuzzy QCA would help to structure the empirically rich findings in an elegant and quick-handed way. The provision of a matrix of possible combinations for each case would make the multifaceted and multilayered research easier to follow.

Secondly, other sites of Europeanisation could be explored, other than the Europarties. For example, research could be extended to the impact of EP Groups on party development in the non-EU countries. Since the EP Groups are particularly powerful and influential in terms of the promotion of EU membership perspective, they could possess an additional channel of impact on non-EU parties' behaviour.

Finally, the case selection could be further extended to other countries of the Eastern Partnership. Since the parties of the frontrunners of the Eastern Partnership (EaP) failed to a great extent to adapt their behaviour and implement changes into their party structures, the inclusion of parties from countries that were less aspiring to join the EU, such as Azerbaijan, Armenia, and Belarus, would be of particular interest. Placed in hybrid regimes, which are more exposed to Russia's influence, parties from these countries still actively establish cooperation with the Europarties. Of particular interest here would be the analysis of their incentive structure in terms of whether it is in any respect different from that of the Georgian, Moldovan, and Ukrainian parties. Also, it would be interesting to examine the inter-party cooperation regarding whether the Europarties' calls for cooperation among the sister parties are more effective, considering the increasing authoritarian regimes in Azerbaijan, Armenia, and Belarus. Furthermore, since these countries are located on the boundary between the Middle East and Eurasia, it is harder to find strong European partners in their vicinity. In contrast to Ukraine and Moldova in particular, where neighbouring European partners propelled non-EU parties' applications to the Europarties and assisted in the organisation of trainings and workshops, the absence of strong neighbouring pro-EU countries might change the process of selection and application procedures in these countries.

Bibliography

Interviews

European Union

Interview with the European Forum for Democracy and Solidarity representative, 5 October 2013 (by phone).

Interview with the ALDE representative, Brussels, 7 October 2013.

Interview with the ALDE representative, Brussels, 7 October 2013.

Interview with the YES PES representative, Brussels, 10 October 2013.

Interview with the EPP representative, Brussels, 10 October 2013.

Interview with the PES representative, Brussels, 15 October 2013.

Interview with the EPP representative, Brussels, 15 October 2013.

Interview with the KAS Brussels representative, Brussels, 15 October 2013.

Interview with the LYMEC representative, 18 October 2013 (by phone).

Interview with the YEPP representative, 25 October 2013 (by phone).

Interview with the ALDE Gender Network representative, 2 July 2015 (by phone).

Ukraine

Interview with the former KAS representative, 5 November 2013 (by phone).

Interview with the SPU representative, Kyiv, 18 November 2013.

Interview with the *Batkivshchyna moloda* representative, Kyiv, 18 November 2013.

Interview with expert, Kyiv-Mohyla Academy, Kyiv, 20 November 2013 (by phone).

Interview with expert, Institute for Political Education, Kyiv, 20 November 2013.

Interview with the NDI representatives, Kyiv, 20 November 2013.

Interview with the *Rukh* representative, youth branch, Kyiv, 21 November 2013.

Interview with the former "Our Ukraine" representative, 21 November 2013.

Interview with the UDAR representative, youth branch, 22 November 2013.

Interview with expert, Kyiv, 26 November 2013.

Interview with the SPU representative, 26 November 2013.

Interview with expert, The Jamestown Foundation, Vilnius, 28 November 2013.

Interview with the FES representative, Kyiv, 3 December 2013.

Interview with the FNS representative, Kyiv, 4 December 2013.

Interview with expert, Kyiv-Mohyla Academy, Kyiv, 4 December 2013.

Interview with the KAS Ukraine representative, Kyiv, 5 December 2013.

Interview with the Party of Regions representative, youth branch, Donetsk, 16 December 2013.

Interview with expert, University of Alberta, Donetsk, 19 December 2013.

Moldova

Interview with the LDPM representatives, Chisinau, 13 January 2014.

Interview with the LDYM representative, Chisinau, 14 January 2014.

Interview with the DPM representative, Chisinau, 15 January 2014.

Interview with expert, Moldova State University, Chisinau, 16 January 2014.

Interview with expert, Institute for Development and Social Initiatives *Viitorul*, Chisinau, 16 January 2014.

Interview with the Liberal Reformist Party representative, Chisinau, 18 January 2014.

Interview with the FES representative, Chisinau, 20 January 2014.

Interview with the NDI representative, Chisinau, 20 January 2014.

Interview with the ADEPT representative, Chisinau, 20 January 2014.

Interview with the Liberal Party representative, Chisinau, 21 January 2014.

Interview with the Liberal Party representative, women's branch, Chisinau, 21 January 2014.

Interview with PCRM representative, Chisinau, 22 January 2014.

Interview with the DPM representative, Chisinau, 22 January 2014.

Interview with the CDPP representative, Chisinau, 23 January 2014.

Interview with the Youth of Liberal Party representative, Chisinau, 23 January 2014.

Interview with the PCRM representative, Chisinau, 23 January 2014.

Interview with *transform!* europe representative, 3 February 2014 (by phone).

Interview with the FNS representative, 6 February 2014 (by phone).

BIBLIOGRAPHY 231

Interview with expert, Institute for Security Studies, 14 February 2014 (by phone).

Interview with expert, University of Edinburgh, Birmingham, 16 December 2014.

Interview with the Olof Palme Foundation representative, Stockholm, 2 January 2015.

Interview with the UK Liberal Democrats representative, London, 5 February 2015.

Interview with the LDPM Women representative, 13 July 2015 (by phone).

Georgia

Interview with expert, Zentrum für Demokratie, Aarau, 27 March 2014.

Interview with the New Rights representative, Tbilisi, 14 April 2014.

Interview with the New Rights representative, youth branch, Tbilisi, 14 April 2014.

Interview with the Republican Party representative, Tbilisi, 14 April 2014.

Interview with the UNM representative, youth branch, Tbilisi, 15 April 2014.

Interview with the Swiss Ambassador to Georgia, Tbilisi, 15 April 2014.

Interview with the UNM representative, Tbilisi, 15 April 2014.

Interview with expert, Caucasus Institute for Peace Democracy and Development, Tbilisi, 16 April 2014.

Interview with expert, Center for Social Studies, Tbilisi, 16 April 2014.

Interview with expert, Tbilisi State University, Tbilisi, 16 April 2014.

Interview with the Our Georgia-Free Democrats representative, youth branch, Tbilisi, 17 April 2014.

Interview with the Our Georgia-Free Democrats representative, Tbilisi, 17 April 2014.

Interview with expert, Caucasus Institute for Peace Democracy and Development, Tbilisi, 17 April 2014.

Interview with the NIMD representative, Tbilisi, 17 April 2014.

Interview with the Republican Party representative, youth branch, Tbilisi, 18 April 2014.

Interview with the Republican Party representative, Tbilisi, 18 April 2014.

Interview with the Georgian Dream representative, Tbilisi, 18 April 2014.
Interview with the UNM representative, Tbilisi, 18 April 2014.

Interview with the IRI representative, Tbilisi, 22 April 2014.

Interview with the NDI representative, Tbilisi, 22 April 2014.

Interview with the KAS representative, Tbilisi, 23 April 2014.
Interview with the FNS representative, Tbilisi, 24 April 2014.
Interview with expert, GDSIS, Tbilisi, 24 April 2014.
Interview with the IRI representative, Tbilisi, 24 April 2014.
Interview with the FES representative, Tbilisi, 25 April 2014.
Interview with the CDM representative, 29 April 2014 (by phone).

Official Documents

Commission of the European Communities (CEC) (2003). Regulation No. 2004/2003. Brussels: Official Journal, 2003.

Committee on Constitutional Affairs, "Report on the Application of Regulation (EC) No 2004/2003 on the Regulations Governing Political Parties at European Level and the Rules Regarding Their Funding", Report No. 2010/2201(INI) (2011).

Court of Auditors Special Report No. 13/2000, OJ C181/1 (28 June 2000). EPP Group, Annual Activity Report 2012.

EU Regulation No …/2014.

EU Regulation No. 2004/2003.

European Parliament (1996). "Bericht über die konstitutionelle Stellung der Europäischen Politischen Parteien". Report by Dimitris Tsatsos on behalf of the Institutional Affairs Committee (A4-0342/96), 10 December 1996.

European Scrutiny Committee, House of Commons (2012).

European Union (1992). *Treaty on European Union, Treaty of Maastricht*, 7 February 1992, Official Journal of the European Communities C 325/5; 24 December 2002.

European Union (2000). Treaty of Nice, Amending the Treaty on European Union, the Treaties Establishing the European Communities and Certain Related Acts, 11 December 2000. Official Journal C 80 of 10 March 2001.

Report of the Committee on Constitutional Affairs on the proposal for a European Parliament and Council regulation on the statute and financing of European political parties (A5- 0170/2003), Rapporteur: Jo Leinen, 21 May 2003.

The Law of Moldova on Political Parties and Other Socio-Political Organizations, No 718-XII of 17.09.91. Vestile No 11–12/106, 1991.

The Organic Law of Georgia on Political Unions of Citizens, 1997.

Party Documents

AECR Declaration. Prague: AECR, 2009.

AECR Declaration. Rejkjavik: AECR, 2011.

ALDE News (2013): "European Liberals Call on Moldova to Continue Reform Programme", 6 March 2013.

ALDE News (2012): "Liberals – the engine of European integration of Moldova", 18 December 2012.

ALDE Press Release (2012): "Liberals in the Driving Seat in Peaceful Transition of Power in Georgia", 2 October 2012.

ALDE Press Release (2012): "Peaceful transition of power in Georgia", 26 October 2012.

ALDE Statute, adopted by the ALDE Party Congress, 30 April 2004.

CDPP declaration, 18 June 2012.

Cuvântarea lui Iurie Roşca, Moldova, PPCD, la Congresul PPE, 30 April 2009.

EL Congress Document "Unite for Left Alternative in Europe", adopted at 4th EL Congress, Madrid, 13–15 December 2013.

EL News (2010): "8th March: 100 Year of Struggles for gender equality", 8 March 2010. EL Party Statute, adopted at the Founding Congress in Rome, May 9, 2004

EL Political Theses "Building Alternatives", 2nd EL Congress Document, Prague, November 23- 25, 2007.

EL Press Release (2007): "EL Conference: The EU New Neighbourhood Policy" in Chisinau, 27–28 October 2007.

EL Statute, adopted at the Founding Congress of the Party of the European Left, Rome, 9 May 2004.

ELDR Declaration. Stuttgart, 26 March 1976.

ELDR Statute. Brussels, April 2004.

EPP Action Programme 2004–2009, approved by the EPP Congress, 4–5 February 2004.

EPP Basic Document "A Union of Values", adopted by the Fourteenth EPP Congress in Berlin on 11–13 January 2001.

EPP Basic Programme, adopted by the Ninth EPP Congress in Athens, 12–14 November 1992.

EPP Group Press Release (2010): "Moldova reforms supported by the European Parliament". Joseph Daul MEP, Chairman of the EPP Group and Monica Macovei MEP, 21 October 2010.

EPP Press Release (2005): "EPP Secretary General invites Yushchenko to the next Summit", 15 February 2005.

EPP Press Release (2007): "Elections in Ukraine. Martens and Daul congratulate Yushchenko and Tymoshenko – support orange government coalition", 1 October 2007.

EPP Press Release (2007): "Ukraine: EPP President and EPP-ED Group Chairman congratulate Tymoshenko on election as Prime Minister", 18 December 2007.

EPP Press Release (2008): "EPP congratulates Yushchenko and Tymoshenko for creation of coalition and believes in their joint cooperation for better future of Ukraine", 10 December 2008.

EPP Press Release (2008): "EPP Secretary General meets PM Yulia Tymoshenko", 28 January 2008.

EPP Press Release (2010): "Ukraine: EPP condemns escalation of aggressive, politically motivated pressure on Yulia Tymoshenko", 17 December 2010.

EPP Press Release (2011): "EPP President: "Ukraine moving further away from EU's norms and values", 4 May 2011.

EPP Press Release (2011): "Moldova: EPP President congratulates PM Filat and new Moldovan government for confidence vote", 14 January 2011.

EPP Press Release (2011): "Ukraine: travel ban on Yulia Tymoshenko confirms EPP criticism", 2 February 2011.

EPP Press Release (2013): "Moldova: EPP President expresses full support and trust to renominated Prime Minister Vlad Filat", 17 April 2013.

EPP Press Release (2013): "Moldova: European future in jeopardy; EPP President calls on AIE members to resume dialogue", 7 March 2013.

EPP Press Release (2014): "Moldova: new pro-European parliamentary majority formed led by PM Iurie Leanca", 31 May 2014

EPP Report (Brussels: EPP, January 2005).

EPP Statute, adopted by 7th Congress, Marseille, 7 December 2011.

LDPM Press Release (2010): "Moldova: EPP President congratulates success of Prime Minister Vlad Filat", 30 November 2010.

LDPM Press Release (2010): "Prime Minister of Moldova: "Today, we have a clear European choice"", 1 August 2010.

LDPM Press Release (2010): "The LDPM proposes a compulsory quota of women representation on the candidate lists for elections", 21 September 2010.

LDPM Press Release (2010): "Vlad Filat: the support offered by EPP targeted not only our party, but the whole Republic of Moldova", 2 October 2010.

LDPM Press Release (2011): "Vlad Filat appreciated the significant support provided by the EPP for bringing Moldova closer to EU", 23 May 2011.

LDPM Press Release (2011): "Vlad Filat: EPP values and ideals are an infinite source of optimism and inspiration", 8 December 2011.

LDPM Press Release (2012): "YLDM launched the School of European Studies", 2012. LDPM Press Release (2013): "A successful visit to Brussels for TLDM", June 2012.

LDPM Press Release (2013): "PLDM Secreatry General, Victor Rosca paid a working visit to Austria, 19 September 2013.

LDPM's electoral platform, 2009. LYMEC Statute. Brussels, 2002.

"Our Ukraine's" party program, 2010.

Party Statute of the *Batkivshchyna* party.

Party Statute of the Liberal Democratic Party of Moldova.

PES Declaration "For a modern, pluralist and tolerant Europe", adopted at 5th PES Congress, 7–8 May 2001.

PES General Resolution "Building a fair Europe by and for the people", adopted by the PES Council in Warsaw, 2 December 2010.

PES General Resolution, adopted by the PES Council on 24 November 2011.

PES Joint Declaration "Strategy for jobs, growth, inclusion, fairness and sustainability", adopted by the PES Presidency and the S&D Group in the European Parliament on the Europe 2020 strategy.

PES News (2013): "PES Meets Prime Minister of Georgia", 17 December 2013.

PES News (2015): "PES President: Alliance for a European Moldova 'the Pro-European Government that Moldova needs'", 26 January 2015.

PES Policy Paper (2010): "A European Employment and Social Progress Pact for fair growth", adopted by the PES Council in Warsaw, 2 December 2010.

PES Press Release (2010): "Democratic Party of Moldova welcomed into PES Family", 14 October 2010.

PES Press Release (2014): PES and Democratic Party of Moldova celebrate upcoming agreement of accession agreement, 25 June 2014.

PES Report "Put Europe to Work: The European Employment Initiative" (June 1994 revised version) adopted at the PES Summit in Corfu, December 1993.

Policies of the ELDR Party on Fundamental Freedoms and Human Rights. The ELDR Policy Center, 2010.

Statement by the Republican Party on „The Political Agenda of the Next Two Years", Tbilisi, 26 October 2014.

The Labour's Party International Democratic Programme, Annual Archive, 2014-15.

Literature

"Alasania Sets Up Political Party", *Civil Georgia*, 16 July 2009. http://www.civil.ge/eng/article.php?id=21248

"Alasania's Free Democrats Quit GD Coalition", *Civil Georgia*, 5 November 2014. http://www.civil.ge/eng/article.php?id=27785

Bader, Max (2010): *Against All Odds. Aiding Political Parties in Georgia and Ukraine*. Amsterdam: Amsterdam University Press, 2010.

Bailey, David J. (2009): *The Political Economy of European Social Democracy: A Critical Realist Approach*. Abingdon: Routledge, 2009.

Bardi, Luciano (2004): "European Party Federations' Perspectives," in *The Europarties: Organisation and Influence*, edited by Pascal Delwit, Erol Külahci and Cèdric Van der Walle, 309-322. Brussels: Centre d'étude de la vie politique, CEVIPOL, ULB, 2004.

Barometer of Public Opinion (2001): Public Opinion Poll. Institute for Public Policy, November, 2001. http://www.ipp.md/libview.php?l=en&idc=156&id=470

Barometer of Public Opinion (2002): Public Opinion Poll. Institute for Public Policy, April 2002. http://www.ipp.md/libview.php?l=en&idc=156&id=469

Bartolini, Stefano (2005): *Restructuring Europe: Centre formation, system building and political structuring between the nation-state and the European Union*. Oxford: Oxford University Press, 2005.

Beach, Derek and Pedersen, Rasmus B. (2013): *Process-tracing methods: foundations and guidelines*. Ann Arbor: University of Michigan Press, 2013.

Beyers, Jan (2005): „Multiple Embeddedness and Socialization in Europe: The Case of Council Officials Authors". *International Organization* 59 (4) (2005): 899-936.

"Bidzina Ivanishvili "Progress Through Pragmatism in Georgia," *The Wall Street Journal*, 6 August 2013. http://www.wsj.com/articles/SB10001424127887323681904578639672933623636

Biezen, Ingried van, Mair, Peter and Poguntke, Thomas (2012): "Going, going, ... gone? The decline of party membership in contemporary Europe." *European Journal of Political Research* 51 (2012): 24–56.

Bolkvadze, Ketevan (2013): "Drams, Laris and Politics. Political Funding Regulations in Armenia and Georgia." NIMD Working paper/Clingendael, the Hague.

Booster, F. J. (1995): "Commentary on Compliance-gaining Message Behavior Research", in *Communication and Social Influence Processes*, edited by Charles R. Berger and Michael Burgoon, 91–113. East Lasting: Michigan State University Press, 1995.

Botan, Igor (2008): 6th Congress and its first consequences, *E-democracy.md*, 31 March 2008. http://www.e-democracy.md/en/monitoring/politics/comments/200803311/

Botan, Igor (2015): "Barometer of Public Opinion about the social-cultural situation before the local elections." *E-democracy*, 25 May 2015. http://www.e-democracy.md/en/monitoring/politics/comments/bop-alegeri-locale-2015/

Burnell, Peter (2000): "Democracy Assistance: Origins and Organizations", in *Democracy Assistance: International Cooperation for Democratization*, edited by Peter Burnell, 34–66. London: Frank Cass, 2000.

Burnell, Peter (2006): "Promoting Democracy Backwards", FRIDE Working Paper 28, 2006.

Calus, Kamil (2015): "A captured state? Moldova's uncertain prospects for modernisation." *Center for European Studies*, 22 April 2015 http://www.osw.waw.pl/en/publikacje/osw-commentary/2015-04-22/appropriated-state-moldovas-uncertain-prospects-modernisation

Carothers, Thomas (1996): *Aiding Democracy Abroad: The Learning Curve.* Washington, D.C.: Carnegie Endowment for International Peace, 1996.

Carothers, Thomas (2006): "Examining International Political Party Aid", in *Globalising Democracy*, edited by Peter Burnell. London: Routledge Publishers, 2006.

Carothers, Thomas (2006): *Confronting the Weakest Link: Aiding Political Parties in New Democracies*, Washington, D.C.: Carnegie Endowment for International Peace, 2006.

Carothers, Thomas (2010): "Democracy Support and Development Aid: The Elusive Synthesis." *Journal of Democracy* 21 (1) (2010): 12–26.

Čáslavská, Teresa (2010): *Increasing Women`s Representation in Decision Making Through Political Parties.* Prague: International Gender Policy Network, September 2010.

"CDPP's declaration about withdrawal from the EPP," *Ava.md*, 20 June 2012. http://ava.md/politics/016332-deklaraciya-hdnp-o-vihode-iz-evropeiskoi-narodnoi-partii.html

Checkel, Jeffrey T. (2003): "Going Native" In Europe?: Theorizing Social Interaction in European Institutions." *Comparative Political Studies* 36 (1/2) (2003): 209-231.

Checkel, Jeffrey T. (2005): "International Institutions and Socialization in Europe: Introduction and Framework." *International Organization* 59 (4) (2005): 801-826.

"Christian-Democratic leader quits politics," *Agenda.ge*, 15 March 2014. http://agenda.ge/news/10613/eng

"Christian-Democratic Movement," *Civil Georgia*, 22 May 2008. http://www.civil.ge/eng/article.php?id=17769

Coalson, Robert (2009): "Kremlin's Ruling Party Boots Ties Accross the Former Soviet Union," *Radio Free Europe/Radio Liberty*, 29 September 2009. http://www.rferl.org/content/Kremlins_Ruling_Party_Boosts_Ties_Across_The_Former_Soviet_ Union/2171505.html

Croissant, Aurel and Merkel, Wolfgang (2001): "Political Party Formation in Presidential and Parliamentary System," Institute of Political Science at the University of Heidelberg, Online Papers (2001).

CRRC Caucasus Barometer 2012 Georgia, http://caucasusbarometer.org/en/cb2012ge/TRUPPS/

Dakowska, Dorota (2002): "Beyond Conditionality: EU enlargement, European party federations and the transnational activity of German political foundations." *Perspectives on European Politics and Society* 3 (2) (2002): 271-296.

Day, Stephen (2013): "Between 'Containment' and 'Transnationalization' — Where next for the Europarties?" *Acta Politica* 1 (4) (2013): 5-29.

Delsoldato, Giorgia (2002): "Eastward Enlargement by the European Union and Transnational Parties," *International Political Science Review*, 23 (3), 2002: 269-89.

Delwit, Pascal, Külahci, Erol and Van de Walle, Cédric (2004): "The Europarties: Organisation and Influence," Centre d'étude de la vie politique of the Free University of Brussels (ULB). Brussels: CEVIPOL 2004: 1-322.

Delwit, Pascal (2004): "The European Peole's Party stages and analysis of a transformation", in *The Europarties: Organisation and Influence* edited by Pascal Delwit, Erol Külahci, and Cédric Van Walle. Centre d'étude de la vie politique of the Free University of Brussels (ULB). Brussels: CEVIPOL, 2004: 135-155.

Deutsch, Karl et al. (1957): *Political Community and the North Atlantic Area: International Organisation in the Light of Historical Experience*. Princeton: Princeton University Press, 1957.

Donnelly, Brendan and Jopp, Mathias (2009): "European Political Parties and Democracy in the EU," in *Democracy in the EU and the Role of the European Parliament*, edited by Gianni Bonvicini. Rome: Quaderni IAI, 2009.

Dunphy, Richard, and March, Luke (2013): "Seven Year Itch? The European Left Party: Struggling to Transform the EU." *Perspectives on European Politics and Society* 14 (4) (2013): 520–537.

"Economy Minister Valeriu Lazar to Resign Soon, Democrats to Decide," *Infotag*, 1 July 2014. http://www.infotag.md/politics-en/190170/

Enyedi Zolt and Lewis Paul (2006): "The Impact of the European Union on Party Politics in Central and Eastern Europe," in *The European Union and Party Politics*, edited by Paul Lewis and Zdenka Mansfeldova, 231–49. Basingstoke: Palgrave Macmillan, 2006.

"EPP Adopts Conditional Roadmap for Concluding Association Agreement," *Georgian Journal*, 16 March 2013, http://www.georgianjournal.ge/politics/22643-epp-adopts-conditional-roadmap-for-concluding-association-agreement.html

"EPP and PES welcome formation of governing coalition in Moldova," *Infotag*, 25 January 2015. http://www.infotag.md/politics-en/198554/

"EPP supports unification of Ukraine's UDAR, BPP and PF parties," *UNIAN*, 3 September 2015. http://www.unian.info/politics/1118258-epp-supports-unification-of-ukraines-udar-bpp-pf-parties.html

"EU freezes funding for Moldova," *EurActiv*, 10 July 2015. http://www.euractiv.com/sections/europes-east/eu-freezes-funding-moldova-316202

"European Liberals and Socialists criticize Georgian PM," *Tabula.ge*, 24 June 2013. http://www.tabula.ge/en/story/72358-european-liberals-and-socialists-criticize-georgian-pm

Fearon, James and Wendt, Alexander (2002): "Rationalism vs. constructivism: a skeptical view," in *Handbook of International Relations*, edited by Walter Carlsnaes, Beth A. Simmons and Thomas Risse, 52–72. New York: Sage, 2002.

"Filat reserved some names of parties; Leancă: Let him register "Moldova without PLDM," *Jurnal.md*, 18 March 2015. http://www.jurnal.md/en/politic/2015/3/18/filat-reserved-some-names-of-parties-leanca-let-him-register-moldova-without-pldm/

Finnemore, Martha and Sikkink, Kathryn (1998): "International Norm Dynamics and Political Change." *International Organization* 52 (4) (1998): 887–917.

Flockhart, Trine (2004): "Masters and Novices': Socialization and Social Learning through NATO Parliamentary Assembly." *International Relations* 18 (2004): 361–380.

Gallaher, Tom (2006): "The European Union and Romania: Consolidating Backwardness?" *Open Democracy*, 27 September 2006. https://www.opendemocracy.net/democracy-europefuture/EU_romania_3943.jsp

George, Alexander L. and Bennett, Andrew (2005): *Case Studies and Theory Development in the Social Sciences*. Cambridge: MIT Press, 2005.

"Georgia is much freer than it ever used to be in the past," *Georgian Journal*, 28 March 2013. http://www.georgianjournal.ge/politics/22797-georgia-is-much-freer-than-it-ever-used-to-be-in-the-past.html

"Georgia Nominates Its First Female Defence Minister," *Gender Information Network of South Caucasus*, 5 April 2015. http://www.ginsc.net/home.php?option=article&id=31920&lang=en#.VctZXvlpG74

"Georgia Ratifies EU Association Agreement," *Civil Georgia*, 18 July 2014. http://www.civil.ge/eng/article.php?id=27503

"Georgia's Fragile Democratic Process." *The Wall Street Journal*, 20 August 2013. http://www.wsj.com/articles/SB10001424127887324085304579010553340036852

"Georgian foreign minister lashes out at EU centre-right party," *EurActiv*, 21 December 2012. http://www.euractiv.com/europes-east/georgian-governments-complains-e-news-516814

"Georgian PM Bidzina Ivanishvili's Open Letter to European People's Party," *Civil Georgia*, 14 March 2013. http://www.civil.ge/files/files/2013/IvanishviliOpenLetterToEPP.pdf

Green, Andrew T., Birch, Sarah and Roberts, Sean (2010): *Evaluation of USAID Political Party Program: Ukraine*. Pittsburgh: University of Pittsburgh Press (2010): 11–12.

Haas, Peter M. (1992): "Introduction: Epistemic communities and international policy coordination." *International Organization* 46 (1) (1992): 1–35.

Hale, Henry E. (2011): "Formal Constitutions in Informal Politics: Institutions and Democratization in Post-Soviet Eurasia." *World Politics* 63 (4) (2011): 581–617.

Hanley, David (2002): "Christian democracy and the paradoxes of Europeanization. Flexibility, Competition and Collusion," *Party Politics* 8(4) (2002): 463–481.

Haughton, Tim (2009): "Driver, Conductor or Fellow Passenger? EU Membership and Party Politics in Central and Eastern Europe." *Journal of Communist Studies and Transition Politics* 25 (4) (2009): 413–426.

Herron, Erik S. (2009): *Elections and Democracy After the Communism?*. New York: Palgrave Macmillan, 2009.

Hix, Simon and Lord, Christopher (1997): *Political Parties in the European Union*. Basingstoke: Palgrave Macmillan, 1997.

Hloušek, Vit and Kopeček, Lubomir (2010): *Origin, Ideology and Transformation of Political Parties: East Central and Western Europe Compared*. Surrey: Ashgate Publishing, 2010.

Holmes, Michael and Lightfoot, Simon (2011): "Limited Influence? The Role of the Party of European Socialists in Shaping Social Democracy in Central and Eastern Europe." *Government and Opposition* 46 (1) (2011): 32–55.

Holubov, Oleksandr (2015): "Ukraine's New Party of Power," Carnegie Endowment for International Peace, 31 August 2015. http://carnegieendowment.org/2015/08/31/ukraine-s-new-party-of-power/if dy

Hudson, Kate (2012): *The New European Left: A Socialism for the Twenty-First Century?* Basingstoke: Palgrave Macmillan, 2012.

"IFLRY strengthens Young Republicans in Georgia," IFLRY, 27 February 2014. http://interim.iflry.com/iflry-strengthens-young-republicans-georgia/

"Individual Freedoms are central in our ideology." Exclusive Interview with (Interview) Zinaida Greceanii: "There was an agreement between the Dodon group and some of the AEI parties," *Tribuna.md*, 25 November 2011. http://tribuna.md/en/2011/11/25/interviu-zinaida-greceanii-%E2%80%9Eintre-grupul-dodon-si-unele-partide-din-aie-intr-adevar-a- existat-un-acord%E2%80%9D%E2%80%9D/

"Individual Freedoms are central in our ideology." Exclusive interview with Irakli Iasania. *Caucasus Elections Watch*, 20 September 2012. https://electionswatch.org/2012/09/20/exclusive-interview-with-irakli-alasania-individual-freedoms-are-central-in-our-ideology/

"Irakli Alasania: Ex-official, Free Democrats leader quits politics," *Agenda.ge*, 10 October 2016.

"Is there any ethnic cleavage in the Moldovan society?" *Alianta.md*, 10 March 2009. http://www.alianta.md/uploads/docs/1238017016_0 3.10_Is_there_an_ethnic_cleavage_in_the_Moldovan_electorate.pdf

Ishiyama, John T. and Kennedy, Ryan (2001): "Superpresidentialism and Political Party Development in Russia, Ukraine, Armenia and Kyrgyzstan," *Europe-Asia Studies* 53 (8) (2001): 1177–1191.

"Iurie Roşca: Admiterea în PPE a partidului condus de Vladimir Filat poate aduce grave prejudicii de imagine creştin-democraţilor europeni", *Flux*, 19 November 2010. http://archiva.flux.md/articole/10847/

"Ivanishvili Addresses EPP in Open Letter," *Civil Georgia*, 14 March 2013. http://www.civil.ge/eng/article.php?id=25847

Jansen, Thomas and van Hecke, Steven (2011): *At Europe's Service: The Origins and Evolution of the European People's Party*. Berlin: Springer-Verlag, 2011.

Johansson, Karl Magnus (1997): *Transnational Party Alliances: analysing the hard-won alliance between Conservatives and Christian Democrats in the European Parliament*. Lund: Lund University Press, 1997.

Johansson, Karl Magnus and Raunio, Tapio (2005): "Regulating Europarties: Cross-Party Coalitions Capitalizing on Incomplete Contracts." *Party Politics* 11 (5) (2005): 515–534.

Johnston, Alistair (2001): "Treating International Institutions as Social Environments." *International Studies Quarterly* 45 (2001): 487–515.

Jupille, Joseph, Caporaso, James A. and Checkel, Jeffrey T. (2003): "Integrating Institutions: Rationalism, Constructivism, and the Study of the European Union." *Comparative Political Studies* 36 (7) (2003): 7–40.

Kallakas, Priit (2015): "Membership Developments in Political Parties in Estonia, Moldova and Ukraine." *Politics* (2015): 196–207.

KAS (2009): "Guidelines for Prosperity, Social Justice and Sustainable Economic Activity." Berlin: Konrad-Adenauer-Stiftung, 2009. http://www.kas.de/wf/doc/kas_17025-544-2-30.pdf

KAS (2011): "Christian Democracy: Principles and Policy-Making," *Handbook for European and International Cooperation*. Berlin: Konrad-Adenauer-Stiftung, 2011. http://www.kas.de/wf/doc/kas_21408-1522-2-30.pdf?110620094737

Kirchner, Emil J. (1988): *Liberal Parties in Western Europe*. Cambridge: Cambridge University Press, 1988.

Kitschelt, Herbert and Wilkinson, Steven I. (2007): "Citizen-Politician Linkages: An Introduction," in: *Patrons, Clients, and Policies: Patterns of Democratic Accountability and Political Competition*, edited by Herbert Kitschelt and Steven I. Wilkinson (eds.), 1–49. Cambridge: Cambridge University Press, 2007.

Kitschelt, Herbert et al. (1999): *Post-Communist Party Systems: Competition, Representation and Inter-Party Cooperation*. Cambridge: Cambridge University Press 1999.

Kostadinova, Tatiana and Levitt, Barry (2014): "Towards a Theory of Personalist Parties: Concept Formation and Theory Building." *Politics and Polity* 42 (4) (2014): 490–512.

Kuzio, Taras (2008): "Big in Brussels," *Business Ukraine*, June 30–July 6, 2008: 18–21.

Kuzio, Taras (2010): "Populism in Ukraine in a Comparative European Context." *Problems of Post-Communism* 57 (6), 2010: 3–18.

Ladrech, Robert (2002): "Europeanization and Political Parties. Towards a Framework for Analysis." *Party Politics* 8 (4) (2002): 289–403.

Ladrech, Robert (2003): "The Party of European Socialists: Networking Europe's Social Democrats." *Journal of Policy History* 15 (1) (2003): 113–129.

Ladrech, Robert (2004): "The European Union and Political Parties," in *Handbook of Party Politics*, edited by Richard S. Katz and William J. Crotty, 492–499. London: Sage Publications, 2004.

Ladrech, Robert (2005): "Programmatic Change in the Party of European Socialists," in *Social Democracy in Europe*, edited by Pascal Delwit, 49–58. Brussels: ULB, 2005.

Ladrech, Robert and Marlière, Phillippe (eds.) (1999): *Social Democratic Parties in the European Union*. Basingstoke: Palgrave Macmillan, 1999.

Lebow, Richard Ned (2008): *A Cultural Theory of International Relations*. Cambridge: Cambridge University Press, 2008.

Lewis, Paul (2008): "Changes in the party politics of the new EU member states in Central Europe: patterns of Europeanization and democratization." *Journal of Southern Europe and the Balkans Online* 10 (2) (2008): 151–165.

Lightfoot, Simon (2006): "The Consolidation of Europarties? The "Party Regulation" and the Development of Political Parties in the European Union," *Representation* 42 (4), 2006: 303–314.

Lista candidaților la funcția de deputat în Parlamentul Republicii Moldova pentrualegerile parlamentare din 30 noiembrie 2014 din partea Partidului Liberal Democrat din Moldova, *E-democracy.md*, November 2014. http://www.e-democracy.md/elections/parliamentary/2014/opponents/pldm/list/

Local Elections 2007, *E-democracy*. http://www.e-democracy.md/en/monitoring/politics/comments/20070406/

Mair, Peter (2000): "The limited impact of Europe on national party systems." *West European Politics* 23 (4) (2000): 27–51.

Mair, Peter (2009): "Representative versus Responsible Government." *MPIfG Working Paper* 09/8. Cologne: Max Planck Institute for the Study of Societies, 2009. http://www.mpifg.de/pu/workpap/wp09-8.pdf

Mair, Peter and Mudde, Cas (1998): "The Party Family and Its Study." *Annual Review Political Science* 1 (1998): 211–229.

Manners, Ian (2002): "Normative Power Europe: A Contradiction in Terms?" *Journal of Common Market Studies* 40 (2) (2002): 235–258.

March, James G. and Olsen, Johan P. (1984): "The New Institutionalism: Organizational Factors in Political Life." *The American Political Science Review* 78 (3) (1984): 734–749.

March, James G. and Olsen, Johan P. (1989): *Rediscovering Institutions: The organizational basis of politics*. New York: Basic Books, 1989.

March, James G. and Olsen, Johan P. (1998): "The Institutional Dynamics of International Political Orders." *International Organization* 52 (4) (1998): 943–969.

March, James G. and Olsen, Johan P. (2009): "The logic of appropriateness." *ARENA Working Paper* 04/09. Center for European Studies. University of Oslo (2009): 1–28.

March, Luke (2005): "The Moldovan Communists: from Leninism to Democracy?" *Eurojournal.org*, September 2005.

March, Luke (2007): "From Moldovanism to Europeanization? Moldova's Communists and Nation Building." *Nationalities Papers: The Journal of Nationalism and Ethnicity* 35 (4) (2007): 601–626.

March, Luke and Mudde, Cas (2005): "What's Left of the Radical Left? The European Radical Left after 1989: Decline and Mutation." *Comparative European Politics* 3 (2005): 23–49.

Marchuk, Anton (2015): "The Law on Financing of Political Parties: Changing the Rules of Political Game," *VoxUkraine*, December 2015. http://voxukraine.org/2015/12/08/changing-the-rules-of-political-game-en/

"Marian Lupu's bifurcates: Moldova to have visa-free travel with the EU, Russia and CIS in the same time," *Moldova.org*, 6 January 2011. http://www.moldova.org/marian-lupus-bifurcatus-moldova-to-have-visa-free-travel-with-the-eu-russia-and-cis-in-the-same-time-215823-eng/

Martens, Wilfried (2008): *Europe: I Struggle, I Overcome*. Brussels: Springer, 2008.

Martens, Wilfried (2012): "Confortons la démocratie in Géorgie," *Le Monde*, 4 July 2012. http://www.lemonde.fr/idees/article/2012/07/04/confortons-la-democratie-en- georgie_1728848_3232.html

Matuszak, Slawomir (2012): *The oligarchic democracy. Influence of business groups on Ukrainian politics*. Center for European Studies 42, September 2012: 1–112.

"MEPs Sum Up Georgia Visit," *Civil Georgia*, 4 June 2013. http://www.civil.ge/eng/article.php?id=26145

Mittag, Jürgen and Steuwer, Janosch (2008): *Politische Parteien in der EU*. Facultas Verlag- und Buchhandels AG, Wien 2010.

"Moldovan Premier Warns Church Against Political Meddling," *Radio Free Europe/Radio Liberty*, 25 September 2011. http://www.rferl.org/content/moldovan_premier_warns_against_political_meddling/24339243.html

Munteanu, Iurie (2010): *Political Parties Legislation in Moldova: Review and Recommendations for Reform*. Chisinau: IDIS "Viitorul", 2010.

National Democratic Institute, "Low Trust in Parliament and Political Figures; Most Georgians Politically Undecided", 13 April 2016, CRRC Georgia. https://www.ndi.org/March- 2016-Public-Opinion-Political-Press-Release-Georgia

Nemyria, Hryhoriy (2009): "EU integration: a healthy dose of realism," *Business Ukraine*, 8 August 2009. http://www.bunews.com.ua/index.php?option=com_content&view=article&id=45:eu-integration&catid=22:opinion-&Itemid=31

Nichols, Dick (2014): "Party of the European Left's fourth Congress: Building Unity to Build Hope," *LINKS International Journal of Socialist Renewal*, February 2014. http://links.org.au/node/3726

Niedermayer, Oskar (1983): *Europäische Parteien? Zur grenzüberschreitenden Interaktion politischer Parteien im Rahmen der Europäischen Gemeinschaft*. Frankfurt: Campus, 1983.

Niemann, Arne (2006): *Explaining Decisions in the European Union*. Cambridge. Cambridge University Press, 2006.

Nodia, Ghia and Scholtbach, Àlvaro Pinto (2006): *The Political Landscape of Georgia: Political Parties: Achievements, Challenges and Prospects*. Eburon: Delft 2006.

Olof Palme International Center (2014): *Report on Gender Evaluation*. Stockholm: Olof Palme International Center, 2014. http://www.palmecenter.se/wp-content/uploads/2014/12/ToR-PAO-Gender-evaluation.pdf

"Parliament Speaker Responds to MEPs' Letter to PM," *Civil Georgia*, 12 March 2013. http://www.civil.ge/eng/article.php?id=25838

Parliamentary Elections in Moldova on April 5 2009, E-democracy. http://www.e-democracy.md/en/elections/parliamentary/2009/

Parliamentary Elections in the Republic of Moldova. *E-democracy.md*. http://www.e-democracy.md/en/elections/parliamentary/

Pennings, Paul (2008): "An Empirical Analysis of the Europeanization of National Party Manifestos, 1960-2003." *European Union Politics* 7 (2) (2008): 257-270.

Poguntke, Thomas et al. (2007): "Europeanization of national party organizations: a conceptual analysis." *European Journal of Political Research* 46 (6) (2007): 747–771.

Pridham, Geoffrey (1999): "Patterns of Europeanization and Transnational Party Cooperation: Party Development in Central and Eastern Europe." Paper for Workshop on European Aspects of Post-Communist Party Development, *ECPR Sessions*. Mannheim: University of Mannheim, 26- 31 March 1999: 1–17.

Pridham, Geoffrey (1999): "Complying with the European Union's Conditionality: Transnational Party Linkages and Regime Change in Slovakia," 1993–1998. *Europe-Asia Studies* 51 (7) (1999): 1221–1244.

Pridham, Geoffrey (2002): "The European Union's Democratic Conditionality and Domestic Politics in Slovakia: The Meciar and Dzurinda Governments Compared." *Europe-Asia Studies* 54 (2) (2002): 203–227.

Pridham, Geoffrey (2014): "Comparative perspectives on transnational party-building in new democracies: The case of Central and Eastern Europe." *Acta Politica* 49 (1) (2014): 30–50.

Pridham, Geoffrey and Pridham, Pippa (1981): *Transnational Party Cooperation and European Integration: The Process towards Direct Elections*. Boston: George Allen & Unwin, 1981.

Prodi, Romano (2002): "A Wider Europe—A Proximity Policy as the key to stability," "Peace, Security and Stability—International Dialogue and the Role of the EU," *Sixth ECSA-World Conference*. Jean Monnet Project, Brussels, 5–6 December 2002.

Przeworski, Adam and Teune, Henry (1970): *The Logic of Comparative Social Inquiry*. New York: Wiley-Interscience, 1970.

Reid, Mary (2013): "LibDems International Office: strengthening liberal democracies," *Liberal Democrat Voice*, 29 January 2013. http://www.libdemvoice.org/training-our-sister-parties- 32913.html

Reif, Karl Heiz and Schmitt, Hermann (1980): "Nine Second-Order National Elections. A Conceptual Framework for the Analysis of European Election Results." *European Journal for Political Research* 8 (1980): 3–44.

Report on the use of homophobic language by politicians in Moldova, GenderDoc-M and ILGA Europe. http://old.ilgaeurope.org/home/guide_europe/country_by_country/moldova/report_on_homophobic_speech_by_members_of_moldova_s_parliament

"Republican Party Condemns Minaret Removal," *Civil Georgia*, 30 August 2013. http://www.civil.ge/eng/article.php?id=26400

"Republicans Want GD to Turn into 'European Style Coalition'," *Civil Georgia*, 29 October 2014. http://www.civil.ge/eng/article.php?id=27754

Rinnert, David (2013): "The Republic of Moldova in the Eastern Partnership: from "Poster Child" to "Problem Child," *Friedrich Ebert Stiftung*, 2013: 1–8.

"Romanian liberals seek EPP affiliation," *EurActiv*, 26 May 2014. http://www.euractiv.com/sections/eu-elections-2014/romanian-liberals-seek-epp-affiliation- 302401

Samnidze, Khatuna (2013): "Georgia stays firm on its way to European integration," Friedrich Naumann Foundation Georgia, 13 November 2013. http://www.msoe.fnst.org/Artikel-Newsletter-16/2015c28178i1p/index.html

Sandström, Camilla (2004): "The European Liberal, Democrat and Reform Party: From Co- operation to Integration," in *The Europarties: Organisation and Influence*, edited by Pascal Delwit, Erol Külahci and Cèdric Van de Walle, Brussels, 157–184. Belgium: ULB, 2004.

Skrzypek, Ania (2013): *Europe – Our Common Future. Celebrating 20 Years of PES*. FEPS, 2013.

Sloam, James (2005): "West European Social Democracy as a Model for Transfer." *Journal of Communist Studies and Transition Politics* 21 (1) (2005): 67–83.

Smith, Julia (2014): "Between ideology and pragmatism: Liberal party politics at the European level." *Acta Politica* 49 (1) (2014): 105–121.

Socor, Vladimir (2005): "The Regional Impact of Moldova's Elections," *Eurasia Daily Monitor*, 9 March 2005. http://www.jamestown.org/news_details.php?news_id=97

Socor, Vladimir (2009): "Moldova's Political Landscape on the Eve of General Elections: Part One," *Eurasia Daily Monitor* 6 (53), 19 March 2009. http://www.jamestown.org/programs/edm/single/?tx_ttnews[tt_news]=34732&tx_ttnews[backPid]=485&no_cache=1#.VmQUQb_MtlI

Socor, Vladimir (2009): "Russia Accepts Pro-Western Candidate for Moldova's Presidency," *Eurasia Daily Monitor*, 4 November 2009. http://www.jamestown.org/single/?tx_ttnews[tt_news]=35694&no_cache=1#.VmQOuL_MtlI

Socor, Vladimir (2013): "Sources of Moldova's Political Chaos: The Parliamentary System," *Eurasia Daily Monitor* 10 (94), 17 May 2013. http://www.jamestown.org/single/?tx_ttnews[tt_news]=40893&no_cache=1#.VzdqCelvvsQ

Socor, Vladimir (2013): "Sources of Moldova's Political Chaos: The Partition of State Institutions," *Eurasia Daily Monitor* 10 (97), 22 May 2013. http://www.jamestown.org/programs/edm/single/?tx_ttnews[tt_news]=40907&tx_ttnews[backPid]=685&no_cache=1#.VmQU2L_M tlI

Spirova, Maria (2008): "Europarties and party development in EU-candidate states: The case of Bulgaria." *Europe-Asia Studies* 60 (5) (2008): 791–808.

Szczerbiak, Alex and Bil, Monika (2008): "When in doubt, (re-) turn to domestic politics? The (non-) impact of the EU on party politics in Poland." *SEI Working Paper No 103, EPERN Working Paper No 20* (2008): 1–38.

Szczerbiak, Alex and Taggart, Paul (eds.) (2008): *Opposing Europe? The Comparative Party Politics of Euroscepticism.* Oxford: Oxford University Press, 2008.

"The Republican party of Georgia Finalized the Strategic Plan Review," *NIMD Archive*, June 2013. http://nimd.ge/mobile/index.php?page=11&news_id=91&lang=eng

Timm, Christian (2013): "Economic Regulations and State Interventions. Georgia's Move from Neoliberalism to State Managed Capitalism," *Research Paper No. 2013/03*, PHG Private Hochschule Göttingen, (2013): 1–41.

Timus, Natalia (2009): "Coming Closer to Europe: Transnational Cooperation between EPFs and Post-Soviet parties." *GARNET Working Paper No 72/09* (2009).

Timus, Natalia (2014): "Transnational Party Europeanization: EPP and Ukrainian Parties." *Acta Politica* 49 (1) (2014): 51–70.

"United National Movement announce Tbilisi Mayoral Candidates," *Agenda.ge*, 1 March 2014. http://agenda.ge/news/9696/eng

"Usupashvili Meets MEPs from Foreign Affairs Committee," *Civil Georgia*, 18 June 2013. http://www.civil.ge/eng/article.php?id=26189

von Beyme, Klaus (1985): *Political Parties in Western Democracies.* Aldershot, United Kingdom: Gower, 1985.

von dem Berge, Benjamin and Poguntke, Thomas (2013): "The influence of Europarties on Central and Eastern European partner parties: a theoretical and analytical model." *European Political Science Review* 5 (2) (2013): 311–334.

Voss, Kathrin (2010): "Hammer, Sichel, heiss. Die 5. Sommeruniversität der Europäischen Linken in der Republik Moldawien," *Die Linke*, 1 August 2010. http://www.dielinkecoburg.de/medien/publikationen_der_partei/disput/ausgaben_2010/2010_08_disput/detail/browse/2/zurueck/2010-08 disput/artikel/hammer-sichel-heiss/

VVD International (2011): *Annual Report 2011*. VVD International/Haya van Somerenfoundation.http://international.vvd.nl/uploaded/international.vvd.nl/files/560be2655bfef/annual-report-matra-2011.pdf

Wachsmuth, Ralf (2006): "Ukraine," in *Parteienzusammenarbeit der KAS in Mittel-, Ost- und Sudosteuropa*, edited by Peter Fischer-Bollin, 66–69. Berlin: Konrad-Adenauer-Stiftung e.V., 2006.

Wheatley, Jonathan (2005): *Georgia from National Awakening to Rose Revolution: Delayed Transition in the Former Soviet Union*. Ashgate: Burlington, 2005.

Whitmore, Sarah (2014): "Political party development in Ukraine." *GSDRC*, Applied Knowledge Service, Helpdesk Research Report (2014): 1–13.

Wilkinson, Cai (2006): "On Not Just Finding What You (Thought You) Were Looking For, Reflections on Fieldwork Data and Theory," in: *Interpretation and Method: Empirical Research Methods and Interpretive Turn*, edited by Dvora Yanow and Peregrine Schwarz-Shea, 387–406. London: Routledge, 2006.

"Women and Political Influence Follow-up: strategic development of the UNM's women organisation," *Robert Schuman Institute*, 26–27 April, Tbilisi, Georgia. http://www.schuman-institute.eu/finished-activities/women-and-political-influence-follow-up-strategic-development-of-the-unm-womens-organisation-26-27-august-2014-tbilisi-georgia

Zürn, Michael and Checkel, Jeffrey T. (2005): "Getting Socialized to Build Bridges: Constructivism and Rationalism, Europe and the Nation-State." *International Organization* 59 (4) (2005): 1045–1079.

Андрей Голубитский, "Виртуальная двухпартийность." *Комментарии.UA*, 2007 [Andrei Golubitskii, "Virtual two-party system." *Kommentarii.UA*, 2007] http://proua.com/accent/2007/04/19/174054.html

"Борис Тарасюк вважає, що опозиції треба об'єднуватися навколо Тимошенко, бо вона найбільш популярна серед громадян," *Політична думка*, 26 січня 2011 ["Borys Tarasuik thinks that opposition should unite around Tymoshenko because she is the most popular among the population," Poitychna dumka, 26 January 2011]. http://www.politdumka.kiev.ua/interview/513-2011-01-26-12-03-17.html

"Доклад председателя ПКРМ Владимира Воронина: почему ПКРМ не признала президента, куда ушел Мишин и что будет дальше," *Комсомольская правда*, 9 June 2012 ["Report of PCRM party leader Vladimir Voronin: why PCRM did not recognise the president, where did Mishin go and what is next?" *Komsomolskaya Pravda*, 9 June 2012]. http://www.kp.ru/online/news/1171901/

Єреміца, Віталій (2013): "У Європі «помінялі» «Нашу Україну» на УДАР і критикують Кремль," *Радіо Свобода*, 6 вересня 2013 [Vitaliy Eremiza, "Europe changed "Our Ukraine" on UDAR and critisises Kremlin'," *Radio Svoboda*, 6 September 2013]. http://www.radio svoboda.org/content/article/25098054.html

"Материалы XIII съезда Христианско-демократической народной партии", *Ava.md*, 24 February 2011 ["Document of XIII Christian-Democratic people's party conference," *Ava.md*, 24 February 2011]. http://ava.md/parties/010489-materiali-xiii-s-ezda-hristiansko--demokraticheskoi-narodnoi-partii.html

"Материалы третьего «круглого стола» из серии «ПКРМ во власти и в оппозиции," *Ava.md*, 23 February 2011 ["Documents of the third round table from a series "PCRM in power and in opposition," *Ava.md*, 23 February 2011]. http://ava.md/politics/010477-materiali-tret-ego-kruglogo-stola-iz-serii-pkrm-vo-vlasti-i-v-oppozicii.html

"Меркель призвала Тимошенко «работать на единство» и предложила лечение." *Українська правда*, 23 February 2014 ["Merkel called on Tymoshenko to work for the unity and offered treatment," *Ukrainska Pravda*, 23 February 2014]. http://www.pravda.com.ua/rus/news/2014/02/23/7015973/

"Про «зміну орієнтації» партії Батьківщина," *Українська правда*, 8 August 2007 ["Of Batkivshchyna's change in orientation," *Ukrainska Pravda*, 8 August 2007]. http://prawda.biz.ua/articles/4b1a9 d82c3988/view_comments/

"Тарасюк не збирається об'єднуватись з Тимошенко," *Корреспондент*, 16 February 2007 ["Tarasuik is not going to unite with Tymoshenko," *Korrespondent*, 16 February 2007]. http://ua.korrespondent.net/u kraine/285313-tarasyuk-ne-zbiraetsya-ob-ednuvatis-z-timoshenko

"Тимошенко змінює орієнтацію," *Українська правда*, 7 August 2007 ["Tymoshenko changes her orientation," *Ukrainska Pravda*, 7 August 2007]. http://www.pravda.com.ua/articles/2007/08/7/3266965/vi ew_print/

Центр Разумкова (2010): "Еволюція партійної системи України: основні етапи." *Національна Безпека і Оборона* 5 (2010): 3–12 [Razumkov Center, "The evolution of party system in Ukraine: the main stages." *National Security and Defense* 5 (2010): 3–12].

Центр Разумкова (2010): "Сучасний стан політичних партій та партійної системи. Головні проблеми та недоліки." *Національна Безпека і Оборона* 5 (2010): 21–31 [Razumkov Center, „The current state of political parties and party system. The main problems and flaws," *National Security and Defense* 2 (2010): 21–31].

Центр Разумкова (2010): "Чинники, що впливають на еволюцію партійної системи України." *Національна Безпека і Оборона* 5 (2010): 12–21 [Razumkov Center, "Factors that influence the elovution of party system in Ukraine." *National Security and Defense* 5 (2010): 12–21].

SOVIET AND POST-SOVIET POLITICS AND SOCIETY

Edited by Dr. Andreas Umland

ISSN 1614-3515

1 Андреас Умланд (ред.)
   Воплощение Европейской
   конвенции по правам человека в
   России
   Философские, юридические и
   эмпирические исследования
   ISBN 3-89821-387-0

2 Christian Wipperfürth
   Russland – ein vertrauenswürdiger
   Partner?
   Grundlagen, Hintergründe und Praxis
   gegenwärtiger russischer Außenpolitik
   Mit einem Vorwort von Heinz Timmermann
   ISBN 3-89821-401-X

3 Manja Hussner
   Die Übernahme internationalen Rechts
   in die russische und deutsche
   Rechtsordnung
   Eine vergleichende Analyse zur
   Völkerrechtsfreundlichkeit der Verfassungen
   der Russländischen Föderation und der
   Bundesrepublik Deutschland
   Mit einem Vorwort von Rainer Arnold
   ISBN 3-89821-438-9

4 Matthew Tejada
   Bulgaria's Democratic Consolidation
   and the Kozloduy Nuclear Power Plant
   (KNPP)
   The Unattainability of Closure
   With a foreword by Richard J. Crampton
   ISBN 3-89821-439-7

5 Марк Григорьевич Меерович
   Квадратные мстры, определяющие
   сознание
   Государственная жилищная политика в
   СССР. 1921 – 1941 гг
   ISBN 3-89821-474-5

6 Andrei P. Tsygankov, Pavel
   A.Tsygankov (Eds.)
   New Directions in Russian
   International Studies
   ISBN 3-89821-422-2

7 Марк Григорьевич Меерович
   Как власть народ к труду приучала
   Жилище в СССР – средство управления
   людьми. 1917 – 1941 гг.
   С предисловием Елены Осокиной
   ISBN 3-89821-495-8

8 David J. Galbreath
   Nation-Building and Minority Politics
   in Post-Socialist States
   Interests, Influence and Identities in Estonia
   and Latvia
   With a foreword by David J. Smith
   ISBN 3-89821-467-2

9 Алексей Юрьевич Безугольный
   Народы Кавказа в Вооруженных
   силах СССР в годы Великой
   Отечественной войны 1941-1945 гг.
   С предисловием Николая Бугая
   ISBN 3-89821-475-3

10 Вячеслав Лихачев и Владимир
   Прибыловский (ред.)
   Русское Национальное Единство,
   1990-2000. В 2-х томах
   ISBN 3-89821-523-7

11 Николай Бугай (ред.)
   Народы стран Балтии в условиях
   сталинизма (1940-е – 1950-е годы)
   Документированная история
   ISBN 3-89821-525-3

12 Ingmar Bredies (Hrsg.)
   Zur Anatomie der Orange Revolution
   in der Ukraine
   Wechsel des Elitenregimes oder Triumph des
   Parlamentarismus?
   ISBN 3-89821-524-5

13 Anastasia V. Mitrofanova
   The Politicization of Russian
   Orthodoxy
   Actors and Ideas
   With a foreword by William C. Gay
   ISBN 3-89821-481-8

14 *Nathan D. Larson*
Alexander Solzhenitsyn and the
Russo-Jewish Question
ISBN 3-89821-483-4

15 *Guido Houben*
Kulturpolitik und Ethnizität
Staatliche Kunstförderung im Russland der
neunziger Jahre
Mit einem Vorwort von Gert Weisskirchen
ISBN 3-89821-542-3

16 *Leonid Luks*
Der russische „Sonderweg"?
Aufsätze zur neuesten Geschichte Russlands
im europäischen Kontext
ISBN 3-89821-496-6

17 *Евгений Мороз*
История «Мёртвой воды» – от
страшной сказки к большой
политике
Политическое неоязычество в
постсоветской России
ISBN 3-89821-551-2

18 *Александр Верховский и Галина
Кожевникова (ред.)*
Этническая и религиозная
интолерантность в российских СМИ
Результаты мониторинга 2001-2004 гг.
ISBN 3-89821-569-5

19 *Christian Ganzer*
Sowjetisches Erbe und ukrainische
Nation
Das Museum der Geschichte des Zaporoger
Kosakentums auf der Insel Chortycja
Mit einem Vorwort von Frank Golczewski
ISBN 3-89821-504-0

20 *Эльза-Баир Гучинова*
Помнить нельзя забыть
Антропология депортационной травмы
калмыков
С предисловием Кэролайн Хамфри
ISBN 3-89821-506-7

21 *Юлия Лидерман*
Мотивы «проверки» и «испытания»
в постсоветской культуре
Советское прошлое в российском
кинематографе 1990-х годов
С предисловием Евгения Марголита
ISBN 3-89821-511-3

22 *Tanya Lokshina, Ray Thomas, Mary
Mayer (Eds.)*
The Imposition of a Fake Political
Settlement in the Northern Caucasus
The 2003 Chechen Presidential Election
ISBN 3-89821-436-2

23 *Timothy McCajor Hall, Rosie Read
(Eds.)*
Changes in the Heart of Europe
Recent Ethnographies of Czechs, Slovaks,
Roma, and Sorbs
With an afterword by Zdeněk Salzmann
ISBN 3-89821-606-3

24 *Christian Autengruber*
Die politischen Parteien in Bulgarien
und Rumänien
Eine vergleichende Analyse seit Beginn der
90er Jahre
Mit einem Vorwort von Dorothée de Nève
ISBN 3-89821-476-1

25 *Annette Freyberg-Inan with Radu
Cristescu*
The Ghosts in Our Classrooms, or:
John Dewey Meets Ceauşescu
The Promise and the Failures of Civic
Education in Romania
ISBN 3-89821-416-8

26 *John B. Dunlop*
The 2002 Dubrovka and 2004 Beslan
Hostage Crises
A Critique of Russian Counter-Terrorism
With a foreword by Donald N. Jensen
ISBN 3-89821-608-X

27 *Peter Koller*
Das touristische Potenzial von
Kam''janec'-Podil's'kyj
Eine fremdenverkehrsgeographische
Untersuchung der Zukunftsperspektiven und
Maßnahmenplanung zur
Destinationsentwicklung des „ukrainischen
Rothenburg"
Mit einem Vorwort von Kristiane Klemm
ISBN 3-89821-640-3

28 *Françoise Daucé, Elisabeth Sieca-
Kozlowski (Eds.)*
Dedovshchina in the Post-Soviet
Military
Hazing of Russian Army Conscripts in a
Comparative Perspective
With a foreword by Dale Herspring
ISBN 3-89821-616-0

29 *Florian Strasser*
    Zivilgesellschaftliche Einflüsse auf die Orange Revolution
    Die gewaltlose Massenbewegung und die ukrainische Wahlkrise 2004
    Mit einem Vorwort von Egbert Jahn
    ISBN 3-89821-648-9

30 *Rebecca S. Katz*
    The Georgian Regime Crisis of 2003-2004
    A Case Study in Post-Soviet Media Representation of Politics, Crime and Corruption
    ISBN 3-89821-413-3

31 *Vladimir Kantor*
    Willkür oder Freiheit
    Beiträge zur russischen Geschichtsphilosophie
    Ediert von Dagmar Herrmann sowie mit einem Vorwort versehen von Leonid Luks
    ISBN 3-89821-589-X

32 *Laura A. Victoir*
    The Russian Land Estate Today
    A Case Study of Cultural Politics in Post-Soviet Russia
    With a foreword by Priscilla Roosevelt
    ISBN 3-89821-426-5

33 *Ivan Katchanovski*
    Cleft Countries
    Regional Political Divisions and Cultures in Post-Soviet Ukraine and Moldova
    With a foreword by Francis Fukuyama
    ISBN 3-89821-558-X

34 *Florian Mühlfried*
    Postsowjetische Feiern
    Das Georgische Bankett im Wandel
    Mit einem Vorwort von Kevin Tuite
    ISBN 3-89821-601-2

35 *Roger Griffin, Werner Loh, Andreas Umland (Eds.)*
    Fascism Past and Present, West and East
    An International Debate on Concepts and Cases in the Comparative Study of the Extreme Right
    With an afterword by Walter Laqueur
    ISBN 3-89821-674-8

36 *Sebastian Schlegel*
    Der „Weiße Archipel"
    Sowjetische Atomstädte 1945-1991
    Mit einem Geleitwort von Thomas Bohn
    ISBN 3-89821-679-9

37 *Vyacheslav Likhachev*
    Political Anti-Semitism in Post-Soviet Russia
    Actors and Ideas in 1991-2003
    Edited and translated from Russian by Eugene Veklerov
    ISBN 3-89821-529-6

38 *Josette Baer (Ed.)*
    Preparing Liberty in Central Europe
    Political Texts from the Spring of Nations 1848 to the Spring of Prague 1968
    With a foreword by Zdeněk V. David
    ISBN 3-89821-546-6

39 *Михаил Лукьянов*
    Российский консерватизм и реформа, 1907-1914
    С предисловием Марка Д. Стейнберга
    ISBN 3-89821-503-2

40 *Nicola Melloni*
    Market Without Economy
    The 1998 Russian Financial Crisis
    With a foreword by Eiji Furukawa
    ISBN 3-89821-407-9

41 *Dmitrij Chmelnizki*
    Die Architektur Stalins
    Bd. 1: Studien zu Ideologie und Stil
    Bd. 2: Bilddokumentation
    Mit einem Vorwort von Bruno Flierl
    ISBN 3-89821-515-6

42 *Katja Yafimava*
    Post-Soviet Russian-Belarussian Relationships
    The Role of Gas Transit Pipelines
    With a foreword by Jonathan P. Stern
    ISBN 3-89821-655-1

43 *Boris Chavkin*
    Verflechtungen der deutschen und russischen Zeitgeschichte
    Aufsätze und Archivfunde zu den Beziehungen Deutschlands und der Sowjetunion von 1917 bis 1991
    Ediert von Markus Edlinger sowie mit einem Vorwort versehen von Leonid Luks
    ISBN 3-89821-756-6

44 Anastasija Grynenko in
    Zusammenarbeit mit Claudia Dathe
    Die Terminologie des Gerichtswesens
    der Ukraine und Deutschlands im
    Vergleich
    Eine übersetzungswissenschaftliche Analyse
    juristischer Fachbegriffe im Deutschen,
    Ukrainischen und Russischen
    Mit einem Vorwort von Ulrich Hartmann
    ISBN 3-89821-691-8

45 Anton Burkov
    The Impact of the European
    Convention on Human Rights on
    Russian Law
    Legislation and Application in 1996-2006
    With a foreword by Françoise Hampson
    ISBN 978-3-89821-639-5

46 Stina Torjesen, Indra Overland (Eds.)
    International Election Observers in
    Post-Soviet Azerbaijan
    Geopolitical Pawns or Agents of Change?
    ISBN 978-3-89821-743-9

47 Taras Kuzio
    Ukraine – Crimea – Russia
    Triangle of Conflict
    ISBN 978-3-89821-761-3

48 Claudia Šabić
    "Ich erinnere mich nicht, aber L'viv!"
    Zur Funktion kultureller Faktoren für die
    Institutionalisierung und Entwicklung einer
    ukrainischen Region
    Mit einem Vorwort von Melanie Tatur
    ISBN 978-3-89821-752-1

49 Marlies Bilz
    Tatarstan in der Transformation
    Nationaler Diskurs und Politische Praxis
    1988-1994
    Mit einem Vorwort von Frank Golczewski
    ISBN 978-3-89821-722-4

50 Марлен Ларюэль (ред.)
    Современные интерпретации
    русского национализма
    ISBN 978-3-89821-795-8

51 Sonja Schüler
    Die ethnische Dimension der Armut
    Roma im postsozialistischen Rumänien
    Mit einem Vorwort von Anton Sterbling
    ISBN 978-3-89821-776-7

52 Галина Кожевникова
    Радикальный национализм в России
    и противодействие ему
    Сборник докладов Центра «Сова» за 2004-
    2007 гг.
    С предисловием Александра Верховского
    ISBN 978-3-89821-721-7

53 Галина Кожевникова и Владимир
    Прибыловский
    Российская власть в биографиях I
    Высшие должностные лица РФ в 2004 г.
    ISBN 978-3-89821-796-5

54 Галина Кожевникова и Владимир
    Прибыловский
    Российская власть в биографиях II
    Члены Правительства РФ в 2004 г.
    ISBN 978-3-89821-797-2

55 Галина Кожевникова и Владимир
    Прибыловский
    Российская власть в биографиях III
    Руководители федеральных служб и
    агентств РФ в 2004 г.
    ISBN 978-3-89821-798-9

56 Ileana Petroniu
    Privatisierung in
    Transformationsökonomien
    Determinanten der Restrukturierungs-
    Bereitschaft am Beispiel Polens, Rumäniens
    und der Ukraine
    Mit einem Vorwort von Rainer W. Schäfer
    ISBN 978-3-89821-790-3

57 Christian Wipperfürth
    Russland und seine GUS-Nachbarn
    Hintergründe, aktuelle Entwicklungen und
    Konflikte in einer ressourcenreichen Region
    ISBN 978-3-89821-801-6

58 Togzhan Kassenova
    From Antagonism to Partnership
    The Uneasy Path of the U.S.-Russian
    Cooperative Threat Reduction
    With a foreword by Christoph Bluth
    ISBN 978-3-89821-707-1

59 Alexander Höllwerth
    Das sakrale eurasische Imperium des
    Aleksandr Dugin
    Eine Diskursanalyse zum postsowjetischen
    russischen Rechtsextremismus
    Mit einem Vorwort von Dirk Uffelmann
    ISBN 978-3-89821-813-9

60   Олег Рябов
     «Россия-Матушка»
     Национализм, гендер и война в России XX
     века
     С предисловием Елены Гощило
     ISBN 978-3-89821-487-2

61   Ivan Maistrenko
     Borot'bism
     A Chapter in the History of the Ukrainian
     Revolution
     With a new introduction by Chris Ford
     Translated by George S. N. Luckyj with the
     assistance of Ivan L. Rudnytsky
     ISBN 978-3-89821-697-5

62   Maryna Romanets
     Anamorphosic Texts and
     Reconfigured Visions
     Improvised Traditions in Contemporary
     Ukrainian and Irish Literature
     ISBN 978-3-89821-576-3

63   Paul D'Anieri and Taras Kuzio (Eds.)
     Aspects of the Orange Revolution I
     Democratization and Elections in Post-
     Communist Ukraine
     ISBN 978-3-89821-698-2

64   Bohdan Harasymiw in collaboration
     with Oleh S. Ilnytzkyj (Eds.)
     Aspects of the Orange Revolution II
     Information and Manipulation Strategies in
     the 2004 Ukrainian Presidential Elections
     ISBN 978-3-89821-699-9

65   Ingmar Bredies, Andreas Umland and
     Valentin Yakushik (Eds.)
     Aspects of the Orange Revolution III
     The Context and Dynamics of the 2004
     Ukrainian Presidential Elections
     ISBN 978-3-89821-803-0

66   Ingmar Bredies, Andreas Umland and
     Valentin Yakushik (Eds.)
     Aspects of the Orange Revolution IV
     Foreign Assistance and Civic Action in the
     2004 Ukrainian Presidential Elections
     ISBN 978-3-89821-808-5

67   Ingmar Bredies, Andreas Umland and
     Valentin Yakushik (Eds.)
     Aspects of the Orange Revolution V
     Institutional Observation Reports on the 2004
     Ukrainian Presidential Elections
     ISBN 978-3-89821-809-2

68   Taras Kuzio (Ed.)
     Aspects of the Orange Revolution VI
     Post-Communist Democratic Revolutions in
     Comparative Perspective
     ISBN 978-3-89821-820-7

69   Tim Bohse
     Autoritarismus statt Selbstverwaltung
     Die Transformation der kommunalen Politik
     in der Stadt Kaliningrad 1990-2005
     Mit einem Geleitwort von Stefan Troebst
     ISBN 978-3-89821-782-8

70   David Rupp
     Die Rußländische Föderation und die
     russischsprachige Minderheit in
     Lettland
     Eine Fallstudie zur Anwaltspolitik Moskaus
     gegenüber den russophonen Minderheiten im
     „Nahen Ausland" von 1991 bis 2002
     Mit einem Vorwort von Helmut Wagner
     ISBN 978-3-89821-778-1

71   Taras Kuzio
     Theoretical and Comparative
     Perspectives on Nationalism
     New Directions in Cross-Cultural and Post-
     Communist Studies
     With a foreword by Paul Robert Magocsi
     ISBN 978-3-89821-815-3

72   Christine Teichmann
     Die Hochschultransformation im
     heutigen Osteuropa
     Kontinuität und Wandel bei der Entwicklung
     des postkommunistischen Universitätswesens
     Mit einem Vorwort von Oskar Anweiler
     ISBN 978-3-89821-842-9

73   Julia Kusznir
     Der politische Einfluss von
     Wirtschaftseliten in russischen
     Regionen
     Eine Analyse am Beispiel der Erdöl- und
     Erdgasindustrie, 1992-2005
     Mit einem Vorwort von Wolfgang Eichwede
     ISBN 978-3-89821-821-4

74   Alena Vysotskaya
     Russland, Belarus und die EU-
     Osterweiterung
     Zur Minderheitenfrage und zum Problem der
     Freizügigkeit des Personenverkehrs
     Mit einem Vorwort von Katlijn Malfliet
     ISBN 978-3-89821-822-1

75 Heiko Pleines (Hrsg.)
Corporate Governance in postsozialistischen Volkswirtschaften
ISBN 978-3-89821-766-8

76 Stefan Ihrig
Wer sind die Moldawier?
Rumänismus versus Moldowanismus in Historiographie und Schulbüchern der Republik Moldova, 1991-2006
Mit einem Vorwort von Holm Sundhaussen
ISBN 978-3-89821-466-7

77 Galina Kozhevnikova in collaboration with Alexander Verkhovsky and Eugene Veklerov
Ultra-Nationalism and Hate Crimes in Contemporary Russia
The 2004-2006 Annual Reports of Moscow's SOVA Center
With a foreword by Stephen D. Shenfield
ISBN 978-3-89821-868-9

78 Florian Küchler
The Role of the European Union in Moldova's Transnistria Conflict
With a foreword by Christopher Hill
ISBN 978-3-89821-850-4

79 Bernd Rechel
The Long Way Back to Europe
Minority Protection in Bulgaria
With a foreword by Richard Crampton
ISBN 978-3-89821-863-4

80 Peter W. Rodgers
Nation, Region and History in Post-Communist Transitions
Identity Politics in Ukraine, 1991-2006
With a foreword by Vera Tolz
ISBN 978-3-89821-903-7

81 Stephanie Solywoda
The Life and Work of Semen L. Frank
A Study of Russian Religious Philosophy
With a foreword by Philip Walters
ISBN 978-3-89821-457-5

82 Vera Sokolova
Cultural Politics of Ethnicity
Discourses on Roma in Communist Czechoslovakia
ISBN 978-3-89821-864-1

83 Natalya Shevchik Ketenci
Kazakhstani Enterprises in Transition
The Role of Historical Regional Development in Kazakhstan's Post-Soviet Economic Transformation
ISBN 978-3-89821-831-3

84 Martin Malek, Anna Schor-Tschudnowskaja (Hrsg.)
Europa im Tschetschenienkrieg
Zwischen politischer Ohnmacht und Gleichgültigkeit
Mit einem Vorwort von Lipchan Basajewa
ISBN 978-3-89821-676-0

85 Stefan Meister
Das postsowjetische Universitätswesen zwischen nationalem und internationalem Wandel
Die Entwicklung der regionalen Hochschule in Russland als Gradmesser der Systemtransformation
Mit einem Vorwort von Joan DeBardeleben
ISBN 978-3-89821-891-7

86 Konstantin Sheiko in collaboration with Stephen Brown
Nationalist Imaginings of the Russian Past
Anatolii Fomenko and the Rise of Alternative History in Post-Communist Russia
With a foreword by Donald Ostrowski
ISBN 978-3-89821-915-0

87 Sabine Jenni
Wie stark ist das „Einige Russland"?
Zur Parteibindung der Eliten und zum Wahlerfolg der Machtpartei im Dezember 2007
Mit einem Vorwort von Klaus Armingeon
ISBN 978-3-89821-961-7

88 Thomas Borén
Meeting-Places of Transformation
Urban Identity, Spatial Representations and Local Politics in Post-Soviet St Petersburg
ISBN 978-3-89821-739-2

89 Aygul Ashirova
Stalinismus und Stalin-Kult in Zentralasien
Turkmenistan 1924-1953
Mit einem Vorwort von Leonid Luks
ISBN 978-3-89821-987-7

90 *Leonid Luks*
Freiheit oder imperiale Größe?
Essays zu einem russischen Dilemma
ISBN 978-3-8382-0011-8

91 *Christopher Gilley*
The 'Change of Signposts' in the
Ukrainian Emigration
A Contribution to the History of
Sovietophilism in the 1920s
With a foreword by Frank Golczewski
ISBN 978-3-89821-965-5

92 *Philipp Casula, Jeronim Perovic
(Eds.)*
Identities and Politics
During the Putin Presidency
The Discursive Foundations of Russia's
Stability
With a foreword by Heiko Haumann
ISBN 978-3-8382-0015-6

93 *Marcel Viëtor*
Europa und die Frage
nach seinen Grenzen im Osten
Zur Konstruktion ‚europäischer Identität' in
Geschichte und Gegenwart
Mit einem Vorwort von Albrecht Lehmann
ISBN 978-3-8382-0045-3

94 *Ben Hellman, Andrei Rogachevskii*
Filming the Unfilmable
Casper Wrede's 'One Day in the Life
of Ivan Denisovich'
Second, Revised and Expanded Edition
ISBN 978-3-8382-0044-6

95 *Eva Fuchslocher*
Vaterland, Sprache, Glaube
Orthodoxie und Nationenbildung
am Beispiel Georgiens
Mit einem Vorwort von Christina von Braun
ISBN 978-3-89821-884-9

96 *Vladimir Kantor*
Das Westlertum und der Weg
Russlands
Zur Entwicklung der russischen Literatur und
Philosophie
Ediert von Dagmar Herrmann
Mit einem Beitrag von Nikolaus Lobkowicz
ISBN 978-3-8382-0102-3

97 *Kamran Musayev*
Die postsowjetische Transformation
im Baltikum und Südkaukasus
Eine vergleichende Untersuchung der
politischen Entwicklung Lettlands und
Aserbaidschans 1985-2009
Mit einem Vorwort von Leonid Luks
Ediert von Sandro Henschel
ISBN 978-3-8382-0103-0

98 *Tatiana Zhurzhenko*
Borderlands into Bordered Lands
Geopolitics of Identity in Post-Soviet Ukraine
With a foreword by Dieter Segert
ISBN 978-3-8382-0042-2

99 *Кирилл Галушко, Лидия Смола
(ред.)*
Пределы падения – варианты
украинского будущего
Аналитико-прогностические исследования
ISBN 978-3-8382-0148-1

100 *Michael Minkenberg (ed.)*
Historical Legacies and the Radical
Right in Post-Cold War Central and
Eastern Europe
With an afterword by Sabrina P. Ramet
ISBN 978-3-8382-0124-5

101 *David-Emil Wickström*
Rocking St. Petersburg
Transcultural Flows and Identity Politics in
the St. Petersburg Popular Music Scene
With a foreword by Yngvar B. Steinholt
Second, Revised and Expanded Edition
ISBN 978-3-8382-0100-9

102 *Eva Zabka*
Eine neue „Zeit der Wirren"?
Der spät- und postsowjetische Systemwandel
1985-2000 im Spiegel russischer
gesellschaftspolitischer Diskurse
Mit einem Vorwort von Margareta Mommsen
ISBN 978-3-8382-0161-0

103 *Ulrike Ziemer*
Ethnic Belonging, Gender and
Cultural Practices
Youth Identitites in Contemporary Russia
With a foreword by Anoop Nayak
ISBN 978-3-8382-0152-8

104 Ksenia Chepikova
,Einiges Russland' - eine zweite KPdSU?
Aspekte der Identitätskonstruktion einer postsowjetischen „Partei der Macht"
Mit einem Vorwort von Torsten Oppelland
ISBN 978-3-8382-0311-9

105 Леонид Люкс
Западничество или евразийство? Демократия или идеократия?
Сборник статей об исторических дилеммах России
С предисловием Владимира Кантора
ISBN 978-3-8382-0211-2

106 Anna Dost
Das russische Verfassungsrecht auf dem Weg zum Föderalismus und zurück
Zum Konflikt von Rechtsnormen und -wirklichkeit in der Russländischen Föderation von 1991 bis 2009
Mit einem Vorwort von Alexander Blankenagel
ISBN 978-3-8382-0292-1

107 Philipp Herzog
Sozialistische Völkerfreundschaft, nationaler Widerstand oder harmloser Zeitvertreib?
Zur politischen Funktion der Volkskunst im sowjetischen Estland
Mit einem Vorwort von Andreas Kappeler
ISBN 978-3-8382-0216-7

108 Marlène Laruelle (ed.)
Russian Nationalism, Foreign Policy, and Identity Debates in Putin's Russia
New Ideological Patterns after the Orange Revolution
ISBN 978-3-8382-0325-6

109 Michail Logvinov
Russlands Kampf gegen den internationalen Terrorismus
Eine kritische Bestandsaufnahme des Bekämpfungsansatzes
Mit einem Geleitwort von Hans-Henning Schröder und einem Vorwort von Eckhard Jesse
ISBN 978-3-8382-0329-4

110 John B. Dunlop
The Moscow Bombings of September 1999
Examinations of Russian Terrorist Attacks at the Onset of Vladimir Putin's Rule
Second, Revised and Expanded Edition
ISBN 978-3-8382-0388-1

111 Андрей А. Ковалёв
Свидетельство из-за кулис российской политики I
Можно ли делать добро из зла? (Воспоминания и размышления о последних советских и первых послесоветских годах)
With a foreword by Peter Reddaway
ISBN 978-3-8382-0302-7

112 Андрей А. Ковалёв
Свидетельство из-за кулис российской политики II
Угроза для себя и окружающих (Наблюдения и предостережения относительно происходящего после 2000 г.)
ISBN 978-3-8382-0303-4

113 Bernd Kappenberg
Zeichen setzen für Europa
Der Gebrauch europäischer lateinischer Sonderzeichen in der deutschen Öffentlichkeit
Mit einem Vorwort von Peter Schlobinski
ISBN 978-3-89821-749-1

114 Ivo Mijnssen
The Quest for an Ideal Youth in Putin's Russia I
Back to Our Future! History, Modernity, and Patriotism according to Nashi, 2005-2013
With a foreword by Jeronim Perović
Second, Revised and Expanded Edition
ISBN 978-3-8382-0368-3

115 Jussi Lassila
The Quest for an Ideal Youth in Putin's Russia II
The Search for Distinctive Conformism in the Political Communication of Nashi, 2005-2009
With a foreword by Kirill Postoutenko
Second, Revised and Expanded Edition
ISBN 978-3-8382-0415-4

116 Valerio Trabandt
Neue Nachbarn, gute Nachbarschaft?
Die EU als internationaler Akteur am Beispiel ihrer Demokratieförderung in Belarus und der Ukraine 2004-2009
Mit einem Vorwort von Jutta Joachim
ISBN 978-3-8382-0437-6

117 *Fabian Pfeiffer*
Estlands Außen- und Sicherheitspolitik I
Der estnische Atlantizismus nach der
wiedererlangten Unabhängigkeit 1991-2004
Mit einem Vorwort von Helmut Hubel
ISBN 978-3-8382-0127-6

118 *Jana Podßuweit*
Estlands Außen- und Sicherheitspolitik II
Handlungsoptionen eines Kleinstaates im
Rahmen seiner EU-Mitgliedschaft (2004-2008)
Mit einem Vorwort von Helmut Hubel
ISBN 978-3-8382-0440-6

119 *Karin Pointner*
Estlands Außen- und Sicherheitspolitik III
Eine gedächtnispolitische Analyse estnischer
Entwicklungskooperation 2006-2010
Mit einem Vorwort von Karin Liebhart
ISBN 978-3-8382-0435-2

120 *Ruslana Vovk*
Die Offenheit der ukrainischen
Verfassung für das Völkerrecht und
die europäische Integration
Mit einem Vorwort von Alexander
Blankenagel
ISBN 978-3-8382-0481-9

121 *Mykhaylo Banakh*
Die Relevanz der Zivilgesellschaft
bei den postkommunistischen
Transformationsprozessen in mittel-
und osteuropäischen Ländern
Das Beispiel der spät- und postsowjetischen
Ukraine 1986-2009
Mit einem Vorwort von Gerhard Simon
ISBN 978-3-8382-0499-4

122 *Michael Moser*
Language Policy and the Discourse on
Languages in Ukraine under President
Viktor Yanukovych (25 February
2010–28 October 2012)
ISBN 978-3-8382-0497-0 (Paperback edition)
ISBN 978-3-8382-0507-6 (Hardcover edition)

123 *Nicole Krome*
Russischer Netzwerkkapitalismus
Restrukturierungsprozesse in der
Russischen Föderation am Beispiel des
Luftfahrtunternehmens "Aviastar"
Mit einem Vorwort von Petra Stykow
ISBN 978-3-8382-0534-2

124 *David R. Marples*
'Our Glorious Past'
Lukashenka's Belarus and
the Great Patriotic War
ISBN 978-3-8382-0574-8 (Paperback edition)
ISBN 978-3-8382-0675-2 (Hardcover edition)

125 *Ulf Walther*
Russlands "neuer Adel"
Die Macht des Geheimdienstes von
Gorbatschow bis Putin
Mit einem Vorwort von Hans-Georg Wieck
ISBN 978-3-8382-0584-7

126 *Simon Geissbühler (Hrsg.)*
Kiew – Revolution 3.0
Der Euromaidan 2013/14 und die
Zukunftsperspektiven der Ukraine
ISBN 978-3-8382-0581-6 (Paperback edition)
ISBN 978-3-8382-0681-3 (Hardcover edition)

127 *Andrey Makarychev*
Russia and the EU
in a Multipolar World
Discourses, Identities, Norms
With a foreword by Klaus Segbers
ISBN 978-3-8382-0629-5

128 *Roland Scharff*
Kasachstan als postsowjetischer
Wohlfahrtsstaat
Die Transformation des sozialen
Schutzsystems
Mit einem Vorwort von Joachim Ahrens
ISBN 978-3-8382-0622-6

129 *Katja Grupp*
Bild Lücke Deutschland
Kaliningrader Studierende sprechen über
Deutschland
Mit einem Vorwort von Martin Schulz
ISBN 978-3-8382-0552-6

130 *Konstantin Sheiko, Stephen Brown*
History as Therapy
Alternative History and Nationalist
Imaginings in Russia, 1991-2014
ISBN 978-3-8382-0665-3

131 *Elisa Kriza*
Alexander Solzhenitsyn: Cold War
Icon, Gulag Author, Russian
Nationalist?
A Study of the Western Reception of his
Literary Writings, Historical Interpretations,
and Political Ideas
With a foreword by Andrei Rogatchevski
ISBN 978-3-8382-0589-2 (Paperback edition)
ISBN 978-3-8382-0690-5 (Hardcover edition)

132 Serghei Golunov
The Elephant in the Room
Corruption and Cheating in Russian
Universities
ISBN 978-3-8382-0570-0

133 Manja Hussner, Rainer Arnold (Hgg.)
Verfassungsgerichtsbarkeit in
Zentralasien I
Sammlung von Verfassungstexten
ISBN 978-3-8382-0595-3

134 Nikolay Mitrokhin
Die "Russische Partei"
Die Bewegung der russischen Nationalisten in
der UdSSR 1953-1985
Aus dem Russischen übertragen von einem
Übersetzerteam unter der Leitung von Larisa Schippel
ISBN 978-3-8382-0024-8

135 Manja Hussner, Rainer Arnold (Hgg.)
Verfassungsgerichtsbarkeit in
Zentralasien II
Sammlung von Verfassungstexten
ISBN 978-3-8382-0597-7

136 Manfred Zeller
Das sowjetische Fieber
Fußballfans im poststalinistischen
Vielvölkerreich
Mit einem Vorwort von Nikolaus Katzer
ISBN 978-3-8382-0757-5

137 Kristin Schreiter
Stellung und Entwicklungspotential
zivilgesellschaftlicher Gruppen in
Russland
Menschenrechtsorganisationen im Vergleich
ISBN 978-3-8382-0673-8

138 David R. Marples, Frederick V. Mills (eds.)
Ukraine's Euromaidan
Analyses of a Civil Revolution
ISBN 978-3-8382-0660-8

139 Bernd Kappenberg
Setting Signs for Europe
Why Diacritics Matter for
European Integration
With a foreword by Peter Schlobinski
ISBN 978-3-8382-0663-9

140 René Lenz
Internationalisierung, Kooperation
und Transfer
Externe bildungspolitische Akteure in der
Russischen Föderation
Mit einem Vorwort von Frank Ettrich
ISBN 978-3-8382-0751-3

141 Juri Plusnin, Yana Zausaeva, Natalia
Zhidkevich, Artemy Pozanenko
Wandering Workers
Mores, Behavior, Way of Life, and Political
Status of Domestic Russian Labor Migrants
Translated by Julia Kazantseva
ISBN 978-3-8382-0653-0

142 David J. Smith (eds.)
Latvia – A Work in Progress?
100 Years of State- and Nation-Building
ISBN 978-3-8382-0648-6

143 Инна Чувычкина (ред.)
Экспортные нефте- и газопроводы
на постсоветском пространстве
Анализ трубопроводной политики в свете
теории международных отношений
ISBN 978-3-8382-0822-0

144 Johann Zajaczkowski
Russland – eine pragmatische
Großmacht?
Eine rollentheoretische Untersuchung
russischer Außenpolitik am Beispiel der
Zusammenarbeit mit den USA nach 9/11 und
des Georgienkrieges von 2008
Mit einem Vorwort von Siegfried Schieder
ISBN 978-3-8382-0837-4

145 Boris Popivanov
Changing Images of the Left in
Bulgaria
The Challenge of Post-Communism in the
Early 21st Century
ISBN 978-3-8382-0667-5

146 Lenka Krátká
A History of the Czechoslovak Ocean
Shipping Company 1948-1989
How a Small, Landlocked Country Ran
Maritime Business During the Cold War
ISBN 978-3-8382-0666-0

147 Alexander Sergunin
Explaining Russian Foreign Policy
Behavior
Theory and Practice
ISBN 978-3-8382-0752-0

148 *Darya Malyutina*
Migrant Friendships in
a Super-Diverse City
Russian-Speakers and their Social
Relationships in London in the 21st Century
With a foreword by Claire Dwyer
ISBN 978-3-8382-0652-3

149 *Alexander Sergunin, Valery Konyshev*
Russia in the Arctic
Hard or Soft Power?
ISBN 978-3-8382-0753-7

150 *John J. Maresca*
Helsinki Revisited
A Key U.S. Negotiator's Memoirs
on the Development of the CSCE into the OSCE
With a foreword by Hafiz Pashayev
ISBN 978-3-8382-0852-7

151 *Jardar Østbø*
The New Third Rome
Readings of a Russian Nationalist Myth
With a foreword by Pål Kolstø
ISBN 978-3-8382-0870-1

152 *Simon Kordonsky*
Socio-Economic Foundations of the
Russian Post-Soviet Regime
The Resource-Based Economy and Estate-Based Social Structure of Contemporary Russia
With a foreword by Svetlana Barsukova
ISBN 978-3-8382-0775-9

153 *Duncan Leitch*
Assisting Reform in Post-Communist Ukraine 2000–2012
The Illusions of Donors and the Disillusion of Beneficiaries
With a foreword by Kataryna Wolczuk
ISBN 978-3-8382-0844-2

154 *Abel Polese*
Limits of a Post-Soviet State
How Informality Replaces, Renegotiates, and Reshapes Governance in Contemporary Ukraine
With a foreword by Colin Williams
ISBN 978-3-8382-0845-9

155 *Mikhail Suslov (ed.)*
Digital Orthodoxy in the Post-Soviet World
The Russian Orthodox Church and Web 2.0
With a foreword by Father Cyril Hovorun
ISBN 978-3-8382-0871-8

156 *Leonid Luks*
Zwei „Sonderwege"? Russisch-deutsche Parallelen und Kontraste (1917-2014)
Vergleichende Essays
ISBN 978-3-8382-0823-7

157 *Vladimir V. Karacharovskiy, Ovsey I. Shkaratan, Gordey A. Yastrebov*
Towards a New Russian Work Culture
Can Western Companies and Expatriates Change Russian Society?
With a foreword by Elena N. Danilova
Translated by Julia Kazantseva
ISBN 978-3-8382-0902-9

158 *Edmund Griffiths*
Aleksandr Prokhanov and Post-Soviet Esotericism
ISBN 978-3-8382-0903-6

159 *Timm Beichelt, Susann Worschech (eds.)*
Transnational Ukraine?
Networks and Ties that Influence(d) Contemporary Ukraine
ISBN 978-3-8382-0944-9

160 *Mieste Hotopp-Riecke*
Die Tataren der Krim zwischen Assimilation und Selbstbehauptung
Der Aufbau des krimtatarischen Bildungswesens nach Deportation und Heimkehr (1990-2005)
Mit einem Vorwort von Swetlana Czerwonnaja
ISBN 978-3-89821-940-2

161 *Olga Bertelsen (ed.)*
Revolution and War in Contemporary Ukraine
The Challenge of Change
ISBN 978-3-8382-1016-2

162 *Natalya Ryabinska*
Ukraine's Post-Communist Mass Media
Between Capture and Commercialization
With a foreword by Marta Dyczok
ISBN 978-3-8382-1011-7

163 Alexandra Cotofana,
 James M. Nyce (eds.)
 Religion and Magic in Socialist and
 Post-Socialist Contexts I
 Historic and Ethnographic Case Studies of
 Orthodoxy, Heterodoxy, and Alternative
 Spirituality
 With a foreword by Patrick L. Michelson
 ISBN 978-3-8382-0989-0

164 Nozima Akhrarkhodjaeva
 The Instrumentalisation of Mass
 Media in Electoral Authoritarian
 Regimes
 Evidence from Russia's Presidential Election
 Campaigns of 2000 and 2008
 ISBN 978-3-8382-1013-1

165 Yulia Krasheninnikova
 Informal Healthcare in Contemporary
 Russia
 Sociographic Essays on the Post-Soviet
 Infrastructure for Alternative Healing
 Practices
 ISBN 978-3-8382-0970-8

166 Peter Kaiser
 Das Schachbrett der Macht
 Die Handlungsspielräume eines sowjetischen
 Funktionärs unter Stalin am Beispiel des
 Generalsekretärs des Komsomol
 Aleksandr Kosarev (1929-1938)
 Mit einem Vorwort von Dietmar Neutatz
 ISBN 978-3-8382-1052-0

167 Oksana Kim
 The Effects and Implications of
 Kazakhstan's Adoption of
 International Financial Reporting
 Standards
 A Resource Dependence Perspective
 With a foreword by Svetlana Vlady
 ISBN 978-3-8382-0987-6

168 Anna Sanina
 Patriotic Education in
 Contemporary Russia
 Sociological Studies in the Making of the
 Post-Soviet Citizen
 With a foreword by Anna Oldfield
 ISBN 978-3-8382-0993-7

169 Rudolf Wolters
 Spezialist in Sibirien
 Faksimile der 1933 erschienenen
 ersten Ausgabe
 Mit einem Vorwort von Dmitrij Chmelnizki
 ISBN 978-3-8382-0515-1

170 Michal Vít,
 Magdalena M. Baran (eds.)
 Transregional versus National
 Perspectives on Contemporary Central
 European History
 Studies on the Building of Nation-States and
 Their Cooperation in the 20th and 21st Century
 With a foreword by Petr Vágner
 ISBN 978-3-8382-1015-5

171 Philip Gamaghelyan
 Conflict Resolution Beyond the
 International Relations Paradigm
 Evolving Designs as a Transformative
 Practice in Nagorno-Karabakh and Syria
 With a foreword by Susan Allen
 ISBN 978-3-8382-1057-5

172 Maria Shagina
 Joining a Prestigious Club
 Cooperation with Europarties and Its Impact
 on Party Development in Georgia, Moldova,
 and Ukraine 2004–2015
 With a foreword by Kataryna Wolczuk
 ISBN 978-3-8382-1084-1

***ibidem*-Verlag**

Melchiorstr. 15

D-70439 Stuttgart

info@ibidem-verlag.de

www.ibidem-verlag.de
www.ibidem.eu
www.edition-noema.de
www.autorenbetreuung.de